PRAISE FOR *Taking Parenting Public*

"Hats off to Sylvia Hewlett, Nancy Rankin, and Cornel West for urging us to take parenting public. Parenting is highly revered in the U.S.—as long as it's done by women for free. It's high time parents got together to work for the supports they need."

—**Ellen Bravo**, Co-Director, 9to5,
National Association of Working Women

"Reading this book feels like having a rich conversation about raising children in today's world with a group of very impressive thinkers. While they bring diverse points of view about the problems facing parents today, they agree that parents are struggling to meet too many demands with not enough time or support. Despite different views of the solutions, the authors likewise agree that parenting must be seen as a public rather than a private concern of society. These agreements should be a very powerful force in bringing about needed changes that will benefit children and families."

—**Ellen Galinsky**, author of *Ask the Children*
and President of the Families and Work Institute

"This evidence-based book clarifies the causes and grievous consequences of the array of societal changes that have undermined parental authority and family functioning across all sectors of our population. The volume relies on scholarly commissioned papers along with results of focus groups and sophisticated survey data. A persuasive case is made for broad-based commitment to the implementation of sound social policy, both public and private, to address major concerns and needs of parents in the twenty-first century. Doing so will alleviate their personal pain as well as reducing the national losses of human potential and productivity for both parents and their children."

—**Beatrix A. Hamburg**, M.D.,
Cornell Weill Medical College

"Whether you're a feminist, a conservative, a liberal or a troglodyte, you'll find plenty of new ideas in this volume to stir you up—both for and against. Together, these essays argue convincingly that effective parenting must be supported by a substantial public investment."

—**Heidi Hartmann**, President and CEO of
the Institute for Women's Policy Research

"The wonderful thing about *Taking Parenting Public* is that it doesn't just analyze the challenges of parenting in the U.S. today—though it does that, in intelligent and compelling detail—but it actually suggests solutions. This is a must-read for anyone who wants to move beyond the current state."

—**Deborah Holmes**, Ernst & Young,
Americas Director of the Center
for the New Workforce

"An impressive list of contributors raises critical issues in a cogent and persuasive way. I highly recommend this book for leaders in the public and private sectors who must consider both the economic and the social impacts of this issue on our families and our nation."

—**Bob Kerrey**, former U.S. Senator
and President of New School University

"Before September 2001 many of us never really understood the centrality of family in our lives and the value of care-giving in our nation. This strong anthology makes a compelling connection between the spirit of democracy and honoring parenting."

—**Paula M. Rayman**, author of
Beyond the Bottom Line

"A vital volume that illuminates the daily crisis in American life—the chronic tension between work and family that confronts tens of millions of working parents. For all Americans, this book shows the high social costs of raising children with a workforce of dual-career families or single parents in an outdated economic system that presumes a nation of stay-at-home moms. It presents a compelling case for fundamental changes in how we organize work to strike a better balance between job and home. It offers an agenda for reforming public policy and tells why all of us have a stake in reform."

—**Hedrick Smith**, Executive Producer,
PBS "Juggling Work and Family"

"An important and timely book that features thoughtful chapters by a diverse group of writers, including some of the most influential scholars and policy analysts in the nation. Rich substantive arguments and policy insights flow throughout the volume."

—**William Julius Wilson**, Harvard University

Taking Parenting Public

Taking Parenting Public

The Case for a New Social Movement

Edited by
Sylvia Ann Hewlett
Nancy Rankin
Cornel West

ROWMAN & LITTLEFIELD PUBLISHERS, INC.
Lanham • Boulder • New York • Oxford

ROWMAN & LITTLEFIELD PUBLISHERS, INC.

Published in the United States of America
by Rowman & Littlefield Publishers, Inc.
4720 Boston Way, Lanham, Maryland 20706
www.rowmanlittlefield.com

12 Hid's Copse Road
Cumnor Hill, Oxford OX2 9JJ, England

British Library Cataloguing in Publication Information Available

Library of Congress Cataloging-in-Publication Data

Taking parenting public : the case for a new social movement / edited by Sylvia Ann
Hewlett, Nancy Rankin, Cornel West.
   p. cm.
Includes bibliographical references and index.
ISBN 0-7425-2110-9 (alk. paper) — ISBN 0-7425-2111-7 (pbk. : alk. paper)
  1. Parenting—United States. 2. Child welfare—United States. 3. Social values—United
States. I. Hewlett, Sylvia Ann, 1946– II. Rankin, Nancy. III. West, Cornel.

HQ755.8 .T35 2002
649'.1'0973—dc21
                                      2001034621

$\otimes$^{TM} The paper used in this publication meets the minimum requirements of American
National Standard for Information Sciences—Permanence of Paper for Printed Library
Materials, ANSI/NISO Z39.48-1992.

To Richard and our children,
for their inspiration and support.
Sylvia Ann Hewlett

To my husband, Paul,
my partner in love and parenting.
Nancy Rankin

To my family,
who share this labor of love.
Cornel West

Contents

Boxes, Figures, and Tables

Acknowledgments

This book grew out of papers presented at meetings of the National Parenting Association Task Forces from 1996 to 2000.

Chaired by Sylvia Ann Hewlett and Cornel West, the task force sessions brought together a diverse group of respected scholars, media and corporate leaders, policymakers, and parents to talk about forces that have undermined parenting—and strategies to turn that around. The papers were often provocative and presented a wide range of perspectives. They challenged us to think about what we can and should do to value, strengthen, and support parenting. And the ensuing discussions have helped guide our mission to make parenting a higher priority in our personal lives and on the public agenda.

We are grateful to the funders of this project, whose support and advice were so critical throughout each stage of our work. We would like to thank Ralph Smith, Paula Dressel, and Janice Nittoli of the Annie E. Casey Foundation and Benita Melton and Lorin Harris of the Charles Stewart Mott Foundation, who provided major financial support. In addition, we thank the American Express Foundation, Carnegie Corporation, Aaron Diamond Foundation, Robert Wood Johnson Foundation, McKnight Foundation, David and Lucile Packard Foundation, Surdna Foundation, and Unitarian Universalist Veatch Program at Shelter Rock, whose generous support made additional research possible.

Special thanks are due to all who participated in the meetings for contributing their expertise, wisdom, and passionate commitment to the work of nurture and care in American society. We are especially indebted to the core group that planned the sessions, identified key research issues, and contributed chapters to this volume, Enola G. Aird and David Elkind, project advisers; and Nancy Rankin, project director. We are indebted to Craig Charney, our pollster, whose expertise was invaluable in carrying out our surveys of parents. Most especially, we would like to thank Peggy Shiller for her extraordinary staff support throughout every phase of work, from the research and task force sessions to the editing and preparation of this volume.

Our profound thanks to each of the authors and discussants: Charles Ballard, David Blankenhorn, Derrick Bell, Andrew Billingsley, John A. Buehrens, Sara Moores Campbell, Geoffrey Canada, Allan C. Carlson, Renée Cherow-O'Leary, James D. Cox, Winston H. (Tony) Cox, Linda DeCarlo, John Demos, Jean Bethke Elshtain, Celeste Estrella, Amitai Etzioni, Steve Farkas, Judy A. Farrell, Sandra Feldman, Shelley Fischel, Judith Flores, Roxanna Foster, Hyman Frankel, Lucy N. Friedman, Vivian Gadsden, William A. Galston, Carol Gilligan, Patricia Girardi, Tracy and Marcus Glover, Michael Goldstein, Roger S. Glass, Stacy Hanley, David A. Harris, Peter Herbst, Janet Heroux, S. Jody Heymann, Betty Holmes, Wade F. Horn, Lou Iacovelli, Ann Jackson, Sean Joe, Philip W. Johnston, Barbara M. Jones, William Kessen, Julia Kristeller, Joyce S. Lapenn, Father Robert Lauder, James Levine, Stephen Manchester, Jake Mascotte, Mark Mauer, Hope Melton, John Modell, Frank Moretti, Mary B. Mulvihill, Essie D. Owens, Jim Papathomas, Samuel P. Peabody, Hugh Pearson, Sylvia L. Peters, Edward Pitt, David Popenoe, Amina Rachman, Wornie L. Reed, Rabbi Sarah Reines, David G. Richardson, Richard Robinson, Maria E. Rodriguez-Immerman, Esmeralda Santiago, Juliet B. Schor, Raymond Seidelman, Jack Sheinkman, Robert Sherman, Vanessa Sims, Theda Skocpol, Taino Soba, George C. Springer, James P. Steyer, Sonia Taitz, Carl Taylor, Ruy Teixeira, Erica E. Tollett, Stanley Turecki, Amanda Vaill, Judith S. Wallerstein, David Walsh, Christine P. Wasserstein, Russell Weatherspoon, Burley Leon Whitten, Helen Wilkinson, Peter Winn, Edward N. Wolff, Ira Wolfman, and Ruth A. Wooden. We are enormously indebted to each of them.

Preface: The Challenge

Sylvia Ann Hewlett and Cornel West

Across the face of this nation children are failing to thrive. Despite an un-precedented run of prosperity, 18 percent of American children still live in poverty (compared with 8 percent in western Europe).[1] Youth suicide rates are up and test scores are down. The incidence of young people taking their own lives has tripled since the 1950s and only a quarter of American high school students can write at a proficient level.[2] According to a report published by the Carnegie Corporation, "nearly half of American adolescents are at high or moderate risk of seriously damaging their life chances."[3]

Behind these troubling statistics lies one all-important fact. Increasingly, parents are unable to come through for their children. Due to a variety of factors that include lengthening workweeks and our government's failure to create paid parenting leave, the amount of time parents spend with their children has shrunk dramatically. In a 1999 study, the Council of Economic Advisers reported that over the past three decades the average American family has lost twenty-two hours a week of parenting time. The end result: stressed-out parents and underachieving, unhappy kids. Too many children are left "home alone," raising themselves on a thin and meager diet of junk food, gangster rap, and violence-laden TV. These are the seedbeds of Littleton, West Paducah, and Jonesboro.

In a nation of sagging blue-collar wages and threadbare social supports, hundreds of thousands of Americans are seriously disadvantaged when they embark on the serious business of raising a child. Unlike new parents in other

Sylvia Ann Hewlett, an economist, is founder and chairman of the National Parenting Association. Cornel West is the Alphonse Fletcher Jr. University Professor at Harvard University. They are co-authors of *The War Against Parents*.

rich nations, American moms and dads are expected to do a stellar job without the benefits of a living wage, medical coverage, or parenting leave. In the late 1990s there were six million American families where two adults held four jobs in order to keep the show on the road. Stagnant wages and increased child-raising costs—from day care to college tuition—are forcing more and more parents to work longer and harder. Like hamsters on a wheel, they are running harder and harder to stay even.

When parents are displaced or disabled, there is a huge fallout in society, because, acknowledged or not, parenting matters. Whether Johnny can read; whether Johnny knows right from wrong; whether Johnny is a happy, well-adjusted kid or sullen, self-destructive, and violent has a whole lot to do with the kind of parenting Johnny has received. If Johnny's mom and dad have been able to come through with sustained, steadfast, loving attention, the odds are Johnny is on track to become a productive, compassionate citizen. If they have not, Johnny is in trouble—and so is our nation.

Thirty years ago Chicago sociologist James S. Coleman showed that parental involvement was more important in determining school success than any attribute of the formal education system. Across a wide range of subject areas, in literature, science, and reading, Coleman demonstrated that the parent was twice as powerful as the school in determining achievement at age fourteen.[4] Psychologist Laurence Steinberg, who recently completed a six-year study of 20,000 teenagers in nine different communities, confirms the importance of parents. Steinberg shows that one out of three parents is "seriously disengaged" from his or her adolescent's education, and this is the primary reason why so many American students perform below their potential— and below students in other rich countries.[5]

A weight of evidence now demonstrates ominous links between absentee parents and a wide range of behavioral and emotional problems in children. A study that surveyed 5,000 eighth-grade students in southern California found that the more hours children were left by themselves after school, the greater the risk of substance abuse. In fact, home-alone children as a group were twice as likely to drink alcohol and take drugs as children who were supervised by a parent or another adult family member after school. The study found that this increased risk of substance abuse held true regardless of the child's sex, race, or economic status.[6]

In a similar vein, a 1997 study of 90,000 teenagers—the ADD Health Project undertaken by the Carolina Population Center and the Adolescent Health Program at the University of Minnesota—found that youngsters are less likely to get pregnant, use drugs, or become involved in crime when they spent significant time with their parents. This study found that the mere physical presence of a parent in the home after school, at dinner, and at bedtime significantly reduces the incidence of risky behavior among teenagers.[7] These findings are confirmed by recent research at the Harvard School of Public Health by Jody Heymann and Alison Earle that demonstrates that a parent's evening work has extremely negative effects on children's cognitive and emotional development.[8]

Finally, a report prepared for the Department of Justice shows that the peak hours for juvenile crime are now 3 P.M. to 8 P.M.[9] This can be attributed to a huge drop-off in the number of parents available to supervise their children after school. In 1970, 57 percent of school-age children had at least one parent at home on a full-time basis; by 1995 this figure had fallen to 29 percent.[10] Millions of latchkey children now go home to an empty house after school, and these children are at significantly greater risk of truancy, school failure, substance abuse, and violent behavior than children who have a parent at home.

Despite the enormous importance of parenting, American society has made it increasingly difficult for moms and dads to come through for their kids. As we shall see in subsequent chapters of this book, over the past thirty years mothers and fathers have been hurt by stagnant wages, pounded by tax and transfer policy, and invaded and degraded by the media. Our leaders talk as though they value families, but act as though families were a last priority. We live in a nation where market work, centered on competition, profits, and greed, increasingly crowds out nonmarket work, centered on sacrifice, care, and commitment. What really counts in America is how much you get paid and what you can buy. Small wonder, then, that parenting is a dying art. Small wonder that parents have less and less time for their children. And time is, of course, at the heart of the child-raising enterprise. As Enola Aird has said, "Being a good parent requires providing a child with the gifts of love, attention, energy, and resources, generously and unstintingly over a long period of time. It involves nourishing a small body, but it also involves growing a child's soul—sharing the stories and rituals that awaken a child's spirit and nurturing the spiritual bonds that create meaning and morality in that child's life." None of these tasks are easily undertaken by overburdened contemporary parents.

Parents are not less well intentioned than they used to be. They do not love their children less. They are as passionately attached to their children as they have ever been. Like Vicki Parker, they strain and stretch to buck the trends and be there for their kids:

Vicki Parker, a single mom, has a punishing schedule. During the day, from 8:30 A.M. to 4:30 P.M., she works in the drug treatment program of the New York City Housing Authority. Her job is to be out in the field locating drug abusers, persuading them to enroll in some kind of treatment. During the night, from 11:00 P.M. to 7:30 A.M., she works as a counselor at the Good Shepherd—a group home for runaway teenagers. Her task here is to make sure the kids make it back to their rooms at night, listen to their troubles, and ward off self-destructive acts. Vicki goes from her night-time job straight to her daytime job. When she arrives home at 5:30 P.M. she has put in a nineteen-hour day.

"It's hard to describe how bone tired I am at the end of the afternoon. Sometimes my legs are trembling with the effort of walking those last few blocks from the sub-way; other times I catch myself moaning aloud, I am so out of my skull with ex-haustion. Most days I walk into my house knowing there's not a prayer I can be a good parent to my kids. First off, in my weary state it's all too easy to find fault: why hasn't Tiffany (ten) stacked the dirty dishes? why didn't Tyrone (sixteen) pick up the groceries? or worse still, how come Jasmine (fourteen) forgot to pick up her little sis-ter from school and left her stranded with an annoyed teacher? Seems like I am al-ways chewing them out for something or other. They're good kids, but the resent-ment builds when I pile so many responsibilities on them.

"I know they need me to fix dinner and help with homework, but more often or not I just collapse on the sofa and wave them away, saying, 'Not now, give me an hour.' Of course, in an hour or so I need to leave for my second job, which is all the way down on 17th Street, an hour's subway ride away."

At the nub of Vicki's problems is her struggle to earn enough money to support her kids. Her day job pays $26,000 a year, which boils down to $224 a week in dis-posable income once taxes ($402 a month), rent ($624 a month) and her college loan repayment ($168 a month) are taken out. This simply is not enough to cover basic living costs—utilities, food, clothing, transportation, school supplies—for Vicki and her three children. Last winter when Con Edison turned off her electricity and Vicki found herself too deeply in debt to borrow the additional $80 it would take to pay her bill, she figured the time had come to take a second job.

Vicki did not plan on life turning into such a treadmill. She spent five difficult years, from 1985 to 1990, going to school at night so that she could earn that college degree she thought would get her a well-paid job. Well, she got the job she was af-ter—she had always wanted to be a social worker and help kids—but there was no way it paid enough to live on.

Vicki has also tried really hard to build a relationship with a man; she knows that her kids need a dad. Her first husband, the father of her two oldest children, was shot dead at age thirty—he was an innocent bystander in a shoot-out between rival gangs. More recently, she has tried to construct a long-term relationship with the father of her third child, but as luck would have it, he was recently let go from a job he had held for fourteen years. According to Vicki, "He doesn't come around as much any more. I figure he's ashamed that he can't contribute as he knows he ought. But he's a beautiful person. When Tiffany wants something bad, he puts away a dollar a day toward it. He can manage that."

The day we interviewed Vicki, she was worried sick: Jasmine had not been home for three days. Vicki knew that she had gotten into some bad company recently. She was "hanging" with a twenty-one-year-old man who kept her out until all hours. Vicki is desperately concerned that Jasmine not get pregnant. "She's just started high school and she's a real strong student, I can't stand the thought that she might be about to throw her chances away. But I guess my not being there at night has just made it too easy for her to act out."

Vicki had one last bitter comment: "I know what happens to neglected kids. I work with them nineteen hours a day. In fact, I am forced to work with them so long and so hard that I end up doing all kinds of bad stuff to my own kids."[11]

Coming through as a parent these days is not hard just for single moms and those at the low end of the income ladder. It affects us all. Parents like Chris and Mary Sue are an American success story. Happily married, they own their own home and are raising two children in a medium-size middle-American city. They have good careers, including one in a booming sector of the economy. Yet, even for them, parenting is a struggle.

Chris's day starts before dawn, at 4 A.M., when he wakes up in order to arrive at his job as controller of a small North Carolina company by six o'clock. Getting in three hours early allows Chris to leave at 2:15, just in time to pick up his eleven-year-old son, Daniel, from school and spend the afternoon at home. Chris's wife, Mary Sue, works hard, too, as a manager in the high-tech world of a cellular phone company. She sees Daniel and his older sister off to school most mornings. Chris has opted for this sleepless schedule because Daniel was unhappy with the afterschool program available at his school, and after Daniel left the program unnoticed one day, his parents were unhappy with the supervision, too.

But Chris isn't complaining. He says he feels fortunate because he works in a high enough position at a small firm that he can juggle his schedule, as long as he gets his work done. What he really wonders is how single parents do it. Chris knows, because he's had a taste of what it might be like. His wife travels about 25 percent of the time for her job, generally leaving on Sunday and getting home Wednesday. She's part of a six-person team, with members scattered across the country in different time zones. It's not unusual for her to get pulled away from dinner for a half-hour call.

Recently, Chris has come under more pressure at work when salespeople griped that he wasn't always available when they needed him. So the family is shifting to a new routine this fall, now that their son has turned twelve. Chris leaves work to pick Daniel up from school, deliver him home safely, and then returns to work, unless he needs to pick up his daughter after her school band practice ends at five. Chris isn't happy about Daniel being what he calls a "latchkey kid," but it's the best compromise they have for now.[12]

Some five years ago the National Parenting Association created a Task Force on Parenting. The idea was to pull together a diverse group of scholars, policymakers, business leaders, and parent activists from all colors and cultures to help design strategies, policies, and programs that would give new support to the work that parents do.

For two years the task force deliberated, sifting through the relevant research, weighing policy options, and listening to testimony from moms and dads around the country. The group then commissioned a set of papers, whose topics reflected different disciplines and ideological perspectives. The challenge was to figure out how and why parents have become one of the most disadvantaged groups in our nation and how to turn this situation around. Our end goal was ambitious: We wanted to develop the intellectual capital for a new parents' movement. This book pulls together this groundbreaking body of work.

In addition, over the past seven years the NPA has devoted considerable energy to listening to parents. We have conducted focus groups, held innumerable town hall meetings, and conducted three nationwide surveys to determine "What Will Parents Vote For?" The results are powerful. Our research reveals a remarkable degree of consensus among parents. This is contrary to popular opinion, which tends to see American parents as a group divided by schism. Such a perception is encouraged by politicians, who often use parents as political footballs in their ideological games, magnifying differences and dividing a constituency that is already demoralized and vulnerable. Working moms are set against at-home moms, mothers against fathers, urbanites against suburbanites, blacks against whites, and welfare moms against everyone else.

In contrast to this history, our data show that once you get away from "hot button" issues such as gay marriage and school prayer, there is impressive agreement among parents. On the critical issues that underpin and condition daily life—workplace policy, tax policy, child safety—there is *enormous unity across race, class, and gender.* It seems that in these practical arenas blue-collar and professional parents, African American and white parents, mothers and fathers are ready to rally behind a common agenda.

Thus there is healing ground on which to build a parents' movement. Millions of moms and dads across the nation are facing the same set of urgent concerns. If they can somehow band together and find collective strength, they stand a much better chance of persuading political leaders to provide the serious support they so desperately need. So perhaps the time has come for the creation of a national movement that would give mothers and fathers real leverage in the corridors of power.

It is important to stress that we are not talking about narrow interest-group politics here. Parenting is an indispensable civic activity, not simply a set of private joys and responsibilities. For if a mom or a dad is able to cobble together the loving attention and financial resources necessary to be a "good" parent and ensures that a child becomes a well-adjusted person who succeeds in school and graduates college, who benefits?[13] Well, a parent gets hugs and kisses, but the big payoff goes to the nation. This on-track child will then go on to become a productive worker (who will boost the GNP and pay his or her taxes) and a responsible citizen (who will vote and otherwise contribute to community life). The fact is, we are all vested in the well-being of other people's children. We need grown-ups to bear and raise children, and we need them to do it well.

For too long the political invisibility and cultural devaluing of parents has blinded us to their enormously important societal role—and impoverished our notions of citizenship. As we look to the future, a vigorous parents' movement could well create the energy that would reinvent government and banish the apathy and cynicism that haunt our public life. What better project to revitalize our republic than giving strength and succor to parents so that they can weave the web of care that is so vital to our nation?

NOTES

1. Neil G. Bennett and Hsien-Hen Lu, "Child Poverty in the States: Levels and Trends from 1979 to 1998," National Center for Children in Poverty, August 2000, available at http://cpmcnet.columbia.edu/dept/nccp/cprb2txt.html, accessed 12/6/00.

2. Centers for Disease Control, "Suicide in the United States," fact sheet, available at http://www.cdc.gov/ncipc/factsheets/swifacts.html, accessed 12/6/00. U.S. Department of Education, National Center for Education Statistics, "Nation's Report Card Rates Typical Student as Less Than Proficient in Writing," press release, September 28, 1999, available at http://nces.ed.gov/Pressrelease/sep99/9_28_99.asp, accessed 12/6/00.

3. Carnegie Council on Adolescent Development, *Great Transitions: Preparing Adolescents for a New Century* (New York: Carnegie Corporation of New York, October 1995), 10.

4. James S. Coleman, "Effects of School on Learning: The IEA Findings," paper presented at Conference on Educational Achievement, Harvard University, November 1973, 40.

5. Laurence Steinberg, "Failure Outside the Classroom," *Wall Street Journal,* July 11, 1996, A14; Laurence Steinberg et al., *Beyond the Classroom: Why School Reform Has Failed and What Parents Need to Do* (New York: Simon & Schuster, 1996), 119.

6. J. L. Richardson et al., "Substance Abuse among Eighth-Grade Students Who Take Care of Themselves after School," *Pediatrics* 84, no. 3 (September 1989): 556–66.

7. Michael D. Resnick et al., "Protecting Adolescents from Harm," *Journal of the American Medical Association* (September 1997): 823–32.

8. Jody Heymann, *The Widening Gap: Why America's Working Families Are in Jeopardy—And What Can Be Done about It* (New York: Basic Books, 2000), 54–55.

9. James Alan Fox and Sanford A. Newman, "After-School Crime or After-School Programs: Tuning in to the Prime Time for Violent Juvenile Crime and Implications for National Policy," report to the U.S. Attorney General, Department of Justice, September 10, 1997, 3.

10. Howard Hayghe, supervisory economist, Bureau of Labor Statistics, telephone interview, January 13, 1998.

11. Vicki Parker is a pseudonym. Member, parent panel, Task Force on Parenting, interview, October 14, 1997.

12. Interview conducted by Nancy Rankin with a parent, Chris M., September 2000.

13. A two-parent household earning $38,000 to $64,000 a year will spend $165,630 to feed, clothe, and shelter a child until age 18, according to the latest government figures. This figure doesn't even include college tuition. U.S. Department of Agriculture, *Expenditures on Children by Families, 2000 Annual Report* (USDA, Center for Nutrition Policy and Promotion, Misc. Publication No. 1528-2000, May 2001), ii.

Introduction

Nancy Rankin

The Dow Jones has climbed fivefold since 1987, breaking records and rewarding investors with huge gains for much of the nineties. Now imagine if during the same period there had been a similar index measuring parent well-being. The headlines would have looked quite different: *Stocks Soar; Parenting Plummets*. Because despite more than a decade of prosperity, mothers and fathers are struggling to do a good job raising their children.

You need only listen to the language we use to describe the daily dilemmas facing parents today—*the juggling act, the moral meltdown, the time crunch, toxic entertainment, the sandwich generation*—to know that these are stressful times. At home, we see parenting increasingly squeezed into the residual moments of our busy lives and contracted out to others. In the public arena, as well, reality falls short of rhetoric. We hear endless talk from the Republicans about "family values" and from the Democrats about "working families." Yet in the 2000 presidential campaign, as just one example, both parties proposed spending three times as much federal money on buying prescription drug coverage for our oldest citizens as on improving schools for our youngest. Whether personally or as a nation, when we underinvest in parenting, the bottom line cannot be good for our children.

The material drawn together in this volume presents a litany of sobering evidence that parenting today gets too little time and attention and not enough support and status. The essays were originally prepared to provoke debate at a series of roundtable discussions hosted by the National Parenting Association. Parents, academics, and leaders from the worlds of business, labor, government,

---

Nancy Rankin is past executive director of the National Parenting Association and before that, director of research and programs.

religion, and the media were invited to examine the state of parenting at the close of the twentieth century. We deliberately sought out different points of view. The forums were noteworthy because, though parenthood is a defining experience in the lives of nearly all the participants, such a diverse group of men and women almost never comes together to speak publicly about it.

This was brought home to us at one of our first sessions. As is common at meetings of this sort, we began by going around the table and introducing ourselves. One by one, the participants defined themselves with their impressive credentials and titles, until we came to Enola Aird, who stopped us dead in our tracks. She said, "I'd like to introduce myself, first, as a mother." Aird, of course, could have started with other items from her glowing résumé—Yale-educated lawyer, think-tank scholar, radio producer, and so on—but she chose instead to offer, first and foremost among her identities, her role as mother.

"Taking parenting public," then, is about parents, ourselves, giving our roles as mothers and fathers more priority in our personal lives. It is about raising our voices and speaking out loud about our concerns as parents. And it is about creating a sea change in our culture that gives the important work of parenting the recognition it deserves. Deep attitudinal change is needed to drive institutional change—a rethinking of how we organize our work lives, schools, religious and communal groups, and public places and policies to support mothers and fathers in nurturing children. Such change is not meant to undermine the accomplishments of the women's movement. On the contrary, if we really want to give women equal opportunities, then we need to transform other aspects of society to make it succeed. This is not a plea to return to the 1950s. It is a call to imagine new paths for the twenty-first century.

Parents, of course, have a tremendous stake in how well they do at raising their kids. But society has an important stake as well. When children grow up to be productive, caring, and ethical citizens, co-workers, and neighbors, the public reaps the benefits. And, of course, if parents fail to do a good job, society bears many of the costs. "Taking parenting public" recognizes that we are all stockholders in "the next generation."

* * *

The chapters in part one of this book, "The Cultural Marketplace," describe forces undermining mothers and fathers—in particular, assaults from the zeitgeist. Enola Aird remembers a time when parents understood that their primary role, supported by extended family and neighbors, was to imbue children with moral character. She argues that, driven by pressures to achieve material success in contemporary America, we have devoted ourselves too little to our children's spiritual and moral upbringing. Reversing this tide will require concerted efforts to counter the culture and reclaim the sense of moral purpose in parenting.

Delving further into how parental roles have evolved from the heyday of the modern nuclear family to what he calls "the postmodern permeable family," Tufts professor of child development David Elkind examines social forces that have diminished parental authority. Paradoxically, he points out that the very changes that have emptied parental roles of their authority have simultaneously created even greater demands for parental guidance. Elkind concludes by describing what he sees as hopeful signs that we are in transition to a new paradigm, "the vital family." Resting on a foundation of committed love, authentic choices, community involvement, and interdependence, this new model can restore parental authority in ways that are healthy for both children and adults.

The changing parental roles, described by Elkind, are both reflected in and shaped by the popular culture. In recent years the media have been an extremely potent force in undercutting the work that parents do. Marketing expert Bernice Kanner shows how over a forty-five-year period, the television industry has moved from celebrating to denigrating parents. Where once mothers and fathers were portrayed as loving and wise, they are now seen as neglectful, bumbling, or missing from the scene altogether. Sure, there are some exceptions. But overall, parents feel increasingly devalued and demoralized by what they see on the small screen. As Sylvia Hewlett and Cornel West write in *The War Against Parents,* "They listen to Beavis tell Butthead, 'Your mother is a slut' and yearn for a time when television, movies and popular music routinely paid homage to moms and dads and reinforced the values that they taught. Now parents are locked in a daily battle to protect their children from the ugly messages spewed forth by the media."

In part two, we turn to an analysis of the economic status of parents in postwar America. New York University economist Edward Wolff shows that the relative well-being of parents has been continuously eroding over the past three or four decades, especially in comparison to that of the elderly. Though poverty rates overall have fallen, the gap between parents and nonparents has widened. In 1998, 15.1 percent of families with children were poor compared to 4.5 percent of families without children. Between 1974 and 1998 the median income of families without children grew four times faster than the median income of families with children.

So despite a recent unprecedented span of prosperity, parents are in many ways under greater stress than ever. The middle-class lifestyle that one earner could support in the 1950s now requires two incomes to achieve. In half of all families today, both parents work, compared to one of five in the 1950s. Another quarter of families are headed by a single parent, typically a working mother.[1] Not only are more parents on the job, but they are working longer and harder. Americans now work more hours than jobholders anywhere else in the industrialized world. According to a report issued in 2001 by the Geneva-based International Labor Organization, U.S. workers put in an average of 1,979 hours in 2000, up 36 hours since 1990, surpassing the Japanese by the equivalent of about three and one-half weeks a year and the Germans by a whopping twelve and a half weeks.[2] In an analysis of the time crunch facing families, the president's Council of Economic Advisers reports that from 1969 to 1996 the increase in hours mothers spend in paid work, combined with the shift toward single-parent families, has meant an average loss of twenty-two hours a week in parental time for families.[3]

The impact of these trends is not hard to figure out. Parents are struggling to meet too many demands with not enough time. No one argues that work, especially the expanding opportunities for women, has not had huge positive payoffs for the economic and psychological well-being of individuals and children. But the transformation of the workforce has not been matched by a revolution in work norms of comparable magnitude. Yes, we see the growth of helpful trends like flextime. True, e-mail and other new technologies free us from the office, but they also allow work to invade our evenings, weekends, and vacations as we struggle to keep up with an ever faster pace. Fundamentally, we are still trying to fit twenty-first-century dual-career parents into jobs designed for men with stay-at-home wives raising the kids and managing the household. The resulting pressures take a toll on family life and marriages. When the National Parenting Association surveyed parents in 2000, mothers told us that "balancing work and family" was their biggest daily challenge. More surprisingly, fathers said so, too, and by the same high margins.

Work hour trends and the implications for families are examined in detail by Juliet Schor, professor of sociology at Boston College. She finds that "estimates of working hours for American parents suggest a dramatic rise between 1969 and the present, with most of the increase concentrated in the 1980s and 1990s." It appears that parents have tried to compensate, in part, by cutting back on time for themselves and other chores to preserve time with their children. But as a result, parents have experienced high levels of stress and time pressure.

If balancing work and caring for children is a tough act for average families, for low-income parents it can be nearly impossible. Jody Heymann, Harvard faculty member and physician, looks at the working conditions facing low-income parents—in particular, those making the transition from welfare to work. Thirty percent of these mothers, who have left the welfare rolls after less than five years, work at jobs that offer no paid leave for sickness or vacation, not a single day. Another 32 percent have very limited paid leave, adding up to less than two weeks. Making matters worse, low-income workers are also more likely to hold jobs that offer little autonomy and flexibility in how and where work gets done. The family-friendly changes we are starting to see in the workplace have not reached the lower strata, where employees lack a floor of the most minimal basic benefits. Heymann concludes by admonishing, "If as a society we are going to expect parents to be responsible for paid work in the labor force and the unpaid work of caretaking, then society must take responsibility for making it feasible."

We turn then, in part three, to looking at public policy. What is our society, through the instruments of tax and transfer payments, regulation, and government programs doing—or failing to do—to support parenting? In Ruy Teixeira's view, the problems of America's parents, symbolized by the iconic soccer mom, have not lacked for attention. What has been missing is a match between the acknowledged magnitude of parents' problems and a political agenda of sufficient scope to address them. Teixeira, a senior fellow at the Century Foundation, attributes the inadequate response to a combination of trends that, taken together, have diminished the political clout of parents. Parents are politically disadvantaged by their relatively poor voter turnout. Once you control for age, however, parents are actually slightly more likely to vote than nonparents. The bigger story is the demographic shift. Teixeira cites figures showing that parents have declined as a share of the eligible electorate from a majority of 55 percent in 1956 to 36 percent in 1996.

Although it is true that parents are no longer the majority of the electorate, they are still a huge group and one that is substantially larger than other powerful interests. In the 2000 elections, seniors sixty-five and older comprised just 14 percent of voters and union households 26 percent, compared to parents at 39 percent.[4] Teixeira points to signs that parents may be regaining their political voice. Parents, he says, may be poised to lead the country back toward a more activist government agenda. He cites surveys, conducted by Stanley Greenberg for the Campaign for America's Future and by Penn + Schoen and Charney Research for the National Parenting Association, that show that parents support a bold, large-scale investment in education and measures to address issues like balancing work and family and ensuring health coverage for all children.

In the next chapter, social historian Allan Carlson provides a conservative perspective on the impact of federal tax policies on marriage, children, and the nonmarket home economy. He argues that the federal government has "socialized the potential economic gains provided by children," while leaving the kids and the direct costs of raising them in parents' laps. According to Carlson, by the end of the 1940s, the federal government had achieved a solidly promarriage, prochild, profamily income tax structure. Since then, he contends, this structure has been steadily dismantled.

Unwilling to cede the profamily turf to the right, William Galston, domestic policy adviser to the Clinton White House, tackles some of these same issues from a progressive perspective. He looks at familiar topics, like the marriage penalty in the tax code, child tax credits, and housing vouchers, through a liberal lens and offers fresh insights. Then he expands the discussion, raising some more provocative proposals for wage insurance and subsidies that would increase the disposable incomes of working-class and middle-class families with dependent children.

In thinking through the role government can have in creating the conditions for forming and sustaining strong, stable families, Tufts University historian Peter Winn draws lessons from the GI Bill. He demonstrates how the postwar "American dream family" depended on public subsidies for education and housing to an extent that today's conservatives—who espouse family values, but decry government social spending—seem to have forgotten. Winn concludes by proposing an analogous broad-scale public program for our era. He envisions a greatly expanded AmeriCorps. In return for service in this national youth corps, young men and women would be entitled to the GI Bill type of benefits that would give them the economic helping hand to start families that a grateful society gave to their postwar grandfathers.

In the final part of this volume, the authors present ideas for generating the public will needed to transform our society from one that seems stacked against parents to one that stands behind them. Political scientist Raymond Seidelman lays out alternative strategies for building a parents' movement. The first organizing strategy, patterned after conventional interest groups, would rely on the financial contributions of affluent and activist parents to buy the expertise and lobbying power needed to gain access in Washington. Seidelman then contrasts what some might call this "astroturf" approach with a genuine grassroots movement.

Harvard professor Theda Skocpol takes the argument from here, making a strong case for a popularly rooted citizens' movement on behalf of parents. She looks back at our country's history to discover the common elements that underpin "America's finest social policy achievements," counting among them public schools, veterans' benefits, and the Social Security Act. Skocpol argues that our most enduring and popularly accepted social benefits have always been morally justified as given in return for, or prospective supports for, vital contributions to society. Surely, parenting qualifies as deserving of support on these grounds. In addition, our most successful policies have been seen as universal, not as welfare for the poor. And third, in each case voluntary citizens' groups have played an important supporting role. She calls for the creation of a widespread civic movement that, embodying the principles of past American success stories, would advocate a bold agenda of economic, political, and community support for families.

But what motivates a groundswell among the public, demanding action? Historically, social movements have emerged when a problem comes to be perceived as a crisis that threatens the well-being of the nation or a pervasive, moral injustice. Think of the movements that arose in the 1960s and 1970s for environmental protection, civil rights, and women's rights and against the war in Vietnam. Wade Horn argues, in his chapter, that the unprecedented rise of fatherlessness in America—where now nearly one out of the three children do not live in the same home as their father—is just such a crisis, with profound, harmful consequences for children. Deep concern about the erosion of father–child bonds has led to the formation of fatherhood groups around the country. Their agendas range from teaching fathering skills to strengthening marriage to advocating for the rights of divorced and unwed dads. Horn examines whether a united fatherhood movement can be forged out of these efforts.

Building the new coalitions that Horn, Skocpol, Seidelman, and others envision would be immeasurably easier if parents saw themselves as a group with strong common interests—or with a clearly defined cause. But parents are not viewed, at least not yet, as a unified group, nor do they tend to see themselves in this way. Pollsters, press, and politicians splinter mothers and fathers into other demographic categories like women, suburbanites, African Americans, Christian conservatives, or blue-collar men. This renders parents, as a group, invisible. Almost no political analysts have looked at the issues that could unite a cross-cutting swath of the American public because of their deeply emotional, core concerns *as parents*.

To examine exactly this question, the National Parenting Association has conducted a series of focus groups and nationwide surveys of American parents. Our research findings, presented in chapter 14, "The Parent Vote," show that parents are surprisingly unified on issues from improving public schools, to balancing family and work and stemming gun violence. There is widespread agreement—not just on what concerns them the most, but on what to do about it—that cuts across many of the usual divisions of gender, race, income, and political party. Moreover, when mothers and fathers enter the voting booth, they are more likely to think of themselves as parents than as any other facet of their identities, including race and gender.[5] These findings suggest that parents could indeed become a potent force for social and political change.

In recent elections, major party candidates have begun to understand the potential power of the parent vote. Improving education was a central theme of both the Bush and Gore 2000 presidential campaigns, and both spoke out against the marketing of violence-soaked entertainment to our children. A few commentators even ventured that the candidates went too far in directing their appeals to families, leaving out those without children. Yet neither candidate really addressed what both mothers and fathers say is their greatest daily challenge: balancing work and family. To be sure, the Democrats offered up modest expansions of the Family and Medical Leave Act and increased dependent-care tax breaks, while Republicans supported time off for overtime and raising the per-child tax credit. But neither candidate proposed fresh, new solutions on the same scale as the problem. Chapter 15 on "Fixing Social Insecurity" offers one such idea that would provide real help to millions of working parents struggling with the time crunch. Nancy Rankin proposes that working parents should be allowed to draw Social Security benefits for up to three years during their prime child-rearing years. Those electing to "borrow" on their Social Security would be expected to partly repay the system by deferring their retirement or upping their contributions once they returned to work. The intent of Social Security—providing financial security in return for a lifetime of contributions—makes it an appropriate vehicle for helping parents. What work is a more vital contribution to the future health of our nation than raising children?

*   *   *

When the essays in this volume were first presented, our nation was gripped by a budget deficit mentality and the limited vision that seemed realistic. In just the short time since, a burgeoning surplus materialized. Then, almost as quickly the forecast billions all but vanished in the face of tax cuts and a faltering economy. When will we look beyond the economic conditions of the moment to think boldly about the best ways to help parents do a good job raising America's children? Isn't it time to make caring for our youngest citizens as high on the national agenda as caring for our oldest?

The call to take parenting public, however, is not just a call for political action. It is a call for a transformation in attitudes that makes parenting a higher priority in our private lives, as well as on the public agenda. In her closing chapter, social marketing expert Ruth Wooden describes the public perception of the work of parenting today. She writes that given the depth of the challenges, it is essential to embark on a major effort to enhance the cultural value we place on the contribution parents make to our society.

Wooden asks, "What does it mean to 'take parenting public'? Why did we choose the metaphor of capital markets, when we have argued so strongly that, in fact, parenting is the ultimate nonmarket activity in our culture? It is precisely because the metaphor helps us look at parenting through a new lens." In a culture that values building successful business enterprises, the work of parenting is very similar to the classic "undercapitalized" firm. The investment that is needed for a parenting movement is both human and financial. We need to engender greater empathy for mothers and fathers and reinforce parents' understanding of the importance of their roles. And we need to invest greater resources in social supports that can help parents come through for their children. For it is our children's well-being that is at stake here. They will most certainly be the greatest beneficiary of a movement to take parenting public.

NOTES

1. Jeff Madrick, "Economic Scene," *New York Times,* August 31, 2000, C2.

2. Steven Greenhouse, "Americans' International Lead in Hours Worked Grew in the 90's, Report Shows," *New York Times,* September 1, 2001, p. A8.

3. Council of Economic Advisers, "Families and the Labor Market, 1969–1999: Analyzing the 'Time Crunch,'" May 1999.

4. Voter News Service, National Exit Poll, November 7, 2000.

5. National Parenting Association, *The Parent Vote: Moms and Dads Up for Grabs* (New York: National Parenting Association, October 2000).

PART ONE

THE CULTURAL MARKETPLACE

On Rekindling a Spirit of "Home Training": A Mother's Notes from the Front

Enola G. Aird

Africans believe in something that is difficult to render in English. We call it *ubunto, botho*. It means the essence of being human. You know it when it is there and when it is absent. It speaks about humaneness, gentleness, hospitality, putting yourself out on behalf of others, being vulnerable. It embraces compassion and toughness. It recognizes that my humanity is bound up in yours, for we can only be human together.

—Archbishop Desmond Tutu, *The Words of Desmond Tutu,* 1989, p. 71.

They were cultural ambassadors—teenagers from Colegio Princeton del Pedregal in Mexico City—visiting a prep school near my home in Connecticut. They represented their country well, leading the audience on a delightful musical and literary tour of their homeland. They also represented their parents well.

Minutes into the performance, the young man who was serving as our guide turned to the audience and, in only slightly accented English, captured my attention when he said with great fanfare, "In Mexico, children are raised to. . . ." He finished the thought by listing a series of striking personal virtues. Among them were "to be respectful of their elders, to take care of younger children, and to be family-oriented."

I have never visited Mexico, nor do I know for sure whether or not this is a universally held view in the country. But as a mother who takes the vocation of mothering seriously, I was deeply moved by the young man and his companions because of their clear sense of the purposes for which they were

---

Enola G. Aird is director of the Motherhood Project at the Institute for American Values, a New York–based nonprofit, nonpartisan organization devoted to research, publication, and public education on family and civil society.

being raised and their strong feelings of pride in knowing and claiming those purposes.

I wondered about the children of the United States. Would most children from our country, in a similar situation, even think to include such an affirmation as part of a presentation about their culture? And, if they did, what would they say to complete the sentence "In the United States, children are raised to . . ."?

Perhaps they would answer "to be successful." My fear is that a great many American children would be at a loss to articulate with any degree of consensus any other purposes for which they are being raised . . . as would most of their parents.

What are we raising our children to be? What are the purposes for which they are being parented?

As we enter a new century, adults in the United States are, with good reason, filled with anxiety about our children's character and morality. A 1999 survey found that a majority of adults in the United States believe that "too many children and teens are not absorbing the moral lessons that will allow them to grow into respectable, respectful, compassionate, and honorable human beings."[1] The same study concluded that "neither adults nor teens believe the next generation will make America a better place."[2] Americans are deeply troubled by the "lack of values such as honesty, civility, and responsibility" among our young people.[3]

The concerns are well justified. In a 1998 survey of over 20,000 high school and middle school students, almost half of the high school students admitted to stealing, and 70 percent admitted to cheating on an exam in the previous year. Almost all the teenagers admitted to lying. Some 92 percent of the high school students said that they lied at least once in the past year; 78 percent said they lied two or more times.[4]

In a 1999 poll of students, 76 percent of males and 63 percent of females in high school said they "hit a person in the last twelve months because they were angry." Forty-seven percent of all high school males, 39 percent of middle school boys, 25 percent of high school females, and 24 percent of middle school young women "believe that it is sometimes OK to hit or threaten a person who makes them angry." And 24 percent of male high school students and 18 percent of male middle school students "say they took a weapon to school at least once in the past year."[5]

People in the United States are more worried about moral values today than they were some thirty years ago. In 1952, 34 percent of Americans thought that the young people of their time did not have as strong a sense of right and wrong as young people did fifty years earlier. In a recent survey, however, 78 percent of respondents reported that they feel that the morals of young people have deteriorated since the 1960s.[6]

Many Americans blame parents for the moral crisis facing today's children.[7] Although they acknowledge the challenges facing parents, Americans believe that too many parents are failing at the job of raising their children. They believe that many parents are not good role models, are not teaching their children the difference between right and wrong, are irresponsible, and "think buying things for kids means the same thing as caring for them."[8]

In a Gallup poll released in 1999, ethics, morality, and family decline topped the list of concerns raised in answer to the question "What do you think is the most important problem facing the country today?"[9]

It is a problem that crosses racial and class lines. It finds its expression in the small, intimate spaces of everyday life: children who seem to have few manners or social graces, who seem to have little sense for appropriate behavior in public places; children who disrespect adults; children who take shortcuts on homework and cheat on quizzes; children who are undisciplined and rude; children who seem increasingly alienated from our society.

In the vernacular of the West Indian and African American communities in which I grew up in the 1950s and the early 1960s,[10] these are children with "no home training."

I want to defend three propositions:

- that the primary role of parents is to shape the spiritual and moral character of their children;
- that the crisis of morals and character that has befallen America's children is due in large part to the fact that too many parents are not sufficiently attentive to the project of forming the character and morality of their children, losing touch with the spirit of "home training"; and
- that if a society is to be civilized, parents must agree on—and be prepared to defend—an irreducible minimum of common moral values that are indispensable for the raising of children of good character.

A PRELIMINARY DEFINITION

The term "home training" is not used much these days. But it was an important idea when I was growing up. It is a vivid part of my memories of a not-so-distant past.

I am not a nostalgist. I am not arguing for a return to the 1950s. But as the author Mary Pipher has put it, "Must we doubt everyone who speaks positively about the past? . . . Rather, a healthy appreciation for what worked in previous eras can inspire action. We can examine what worked well and what didn't and use this knowledge in planning for a better world."[11]

As a black woman, I know all too well that the 1950s and the early 1960s were not as virtuous as some would paint them. But I also know that life for many children then was radically different and—in important ways—markedly better than it is for a great number of children today. I know that I am not deluded in remembering a time when many parents considered it their duty to watch out for and watch over each other's children; when adults felt free to discipline and correct children who were not their own; and when if I did something wrong on the street, by the time I got home my mother and my father, my aunts and uncles often already knew all about it because some nosy neighbor had taken it upon herself to report to them.

Adults tended to watch what they said and what they did in front of children. Certain subjects were considered unsuitable for children's ears and eyes. Television was still young, innocent, and tame. There was no communications technology explosion, no Internet. There was a remarkable consensus about the fundamentals of right and wrong and how children were to behave. There was considerable agreement on the basic values that children were to be taught—so that many of my neighbors and my parents' friends could honestly say to me: "I know your parents, I know that they would not approve of your behavior, young lady." And if I dared to complain to my parents, they would confirm for me that yes, indeed, Miss So-and-So did have it right, my behavior was absolutely unacceptable. I was a part of a local community of people, but just as important, I was part of a local community of shared moral values. What I learned at home was generally reinforced as I went out onto the streets of my neighborhood, into church, and almost everywhere else.

My parents (and later my aunt and uncle who became my guardians) seemed to know more or less what their job was. They did not seem doubtful or insecure about their responsibilities. What they had learned from their parents they sought to teach me. They assumed authority, set standards, made judgments, and held me accountable when they deemed my conduct unacceptable.

The other day, I did a quick survey of a few of my friends (around my age) to see if they could recall the days when adults were quick to point out that some young person or another was acting as though he or she had "no home training."

Just about everybody remembered. At the same time, my friends and I all agreed that "home training" is in that category of ideas that is very hard to pin down and tough to talk about—a notion that we cannot define with precision. We do know it when we see it, though, and we know it when it is missing.

One of my friends, Curlena, said, "When I think about 'home training' I think about what your parents are supposed to teach you before they send you out into the world." Loretta, a great friend of mine, responded, "Yes, that was a much-used phrase, particularly in the African American community, usually preceded by the word 'no' as in 'that child has no home training.' It meant not knowing how to act, how to carry oneself, how to treat others, how to exercise self-control." She added: "Children today are 'house trained,' but they are not 'home trained.' They have some of the basics, but they are not fully steeped in the training in morals and manners that 'home training' implies."

It is a term deep and rich in meaning—so much so that it is best understood intuitively by those who "know it when they see it." But for those who do not know the term, "home training" implies parenting a young person to take on a specific moral character and a desired moral course in life. It implies focusing the young person on particular goals—on developing the habits and disciplines of a moral life.

It is a term that is audacious about the mission of parenting. It suggests that those raising the child have agreed upon the virtues that he or she should embody. It assumes that there is a right way and a wrong way in which children can be trained. It suggests a teleology of parenting—that the process of parenting ought to be shaped by particular purposes and directed toward specific ends. It is a term that suggests an intuitive sense of what the end result of raising children ought to be—that children should be trained to grow to know, to love, and to embody certain virtues.

The idea of "home training" has a distinctly spiritual and moral character, as it is rooted in the biblical mandate to "train up a child in the way in which he should go."[12] Home training, as the name implies, took place primarily at home, led usually by parents with the help of older brothers and sisters, grandparents, and aunts and uncles. But the home training concept also extended out into the neighborhood and church and even sometimes into school because, on the question of how children were expected to behave, nearly everyone seemed to be singing out of the same hymn book. The cultural ethos of the era supported parents in the work of raising more or less "home trained" children.

I never heard anybody recite an exhaustive list of the specific virtues that the "home trained" child ought to evince. I learned them by osmosis from the Bible and family stories I heard at home, from the lessons of Sunday school, from the conversations that adults allowed me to overhear, from the stern looks that would be shot my way if I did something that did not meet the standards that had been set for me. The "home training" virtues included faith in God, respect for self and others (especially elders), honesty, discipline, self-control, sacrifice, duty, hard work, responsibility. And they included the idea that I was to aspire to be a certain kind of person. As poor as my family was, it was clear to me that there were certain high standards that I, as a member of my family, was expected to uphold. My grandmother would often say, "We just don't do so and so. We do such and such." There were expectations held high for me to reach.

I know many people of different races and backgrounds who remember similar experiences of growing up in the United States in the 1950s and early 1960s, even if they do not know the term "home training." But I do not for one minute want to pretend that this was a universal experience. Nor do I want to suggest that I lived an idyllic existence; I did not. And I am well aware that there were many parental abuses of the privilege of home training.

I am not advocating a return to the past. I am arguing for a revival and an updating of an old idea that once worked fairly well in helping children to learn moral values.

The polls and the surveys and, most important, the anguish that so many of us feel when we hear the latest piece of evidence that something has gone horribly wrong with our children make it quite clear that it is well past time to breathe new life and substantive meaning into some notion of "home training."

PARENTS AND THE RAISING OF MORAL CHILDREN

When our first child, who is now sixteen, was born, there were a few complications. As a result, at discharge time my husband and I, both lawyers, had an excruciatingly long list of questions for our doctor. After patiently answering all our queries, he finally looked at us with all the power of his bedside manner and said, "Remember that the both of you and your daughter are animals and that you have instincts. You must learn to trust those instincts."

That bit of advice ended our inquisition on a sobering but strangely reassuring note. Over the years, it has given us a great deal of confidence to trust our own intuition more than the advice of "experts" when it comes to raising our children. It has also helped us to focus starkly on the primary mission of parents: to civilize, moralize, and humanize their children. As the sociologist Amitai Etzioni has put it, "Infants are born only with a human potential, one that is not self-realizing. They must be made human." Etzioni continues: "Infants are born into *families* that have been entrusted through human history with beginning the process of planting values, launching the moral self."[13]

Psychiatrist and neuroscientist Jeffrey Schwartz has observed that in human beings "a lot of the time, animal drives are *running* the pre-frontal cortex [the front of the front of the human brain] on a sort of 'automatic pilot' using it as nothing more than a very fancy way to get food, sex, belonging, dominance, and security. Many of our most cherished likes and dislikes, fantasies and feelings are actually mental elaborations and justifications of those basic animal drives."[14] Without parents' humanizing work, children may be quite smart, well-educated, and successful but so selfish, self-centered, and uncaring as to be essentially uncivilized—not able to live in a spirit of community with others.

Throughout history, we humans have been deepening our understanding of the role of parents—and our expectations of parents—in raising children. In recent history, parents, in partnership with extended families and communities, have been the first and most important persons charged with the responsibility of showing children how to discipline their basic drives, how to control themselves in order to be civilized. Parents must help their children to become fully human—help them, as social scientist James Q. Wilson suggests, to discover the "oughts" of life.[15]

It is in loving our children that we show them how to love and bind them to us in ways that make them want to respect our authority and follow our example and our leadership. It is by teaching children to care about and care for others as well as themselves—by cultivating feelings such as empathy and virtues such as self-control—that parents help their children to become caring human beings able to love others, make sacrifices, make and keep commitments, act responsibly, and live lives of discipline and moderation.

At the heart of the vocation of parenting is the work of moral education and at the heart of moral education is teaching children how to govern themselves and how to balance self-interest with the interests of others.

Mothers and fathers are called to create, protect, and defend the physical, emotional, and spiritual spaces in which the process of moral development can take place. It is in spaces of love, nurture, security, playfulness, trust, and close human relationship that young people as apprentices to adults can belong, be loved and be taught how to love, learn what is right and what is wrong, and learn how life is to be lived.

From the foundation and security of these spaces, children are equipped and emboldened to grapple with life's most difficult questions, questions of meaning and purpose: *Who am I? Why am I here?* Every child has a purpose in life—some potential to be realized—and it is the job of each mother and father to create a space within which the child can explore, discern, and discover that purpose.

It is in the small, ordinary, unglamorous, and sometimes tedious experiences of everyday family life that our children become anchored, learn who they are, and discover what is truly important in life and what is expected of them. It is in hearing and reading stories, sharing meals, walking hand in hand, visiting with grandparents and extended family and friends, learning and being steeped in traditions and customs, working around the house, sharing thoughts and comparing notes at the end of the day, and taking part in the countless other activities of ordinary life that children discover how to be and how to behave.

It is these experiences that create the childhood memories that help to nourish our children's spirits and awaken within them a sense of awe and gratitude for the gift of life. These experiences can be marvelously enriching . . . or sorely impoverished. If they are done in relative peace and calm, they can offer opportunities for a wonderful companionship through which children can learn from being with and observing their parents. If they are done in a hurried and perfunctory way, they can send a clear and painful message to our children that they are not important enough to us to deserve what is perhaps the most precious gift of all because it cannot be replenished—our time.

Parenting is an awesome responsibility. It is most glorious when it is treated as a calling, a work of stewardship in grateful response to the great blessing—the wondrous gift—of a child. Parenting and creating a family is difficult work, but it is sacred work, and we are most true to our vocation when it is informed by a sense of high purpose and when it seeks to impart to children an equally compelling sense of high purpose and mission. It is in the family that our children should learn that they did not create themselves; that we are all necessarily dependent on others; that we cannot become fully human without strong and enduring relationships with those around us and without a connection to the transcendent. It is in the family that parents should hold up a vision of the good and struggle to help their children understand what it might mean to be a good man and a good woman, to be a good husband and a good wife, to be a good father and a good mother, to live a good life.

In his book *The Moral Intelligence of Children,* the psychiatrist Robert Coles poignantly recalls how, day in and day out, his mother made quite clear to her children what she held "high and dear," how hard she worked to "convey her values" to her children, "how imaginative or inventive she'd try to be, how responsive to our humanity, even as she was putting her own on the line."[16] He observes: "We grow morally as a consequence of learning how to be with others, how to behave in this world, a learning prompted by taking to heart what we have seen and heard. The child is a witness; the child is an ever-attentive witness of grown-up morality—or lack thereof."[17]

Parents in the United States are at a moral crossroads. The central question facing parents today is whether we wish to preserve the idea of childhood as a time when parents, in partnership with other adults, strive to raise moral children by helping them learn how to pursue high ideals . . . or whether we wish to abandon that aspiration altogether.

PARENTING TODAY

Americans are only partly right in holding parents responsible for the moral decline of our nation's children. It is true that too many parents are raising their children carelessly, without a sense of calling and high purpose. But in pointing the finger at parents, Americans fail to see how many fingers are pointing back at themselves and at our culture.

One of the ideas that was planted in the 1950s that has grown in currency since, and now haunts our children, is the notion of "giving our children a better life."[18] In the 1950s, people recovering from World War II with the memories of the Great Depression still alive in their minds, and with an unprecedentedly high standard of living, began to equate the idea of a "good life" with material success. And so began the American quest to work and to provide and to buy. Over the past fifty years, an idea that seemed so reasonable to our parents and grandparents has outgrown us and now threatens to overwhelm us and crush our children.

When I asked my teen-aged daughter, "What are we raising young people in the United States to be?" she answered without hesitation that we are raising them "to compete, to go to school, to get good grades, and to get a good job to make lots of money to buy lots of things so they can have children and raise them to compete, to go to school, to get good grades, to get a good job to make lots of money to buy lots of things."

According to Michael Josephson, head of the Josephson Institute of Ethics, which regularly conducts surveys on the ethical behavior of young people, "When you ask parents whether they'd rather have a good kid or a rich kid, they'll tell you they'd rather have their children be good. But if you look at their behavior—and the children's interpretation of what's important to the parents—it's getting ahead, getting the grades, getting into the best school."[19]

The most powerful and consistent message that our culture sends to young people is that the purpose of life is material success. For middle-class suburban children, the goal may be getting into the best college and getting a good job or striking it rich in the Silicon Valley or buying Polo shirts. For poor inner-city children, the goal may be making it big as a rap star or basketball player or buying FUBU merchandise. But the goal is essentially the same: money to buy things. Our children's idea of the good life is tied inextricably to material things.

Our children today live in a culture that, in the words of Sylvia Ann Hewlett and Cornel West, "venerates the market."[20] The values of the marketplace—a focus on material things, profit maximization, competition, instant gratification—reign above and threaten to destroy such virtues as sacrifice, commitment, dedication, duty, and responsibility. The market thrives on and promotes the exaltation of the self. And increasingly, the market embraces and cultivates the most base and crass aspects of human nature.[21] Increasingly, children are seen as means and not ends. Our children have become the main targets of marketers and advertisers intent on feeding their already well-developed consumer appetites. The problem is that this is not just about buying and selling products and services. It is about cultivating a worldview and a way of life that make the individual sovereign, unconnected in any serious way to any enduring sources of meaning. We have raised a material generation (to paraphrase Madonna, one of its icons) that lives in a material world.

Our veneration of the marketplace has, in effect, so coarsened our children's lives (through a media that has in effect been parenting our children by cultivating within them a voracious appetite for vice) that it is nearly impossible to preserve our children's innocence. My thirteen-year-old son said to my husband a year or so ago that he was sorry that we had sent him to summer camp because he had heard so much bad language there that now he is more tempted "to curse and take the Lord's name in vain."

The predominant and growing values of our age are materialism and self-gratification—the very antithesis of the aims of moral education, the very antithesis of the aims of good parenting. This cultural ethos has already exacted its toll on family life and on children. It has encouraged parents—mothers and fathers alike—to reduce their commitments to family. It has weakened the bonds of family as individual members—mothers and fathers—pursue their own personal fulfillment, leaving behind a growing population of children of divorce. It has encouraged people who are not married to have children without the commitment of marriage, even though they may actually be living together, on the theory, in some cases, that they do not have enough money to get married. It has emptied our homes of parents, as more and more mothers and fathers find the work of caring for, nurturing, and guiding children no match for the excitement and financial enticement of the workplace. Still others work overtime, not out of great affection for their work but in order to be able to afford the material things that the market tells them they must have. It has driven our children to put in their own overtime hours on homework, as the pressure and competition for grades (which are deemed essential for admission to the best schools in order to get the best jobs) send more and more children to special schools to prepare them for the standardized tests on which so much of their future success now seems to rest.

Under the influence of a psychology of self-esteem, many parents have lost sight of their obligation to provide moral leadership to their children, opting instead to live by the rules of what sociologist William Doherty has called a "consumer culture of childhood and a therapeutic culture of parenthood," in which parenting is focused on satisfying children's wants and desires, and parents substitute money spent on children for time spent with children.

There can be no greater indictment of our market veneration than a recent survey in which children were asked whether they wished their parents would spend more time with them. The result: "What the largest proportion of children [say] that they want is for their mothers and their fathers to make more money."[22] In too many cases we have made the market our god and material success our religion.

But our children are not just material beings; they are also spiritual beings. This is why, notwithstanding our nation's material progress, there is a deep sadness and sickness in the souls of so many of our children. It is this sadness and sickness that the surveys and polls are diagnosing.

In such a world, it is no surprise that our children have such difficulty doing the right thing—that they do not know how to behave. Every day, most of us vote against our children by going along with the tide—by watching silently as our culture and our children slide away from morality.

Our children simply reflect our culture. They reflect the adults who are around them and who have no moral right to point fingers at their children unless and until they change their own lives. And therein lies the most important challenge that faces us as parents.

Former White House speechwriter Peggy Noonan, in a *Wall Street Journal* article entitled "The Culture of Death," described the conditions that gave rise to the tragedy at Columbine High School: "[M]ost of the children who get into terrible trouble and wind up with guns in their hands don't have anyone to counter the culture. There are a number of reasons. But lately, I think that a great one is this: So many parents themselves are bound down by the culture, by the sickness of it, which they bear as a weight on their shoulders."[23]

The goal of giving our children a "good life" has been perverted and is now deeply entangled with a cultural ethos that is causing our children profound harm. But parents themselves are deeply entangled as well. The question is whether we have been so desensitized by the culture that we cannot see the need to extricate ourselves and our children from it.

This is a defining moment for parents. Can we muster the courage and the strength to rescue ourselves and our children?

What is at stake is nothing less than our ability to raise fully "human" beings.

REVIVING A SPIRIT OF "HOME TRAINING" FOR THE TWENTY-FIRST CENTURY

The stakes that are now so high are getting higher. The forces that are promoting the moral slide of our children will only intensify in the coming century as new, more intrusive, and pervasive technologies are used to advance the reign of marketplace values. All the corporate players who have used television so successfully to cultivate the spirit of wanting in our culture are trying hard, despite recent reversals, to figure out how to use the Internet to generate huge profits from e-commerce.[24] As the journalist Thomas Friedman has put it, "When you take such a totally open network, and you combine it with parents' being able to spend less time building their kids' internal codes and filters, and then you add the fact that the Internet is going to become the nervous system of our commerce and society, you have a potentially dangerous cocktail. . . . [U]nless parents are building kids with sound fundamentals—with the individual judgment, values and knowledge skills to handle this technology on their own—Lord only knows what can happen. It can be like everyone letting their kids drive without a license, map or sense of purpose."[25]

To reverse our children's moral slide and to prepare them for the unprecedented moral challenges that the new technologies will foist upon them, parents will need at least five basic resources: (1) a moral purpose in parenting; (2) a willingness to teach and model the virtues we want our children to embody; (3) more time for our children; (4) supportive moral communities; and (5) a readiness to fight back against a culture that is harming our children.

Moral Purpose

As James Q. Wilson has argued, "Most of us have a moral sense, but . . . some of us have tried to talk ourselves out of it."[26] We must talk ourselves back into having a moral sense. We must put ourselves to the task of rediscovering the teleology of parenting.

In *A Call to Civil Society*, a 1998 report to the nation issued by the Council on Civil Society, over twenty leading scholars and activists of diverse backgrounds and varied political views concluded: "What ails our democracy is not simply the loss of certain organizational forms, but also the loss of certain organizing ideals—moral ideals that authorize our civic creed, but do not derive from it. At the end of this century, our most important challenge is to strengthen the moral habits and ways of living that make democracy possible."[27]

In American culture today, there is a profound uneasiness about the public discussion of morality. Our choice of language expresses that discomfort as we shy away from the use of the words *moral* and *virtue,* which suggest binding principles, in favor of the more relativistic word *values,* which suggests more malleable preferences. One reason for our reluctance to speak in moral terms may be what has become a profound national wariness of religion, prompted in part by constitutional concerns and in part by a widespread desire in our culture not to be bound by any rules other than those of our own choosing. But our reluctance to use moral language has left our children profoundly confused and morally adrift. We ignore the resources of our moral vocabulary and the resources of religion at our peril.

In the words of the Council on Civil Society, "If a central task of every generation is moral transmission, religion is a primary force in American life—historically, it has been *the* primary force—that transmits from one generation to another the moral understandings that are essential to liberal democratic institutions. Religion is especially suited to this task because it focuses our minds and hearts on obligations to each other that arise out of our shared createdness. By elevating our sights toward others and toward ultimate concerns, religious institutions help us turn away from self-centeredness, or what Tocqueville terms 'egotism,' democracy's most dangerous temptation, through which 'citizens have no sympathy for any but themselves.'"[28]

Our children need a strong, well-developed moral sense and a captivating vision of the "good," as it has been understood through time, to serve as antidotes to all that is morally debasing in our culture. If we are to rescue our children, we must be prepared to share with them a morally robust vocabulary drawing on the rich resources of the world's great religions.

A Willingness to Struggle to Teach and Model Virtues

With children, much more is caught than taught. As every parent knows, children learn more from what we do than what we say. When we look at our children, if we are honest we must see ourselves. They reflect us and what we truly value, as opposed to what we say we value. If we really want our children to change, we must change. If we want them to be virtuous, we must make the sacrifices in our own lives that enable our children to see how it is done. We ourselves must first become what we wish our children to become.

Time

Moral education takes time. Time is the resource that enables us to walk with our children—to be in companionship with them so that they will know that we love them and so that they can be our apprentices, witnesses to our struggle to live the virtues we espouse.

Supportive Moral Communities

Strong families alone cannot stand against the cultural tide that is engulfing our children. As sociologist David Popenoe has observed: "For the moral development of children, no aspect of community support is more important than the community's ability to reinforce the social expectations of parents; that is to express a consensus of shared values. . . . [Children] need not only a social community but a *moral* community."[29] Parents will need to join with other parents and extended family, neighbors, friends, faith communities, and the larger community to negotiate new social understandings and new commitments to each other and to each other's children.[30]

Parents must join together in community centers and churches, synagogues, and mosques throughout the nation and struggle to come to agreement on a core of moral values that can guide them in establishing new moral communities for the children of their neighborhoods, so that they will be able to say to their children in good conscience, "go outside and play."[31]

A Readiness to Do Battle with the Culture

The battle lines should by now be clear. Parents are facing a culture that is driven by what is among the most powerful drives: greed. We, too, are bound up in it. We must somehow summon the courage and the resources to free ourselves from it. We need to discern anew what the mission of parenting is and we must bring to that mission as much creativity and relentlessness as the best advertisers and marketers bring to their mission of cultivating a taste for self-centeredness and materialism among our children.

Here is our advantage: Parents are everywhere in this culture. Parents are in the corporations that are polluting our children's minds and souls. We are in the growing standardized testing industry that is driving our children to judge their worth based on how well they can score on tests. Parents hold powerful positions in the corporations that are supporting early childhood education, school vouchers, scholarships for minority students, chiefly as a means of guaranteeing a supply of good workers. Our challenge is to figure out how to use our well-earned positions in these places to rescue our children.

It is time for parents to fight back. We were not given the blessing of children to deliver them unto the marketplace. In our hearts and in our souls we know that they are in our care for better and higher purposes.

CONCLUSION

Over the past several years, every time children have taken up arms and engaged in some act of terror and violence, politicians and other leaders have called for a range of responses and issued calls for parents to "spend more quality time with their children." The devotion of more time—quality or otherwise—is a necessary, but not sufficient, condition for addressing the moral crisis facing our young people. The time spent with children must be intentional and focused on strengthening their moral armor.

Parents must be called back to the home front to secure our children's moral defenses.

I have no desire to undo the gains of the women's movement; I am simply arguing that *someone*—father, mother, guardian, mentor—must make it his or her business to secure the children's moral foundations. In every home, someone must make it his or her first and most important job to revive some notion of "home training." Someone must take responsibility for protecting and defending the physical, emotional, and spiritual spaces in which our children can be grounded morally and grow spiritually. In every neighborhood, parents must come together to create larger and larger protected spaces—spaces of shared values where adults can once again watch out for and watch over each other's children. And parents must venture out to do battle with a culture that seems more and more intent on destroying our children's humanity.

On this earth, we are our children's best—and only—hope.

NOTES

1. Public Agenda, *Kids These Days '99: What Americans Really Think about the Next Generation* (New York: Public Agenda, 1999), 2.

2. *Kids These Days '99*, 3.

3. *Kids These Days '99: Online Press Release* (Public Agenda, 1999), 9.

4. Character Counts, *1998 Report Card on the Ethics of American Youth* (Josephson Institute of Ethics, 1998), 1.

5. *Nationwide Survey on Youth Violence and Ethics* (Josephson Institute of Ethics, 1999).

6. See Robert Blendon et al., "The 60's and the 90's," *Brookings Review* (Spring 1999): 14–17.

7. *Kids These Days '99: What Americans Really Think*, 5.

8. *Kids These Days '99*, 5.

9. "What's the Problem?" *New York Times*, Week in Review, August 1, 1999, D4.

10. I was born in Panama of West Indian heritage. I left Panama in 1962 to live with my aunts and an uncle in Brooklyn, New York, in a community with a sizable West Indian and African American population.

11. Mary Pipher, *The Shelter of Each Other* (New York: Ballantine Books, 1996), 70, 71.

12. Proverbs 22:6.

13. Amitai Etzioni, *The New Golden Rule: Community and Morality in a Democratic Society* (New York: Basic Books, 1996), 167, 176.

14. Jeffrey M. Schwartz, *A Return to Innocence: Philosophical Guidance in an Age of Cynicism* (New York: Regan Books, 1998), 101.

15. See James Q. Wilson, *The Moral Sense* (New York: Free Press, 1993), xii.

16. Robert Coles, *The Moral Intelligence of Children: How to Raise a Moral Child* (New York: Random House, 1997), 184.

17. *Moral Intelligence of Children,* 5.

18. See Schwartz, *A Return to Innocence.*

19. Quoted in Laura Schlessinger, "Which Are Better: Smart Kids or Good Kids?" *USA Weekend* (January 15–17, 1999), 5.

20. Sylvia Ann Hewlett and Cornel West, *The War Against Parents: What We Can Do for America's Beleaguered Moms and Dads* (New York: Houghton Mifflin, 1998), 36.

21. See, for example, Douglas Rushkoff, *Coercion: Why We Listen to What "They" Say* (New York: Riverhead Books, 1999), and James B. Twitchell, *Lead Us into Temptation: The Triumph of American Materialism* (New York: Columbia University Press, 1999).

22. Ellen Galinsky, "Do Working Parents Make the Grade?" *Newsweek* (August 30, 1999): 52. The children's emphasis on making more money may well be tied to the fact that money issues are a source of great stress for many families.

23. Peggy Noonan, "The Culture of Death," *Wall Street Journal,* April 22, 1999, A22.

24. See Rushkoff, *Coercion,* and Twitchell, *Lead Us into Temptation.*

25. Thomas Friedman, "Are You Ready?" *New York Times,* June 1, 1999, A23.

26. See Wilson, *The Moral Sense,* ix.

27. *A Call to Civil Society: Why Democracy Needs Moral Truths* (New York: Institute for American Values, 1998), 15.

28. *A Call to Civil Society,* 8.

29. David Popenoe, "The Roots of Declining Social Virtue: Family, Community, and the Need for a 'Natural Communities Policy,'" in Mary Ann Glendon and David Blankenhorn, eds., *Seedbeds of Virtue* (Lanham, Md.: Madison Books, 1995), 73.

30. For example, Character Counts, sponsored by the Josephson Institute, promotes six basic pillars of character: trustworthiness, respect, responsibility, fairness, caring, and good citizenship. The goal has been to mobilize communities, adults and children alike, to consider what each pillar means and how it should be manifest in the behavior of members of the community. For example, what does it mean to be trustworthy? Respectful? Responsible? Fair? Caring? And a good citizen? In communities like Albuquerque and Roswell, New Mexico, people struggled to do what might be called personal and community audits to see how their behavior stacks up against the six pillars and to make the personal changes necessary to change community norms. This is not an easy thing to do. But these cities have tried to build a new moral consensus around certain basic values to help bring an end to the moral confusion in the lives of their children.

31. *A Call to Civil Society,* 8.

2

Empty Parenthood: The Loss of Parental Authority in the Postmodern Family

David Elkind

Parenthood, the child-rearing authority with which mothers and fathers are empowered, is always socially determined. The extent of this child-rearing authority must, therefore, reflect the beliefs and values of the society in which it is exercised. When society undergoes a major transformation, parental authority must also be redefined. In the United states, over the past half-century, we have experienced a sea change in the ways in which we see ourselves and our world. This transmutation has been called the movement from the *modern* to the *postmodern.*[1] It has impacted upon all of our social institutions, from science to government and from the arts to religion. It has also changed the character of our families and, in so doing, has emptied parenthood of much of the authority it enjoyed in the modern era.

The very same postmodern innovations that have undermined parental authority have, paradoxically, also created a greater need for the exercise of this authority. In the postmodern world, children and youths have become a niche market for everything from designer clothing to television programs, movies, and video games rife with sex and violence. Today, when young people need parental authority the most, they get it the least. In this chapter, therefore, I want to describe the postmodern paradox of the loss of parental regulatory power at a time when young people are most in need of parental guidance and limit setting. I will also touch on some of the consequences of this paradox for children, for parents, and for the conception of parenthood itself.

David Elkind, professor of child studies at Tufts University, is the author of many books, including *The Hurried Child: Growing Up Too Fast Too Soon* and *Ties That Stress: The New Family Imbalance.*

To accomplish these aims, it is first necessary to describe the movement from modernity to postmodernity and how this has been mirrored by the parallel shift from the modern nuclear family to the postmodern permeable family. In so doing, I will argue that it is the ascendance of the permeable family, as the dominant family structure in America, that accounts for the loss of authority by many contemporary parents. The chapter closes with a description of a new family form, the vital family, that combines the best of modern and postmodern parental authority.

PARENTAL AUTHORITY IN THE MODERN ERA

Modernity emerged in the sixteenth century when the tenets of science, rather than those of a monarchy or the Church, became the guiding principles and model for human thought and action. Modern science was based on the belief in reason as the final arbiter of truth and the conviction that the world was ruled by the principles of progress, universality, and regularity.

With the aid of reason and the scientific method—namely, experimentation—it was believed that we would progressively acquire the knowledge and skills that would lead to fuller and happier lives for the whole of humanity. The knowledge so acquired was thought to be universal and to transcend the time and place where it was first discovered. Newton's laws of gravitation provided the model for such universality. Finally, the natural laws discovered by science were regarded as regular and to brook of no exceptions. As Einstein said, "God does not play dice with the universe."

Because America was founded during the modern period, modern beliefs were reflected in all of its social institutions. Education is a case in point. The age grading of our "universal" free public schools, first mandated in the 1830s, embodied the belief that the accumulation of knowledge and skills by the child paralleled the progressive acquisition of knowledge by science. Likewise, it was believed that the laws of learning, such as formal discipline (the learning of the classics to train the mind to think logically), were universal. And finally, the acquisition of knowledge and skills was regarded as regular and to follow a necessary sequence— say, arithmetic before algebra.

The modern nuclear family incorporated these foundation beliefs as well. The structure of the nuclear family, two parents (one parent working, one parent home to rear the children) was regarded as the end result of an evolutionary progress that overcame such primitive practices as polygamy and polyandry. The nuclear family was also thought to be the universal form toward which all families were evolving. And, finally, the nuclear family was held up to be the social and moral ideal against which all other family forms were to be measured and evaluated.

It was, however, the sentiments of the nuclear family (Shorter 1977)— rather than its structure or functions per se—from which modern parents drew their authority. One of these sentiments was that of *romantic love*. This belief, which emerged in the nineteenth century, was the radical idea that young people should have the freedom to choose their own mates. Up until this time, marriages were arranged by family or the community for social class and/or economic reasons. Romantic love, in contrast, was founded upon the quixotic idea that there was one and only one person in the whole world who was meant for you, and once you found that person you would fall in love, marry, and live happily ever after.

One consequence of the sentiment of romantic love was that young women "saved" themselves for their fated partner. Virginity had value, inasmuch as husbands were duty bound to remain faithful to their wives in return for the wife's chastity prior to marriage. The modern mother's premarital virginity buttressed her parenthood role as the provider of moral and spiritual authority. Fathers, too, gained a quality of moral integrity for their faithfulness to their wives. Romantic love thus gave modern parents a, perhaps unconscious, sense that they were entitled to be the purveyors of manners and morals to their children.

Romantic love, to the extent that it reinforced chastity prior to marriage and fidelity afterward, reinforced and supported religious and spiritual values. In the modern era, in lieu of the many preoccupations of the present day, religion took up much of the recreational time families now spend watching television, going to athletic events, and so on. The Bible was the most read book in the country, and by the time most young people had reached adulthood they had gone through the Bible at least sixteen times. The religious orientation and observances of the modern nuclear family thus lent parents a spiritual as well as a moral authority.

There was also an economic dimension to this moral and religious authority. Although consumerism was well established (e.g., most families had pianos in their homes even if they could ill afford them and even if no one in the family played them), it was not anywhere near as pervasive as it is today. Parents, by and large, did not spend a great deal upon themselves and the craze for designer labels had not yet emerged. Particularly during the Depression and the years during and following the Second World War, parents displayed a financial discipline and restraint that added to their moral and religious authority.

A second sentiment of the modern nuclear family was that of *maternal love*. This was the belief that women had a maternal instinct, an innate need to care for and to nurture their children. The concept of maternal love greatly extended the modern woman's parenthood authority, particularly in the late modern era—after the Civil War. With industrialization, the movement to cities, and the predominance of factory work, women gave up the provider role they had shared with their husbands when the family farmed (Bernard 1981). Child rearing and nurturing now became primarily a maternal task, and mothers took authority for making most of the child-rearing decisions.

The division of labor between mothers and fathers in the nuclear family was emphasized by the third sentiment of the nuclear family—namely, *domesticity* (Matthews 1987). If the father was the provider of food, clothing, and shelter by his labors in the outside world of factories, the mother became the manager of a clean, well-ordered, and nurturing household. The crystallization of these roles around the turn of the century was epitomized both by the identification of home economics (and its spokesperson Betty Crocker) with motherhood and femininity and the identification of the provider role with maleness and masculinity. Through these identifications modern parents assumed the authority to be *gender* and *vocational* role models for their children.

The value of the modern nuclear family was that of *togetherness* (Elkind 1994). In essence, togetherness meant that the family took precedence over the individual. When men filled the provider role, they did this for the family because work was often hard, repetitive, and tedious. Mothers likewise devoted themselves to their families at the expense of pursuing their own talents and interests. A concrete expression of this togetherness was family meal time. Being present at meal times took priority over any other activity. Togetherness meant that individuals had to sacrifice individual needs and interests on behalf of the family. Sacrifice on the part of modern parents yielded still another parenthood regulatory power—namely, emotional authority. Although often unverbalized, the sacrifice of parents on behalf of their children made many children feel (in part unconsciously) emotionally indebted and committed to their parents.

Parenthood in the modern nuclear family was thus empowered with moral and spiritual, child-rearing, gender-vocational role modeling and emotional authority. Society as a whole recognized and supported this authority, and parenthood was highly regarded as the primary means of perpetuating a democratic and moral society. Nonetheless, the clear-cut role differentiation and well-defined parenthood authority of the late modern nuclear family had drawbacks as well as benefits. Having definite and delimited powers and responsibilities removes the need to make choices and to exercise options— both of which can be stressful (Fromm 1941). On the other hand, fixed roles can be confining and debilitating. Women increasingly chafed under the limits of the nuclear family sentiments (Friedan 1963). Fathers who, for whatever reason, could not fulfill the provider role often felt guilty and inadequate and, not infrequently, took their frustration out on their wives and their children.

Put differently, there was often considerable discrepancy between the idealized nuclear family, the proscribed parental roles, and the reality of many modern families. For example, it must be admitted that not all the children for whom parents made material and psychological sacrifices were grateful for what they had received. It must also be said that some modern parents used their emotional authority as a kind of guilt-inducing blackmail: "After all I did for you, you can't even pick up the phone and call," or other similar complaints. Some modern parents therefore abused their emotional authority to bludgeon their children with guilt. For the most part, however, nuclear family sentiments and values bound parents and children together in emotionally healthy ways.

Although mothers and fathers were allotted most of the parenthood authority in the modern era, schools were already taking on some of what were once parental responsibilities. That is to say, the loss of parental authority did not begin during the modern era; it has only accelerated in pace. When America was largely an agrarian society, parents did most of the vocational training. In addition, some young people were apprenticed out to skilled craftsmen with whom the young person lived while he or she was being trained. In most cases it was young men who were apprenticed out, but in poor families young women might train away from home as domestics.

With the movement of farm families to the cities, however, and the employment of parents in factories, there was a new separation between home and workplace, and most parents had neither the skills nor the machines to provide vocational training. To be sure, mothers might teach their daughters some cooking and sewing skills, just as fathers might teach their sons the use of basic tools, but by and large, vocational training was shifted to the schools, where it remains today. For boys, modern schools had wood and machine shops and courses in mechanical drawing. For girls, there were courses in bookkeeping, stenography, typing, and shorthand.

The provision of free public schooling and the schools' assumption of authority for vocational training created a dynamic tension between schools and parents regarding their respective roles in the socialization of the young. Toward the end of the nineteenth century, the schools themselves began to debate their educational mission. Were they to prepare children in the classical manner by teaching them Greek, Latin, and the arts, or were they, as John Dewey (1943) argued, to prepare them to live productively in contemporary society?

The new and growing field of child study contributed to the debate. As more information accrued as to the novel ways in which children understand themselves and the world, the Dewey camp eventually won out. Increasingly, school curricula became progressive, adapted to the developing needs, interests, and abilities of children. Some educators went too far, however, and accommodated to children at the expense of inculcating basic skills and knowledge. By mid-century, progressive education was discredited and the pendulum swung back to a focus upon the basics (Cremin 1961). The debate continues today over those who would have children learn a fixed body of skills and knowledge (e.g., E. D Hirsch 1988) and those who place the encouragement of motivation and interest ahead of curriculum goals (e.g., Elkind 1987).

What is striking about modern educational writers is the fact that they saw the school and the family as distinct and separate institutions. In John Dewey's most comprehensive book on education, *Democracy and Education* (1916), neither parents nor family are to be found in the index. Nor is there any mention of parents or family in Lawrence Cremin's history of the progressive education movement, *The Transformation of the School* (1961). This omission was not a sign of neglect but rather an acknowledgment of their separate spheres of influence and activity. Although Dewey wrote that the school should want for its pupils what every parent wants for his or her child, school and family had different agendas. In many ways, the separation of school and family was an index of the societal respect accorded parental authority in the modern era.

PARENTHOOD IN THE POSTMODERN ERA

Like modernity itself, postmodernity has not happened all at once or all in the same place. It is a movement that began with challenges to the modern faith in reason and the beliefs in progress, universality, and regularity. Modernity was modeled after the physical sciences, within whose confines these principles have a certain validity. When the social sciences emerged in the nineteenth century, they naturally adopted the paradigm of the physical sciences. In many respects, postmodernity can be looked upon as the realization that the principles that hold true for the physical sciences may not hold equally true for the social sciences.

Reason itself is ambiguous, inasmuch as it is mediated by language, which always has multiple levels of meaning (Rorty 1989). Likewise, the principle of progress can hardly be applied to the twentieth century, which was witness to the creation and use of weapons of mass destruction that have killed more people than ever before in history. In addition, while most physical and biological laws are universal, this is much less true for social and psychological principles. The Marxian prophecy of the rise of the proletariat was never fulfilled. In the same way, Freud's postulation of a universal Oedipal conflict hardly seem applicable to single-parent families.

The principle of regularity, in turn, has even been challenged in the physical domain, where the phenomena of indeterminacy and chaos are now recognized. A few physical phenomena, such as the weather, are irregular by nature. Uncertainty, however, is the rule in the realm of social science. A classroom, for example, is a chaotic phenomenon. Each time a class meets, each of its members, thanks to his or her unique experiences in the interim, is different than he or she was at the prior meeting. Social phenomena must thus be studied using different methods than in the physical sciences.

Postmodernity, while recognizing the value and importance of reason and of the principles of progress, universality, and regularity, nonetheless argues that these dicta must be complemented by the additional principles of difference, particularity, and irregularity (Connor 1989). And these postmodern principles are increasingly finding their way into the arts, industry, and technology. They have also become the foundation for what has emerged as the postmodern *permeable* family (Elkind 1994).

As a result of the many changes in our society beginning at mid-century, the boundaries of the nuclear family—the clear separation between home and workplace, between public and private life, and between children and parents—have become increasingly porous. In many instances the homeplace has become the workplace (with 30 million home offices) and the workplace the homeplace (with thousands of companies providing on-site child-care services). Likewise, even the most intimate details of our private lives have become daily media fare. Finally, the difference between children and adults has been obscured by, among other things, dressing children like adults and treating them as competent to deal with all of the stressors of postmodern life.

The boundaries of the postmodern family have not only become permeable, they have also been greatly expanded. That is to say, the permeable family encompasses a number of different family forms. It includes not only the traditional nuclear family, but also two-parent working families, single-parent families, remarried families, adopted families, as well as families whose children have special needs. With the rise of the permeable family, the nuclear family has lost its status as the evolutionary endpoint and moral standard for all families.

As part of this transformation process, the sentiments of the nuclear family have been reconstructed as well. The sexual revolution of the 1960s had the effect of making premarital sex socially acceptable within American society.

This has undermined the sentiment of romantic love and the belief in fated partners. Today it is generally accepted that one has to experiment a bit to find the person to whom one is best suited. The result is the sentiment of *consensual love.* Consensual love is based upon mutual agreement and with the recognition that either person has the option to terminate the relationship. This type of love acknowledges the fact that marriages are not made in heaven and that some trial and error may be necessary in order to find the most compatible marital partner. Computer dating is a case in point. By the time most contemporary young people marry, they have had several sexual relationships and may even have cohabited with several different partners.

Thanks to the sentiment of consensual love, virginity has lost its value. It can no longer be exchanged for a promise of fidelity on the part of the husband. The engagement in consensual love prior to marriage has thus weakened the commitment to marriage itself (Blankenhorn 1995). With the demise in the belief of a fated, one and only partner, it is now entirely conceivable to look elsewhere if you are unhappy with your spouse. As a consequence of this new outlook, the idea of divorce is more socially acceptable and less guilt inducing. Added to this is the passage of no-fault divorce laws that have made divorce much easier than it was in the modern era. Finally, the movement of women into the paid workforce has removed the economic dependence of women as a reason to remain in an unhappy marriage. Taken together, these three changes have made divorce a permanent feature of permeable family life. About 50 percent of marriages will end in divorce.

The prevalence of premarital sexual behavior and of divorce has lessened the moral authority of parenthood. Because the commitment to marriage is less, infidelity among both husbands and wives is more common than it was in the modern era. As a consequence, parents can no longer claim the moral high road if they themselves have been sexually active and perhaps cohabited before marriage. Extramarital affairs and divorce further weaken parental moral authority. At the same time, because adolescents model their behavior after that of adults, they have become more sexually active than ever before.

The economic factor plays a role as well. In the postmodern world, consumerism has become part of the American psyche. It has affected the parent–child relationship in many different ways. For example, a mother told me that she was afraid to take her attractive tow-haired child to the mall for fear he would be abducted. When I suggested that in that case she not go to the mall, she replied, "I can't do that, I'm a shopaholic." In addition, parents find themselves maneuvered by their children into buying products sold to the children via television commercials. Finally, those parents who are victims of consumerism may buy themselves luxuries at the expense of buying necessities for the home or for their children. Parents' acceptance of consumerism contributes to the loss of their moral stature.

As a result of their acceptance of consensual love and consumerism, parents have lost their moral authority at a time in history when their offspring are in desperate need of guidance and limits. Illustrative of this postmodern loss of parental moral authority is the trouble many contemporary parents have in asking their adolescents to refrain from premarital sexual activity and drug use when they themselves have engaged in these activities. Consensual love, together with consumerism, has emptied postmodern parenthood, to some extent, of its privileged position as a purveyor of high moral and spiritual values.

Permeable family parents have also lost much of their spiritual authority as we have become a much more secular society. Until just the past few years, membership in all of the major religious denominations has been declining. For two-working-parent families, for example, Sunday may be the only day for catching up on shopping and other household chores. Most food and many clothing and department stores are now open on Sunday. In many states, liquor is now sold on Sundays as well. The new secularism has, as a consequence, lessened postmodern parents' spiritual authority.

The modern sentiment of maternal love has also been deconstructed. With our movement from an industrial to a postindustrial information society, the nature of the workforce has changed. Factories required male brawn. Information industries, however, require brains. Inasmuch as women have as much or more intelligence than men, women have entered the workforce in increasing numbers, and this is simply a reality of the postmodern world. Today, more than 60 percent of mothers with children under the age of six are in the workforce full or part time. We appreciate today that humans are not ruled by instinct in the sense of following a preprogrammed pattern of behavior. Although many women find child rearing and homemaking totally fulfilling, many others do not. In place of the maternal instinct, we now accept the sentiment of *shared parenting*. This sentiment is to the effect that child-rearing authority must be vested in both parents and may also be shared as well with relatives and with nonparental caregivers.

It is the sentiment of shared parenting that has led to the loss of postmodern parenthood's child-rearing authority for the care of infants and young children. This authority, once the sole province of mothers, is now shared with nonparental caregivers—home care, child-care centers, au pair, and other arrangements. Parents who once had full responsibility for their children's feeding, toileting, dressing, and providing play materials and instruction in manners now share these responsibilities with strangers. As more and more children are in out-of-home settings during the early years, some of the

dynamic tension between school and family that existed at the elementary-
and secondary-school level has now been extended downward to the relations
between parents and child-care providers.

With the emergence of the sentiment of shared parenting, we re-encounter
the paradox of a loss of parental authority at the very time when children are
most in need of its exercise. Television monitoring is a good example. Television is powerfully attractive, indeed addictive, to young children. Yet too
much television (more than two hours a day) induces children to get their information visually and not to develop their auditory and other sensory discrimination skills. Such skills are very important for learning to read. Parents
of young children need to exercise authority over home television watching.
But they have little or no control over how much, or what, their children
watch in out-of-home settings. This is but one example of how decreased
child-rearing authority comes just at the time when such authority is very
much needed to protect children from abuses of our postmodern technologi-
cal innovations.

The third sentiment of the nuclear family, domesticity, has been transformed as well. The advent of television, of jet travel, of superhighways and
the Internet have made families comfortable with the world at large. In addition, the prevalence of many different family forms, of fast-changing technology, and of the exposure of even young children to the worst, as well as to
the best, facets of contemporary society have made family life more hectic
and also more *urbane*. The home today is less like a *Haven in a Heartless
World* (as Christopher Lasch, in 1977, termed the nuclear family) and more
like a busy bus or railway station where people stop off to catch a meal or get
refreshed before going on to another destination.

The urbanity of the postmodern permeable family and the decline of domesticity have brought about a blurring of the once clear-cut identification of
gender and occupational roles. Mothers are no longer simply homemakers,
and fathers are no longer the sole providers. Although parents still model gender in their clothing, interests, and friendship patterns, the occupational gender definitions have become much less clear. Postmodern parenthood has thus
been emptied of some of its gender identification authority. Although this has
real benefits, it is constantly being undermined by merchandisers who wish
to make money by refurbishing stereotypical gender roles. Beauty contests
for little girls are a case in point. Gender authority is usurped by nonparental
agencies.

Finally, the value of the postmodern permeable family has also been rein-
vented. Today, the value of togetherness has been replaced by the value of *autonomy*. Given the other sentiments of the permeable family, the movement to
autonomy is understandable. This value holds that the individual's needs and

interests should take precedence over those of the family. This new family value is illustrated by the fact that now soccer practice or a business meeting may take precedence over a family meal. Similarly, in the modern family when a child returned from a party, parents asked, "Were you good?" Today, however, parents are likely to ask, "Did you have fun?"

One consequence of the value of autonomy is that parents have fewer ways to demonstrate self-sacrifice on behalf of the children and the family. In the modern nuclear family, parental sacrifice in service of the value of togetherness was built into family life. Parents routinely forsook personal interests and made financial sacrifices for the sake of the family. As we saw, this sacrifice gave modern parents emotional authority. When autonomy is the family value, it is harder for parents to demonstrate sacrifice, with the result that their parenthood often loses its emotional authority. To be sure, many contemporary parents make sacrifices about where to live, career opportunities, and the like. Yet these are more likely to be compromises and still reflect autonomy.

Again, this loss of emotional authority comes just at a time in our social history when the young need such authority as never before. From an early age, today's children learn about all the many possible terrible threats to their well-being. They are told about sexual abuse, about the effects of drugs, of the dangers of abduction, and much more. These warnings are aided and abetted by media broadcasts of the most violent examples of child abuse and of students committing murder in the schools. To buffer this onslaught, young people need the unquestioned conviction that they are cared for and that they are important in their parents' lives. Yet this need emerges just when it is a major struggle for fathers and mothers to provide it.

All of these postmodern losses of parental authority have been heralded in our media, and all have contributed to the general devaluation of parenting and parenthood in the society as a whole. In the movie *Home Alone,* the parents lose their son on the way to Europe and he manages very well without them, even outwitting two witless thugs. In the TV series *Married with Children,* the children and mother trash the father, who is presented as a hapless shoe salesman. When an au pair was charged with causing the death of an infant in her care, the child's parents were trashed by the press, while the au pair was given star treatment. When a female CEO of a major firm left to be with her family, commentators often described it as evidence of weakness rather than of courage. These are but a few of the examples of how parenting and parenthood have been devalued in our postmodern society (Mack 1997).

The devaluation of parenthood is also evident in the increasing demand that schools take over what were once parental functions, such as character and sex education. The modern separation between home and school has been replaced by the belief in "parental involvement." The demand for parental involvement reflects the implicit conviction that parents have given over too much authority to the schools and have to become involved with the schools to become reinvolved with their children. In truth, therefore, the much-lauded postmodern concern with parental involvement actually reflects a devaluation and denigration of the parents' role in child rearing. For many parents, this only adds to their anxiety and guilt about not exercising their parental authority.

In summary, the postmodern permeable family has emptied parenthood of much of the moral, spiritual, child-rearing, vocational modeling and emotional authority that it enjoyed in the modern era. The postmodern view of children and adolescents as consumers, who can be sold anything and everything in any way, ignores their innocence and inexperience. This view of young people as a market has made the exercise of parental authority even more necessary than it was in the past. Yet contemporary parents, for all the reasons outlined previously, are too often unable to provide it. The schools and social agencies have tried to fill this parental vacuum, but their staffs are overworked and underpaid. As a result, too many children are growing up without the benefits of guidance and limit setting so essential to a healthy sense of self and of social responsibility.

The end result of growing up without the protection and guidance of parental authority can be seen in behavior patterns that are all too common among young people today. Too many of our children and adolescents give evidence of a lack of a moral and spiritual compass, a deficiency of manners, a gender identity confusion, and a lack of loyalty and commitment to anything beyond a particular lifestyle. Others develop a volcano of anger that can, and unfortunately has, burst into horrifying episodes of murderous violence.

Is there any hope for turning this situation around, for restoring, to some extent, parental authority and societal respect and support for it? I believe that there is and without the necessity of returning to the traditional family. Many of the changes in the family have been extreme, perhaps necessary, to break away from traditional values. Now that most of the battles have been won, it appears that we are moving toward a more middle ground, incorporating the best of both the nuclear and the permeable families. It is hoped that this new, vital family will help restore both parental authority and the social support and respect of that authority.

REFURBISHING PARENTAL AUTHORITY: THE VITAL FAMILY

The postmodern permeable family can be looked at as an extreme, as an overreaction to some of the confinements and restraints of the nuclear family. In many respects modern parenthood had too much authority over children and youth, whereas postmodern parenthood has too little. My sense is that we are slowly moving toward a more balanced position, where parenthood is endowed with sufficient authority to ensure children's healthy growth and development but limited enough so that young people can get on with their lives, unburdened by unnecessary guilt or anxiety about overstepping parental precepts. This is the *vital* family, which meets the authority needs of both parents and children.

In vital families, the parents have moved from consensual love to *committed love*. Even though the parents may have had other sexual partners and may even have cohabited prior to marriage, they nonetheless look upon marriage as a commitment. They see marriage as a partnership that must be constantly worked at, and they are willing to make the effort. This is different from the concept of romantic love, which assumed that once you met your one and only, there was nothing else you had to do but live happily ever after. It is also different from consensual love, which sees every relationship as transitory, no matter how long it lasts.

The participation in committed love restores some of the mother's and father's moral and spiritual authority. Commitment to a relationship and to putting in the ongoing effort to make it work is a moral stance. If parents themselves are working hard at a relationship, they feel entitled to serve as a model that their children can look up to and emulate. Children also believe, quite rightly, that some of these efforts are on their behalf and are willing to invest such parents with moral authority. Children love and respect parents who differ but who can resolve their differences in healthy ways that strengthen, rather than weaken, the relationship.

The conception of shared parenting has been modified as well. Many parents of young children chose to work, even when they did not have to or want to, out of the conviction that shared parenting was the socially correct thing to do. Of course, many other parents of young children went to work out of necessity and were also looked upon as being politically correct. Contrariwise, some fathers stayed home and became house-husbands and child rearers out of a need to demonstrate a man's ability to engage in shared parenting.

More recently, we have moved away from the need to use shared parenting as an index of our position on women's rights and on male sensitivity. We have moved more toward *authentic* behavior, where parents can choose the parenting role they wish to fill on the basis of their own temperament and feelings, rather than in accord with what is politically correct for their gender at that time. We know that mothers who work out of choice are more successful at child rearing than women who work out of necessity. But it is also true that women who stay home out of choice are more successful mothers than those who stay home out of some sense of duty.

When parents feel authentic in their parenting role, they can exercise child-rearing authority with conviction, regardless of whether they are stay-at-home or working parents. It is not working or staying at home that confers true child-rearing authority in parents but, rather, their own sense of authenticity, their sense that they are doing what is best for them and for their children. For authentic parents, working is a little bit like what is advocated for parents in an airplane. They have to put their oxygen mask on before they put on the child's. Parents who authentically want to work are in effect putting on their own oxygen mask to better perform the task on their child. And children know it.

The shift to urbanity was also something of an exaggeration. Even with our busy postmodern lives, we still need a home base that is more like a home than like a busy transit terminal. Indeed, in recent years we have become increasingly aware of the importance of community in our lives. As parents become more community oriented, they also regain some of the gender identity authority. In the community, the father might coach Little League or lead a boy scout group. The mother might coach a girls' soccer team or lead a troop of girl scouts. In their avocations, particularly as evidenced in community service, parents can provide models of gender identity. By participating in community activities, parents often also revive their gender roles' authority, which might have been clouded by the disappearance of vocation as a clear index of gender identity.

Finally, another value of the permeable family, autonomy, was also an extreme. From the time of the founding of the republic, parents have had to deal with the conflicting challenges of teaching children to be individuals in accord with our economic values and to be respectful of the law in accordance with our political values (Rorty 1989). Unhappily, the modern value of togetherness went too far in the direction of community, whereas the postmodern value of autonomy went too far in the direction of individualism. The sentiment that seems most appropriate for the vital family is *interdependence.* We are all both dependent on others and also independent of them. This is true with respect to our children as well; we need them as much as they need us. If we give up something on their behalf, it is because we need them and not because we are being entirely altruistic. When we demonstrate our interdependence in many different ways, we are able to regain our emotional authority without engendering guilt.

CONCLUSION

As we have moved from a modern to a postmodern society and from a nuclear to a permeable family, parental authority has been emptied in significant ways. Modern parenthood was characterized by the exercise of moral and spiritual authority, by child-rearing authority, by the authority of gender modeling, and by emotional authority. These forms of parental authority were recognized, supported, and respected in the larger society. And they afforded young people the limits, values, and motivations they needed to develop healthy personalities. Such authority was essential to children's development as moral, responsible, productive, and caring citizens.

With the rise of the postmodern permeable family, much of the authority of modern parenthood has been lost. Postmodern parenthood is now largely devoid of its moral and spiritual authority, its child-rearing powers, its gender and occupational defining roles, and its emotional authority. As a result, society as a whole has denigrated and devalued parenthood and other social institutions, like the schools, have taken over many parental functions. At the same time, because young people are now seen as a morally unbounded niche market, parental guidance and regulatory power are needed more than they ever were before. This disparity between what young people need and what parents are able to provide has produced a generation of young people, too many of whom are growing up morally and spiritually adrift, lacking in civility, confused as to gender role, self-centered, and, sometimes, even murderously angry.

The permeable family was an extreme reaction to some of the debilitating constraints of the modern nuclear family. As these constraints have been lifted, the permeable family is now itself disappearing. In its stead we are beginning to see evidence of a new, vital family that combines the best of both family forms while discarding some of their less effective features. Parents now engage in committed love and believe in working at the marriage. This has reinvigorated their moral and spiritual authority. Contemporary parents are likely to be more authentic in their parenting and engage in those parenting practices that are genuinely themselves. In this way, they are better child rearers whether they work or stay at home. Vital family parents are also community oriented and in their volunteer actions once again offer children models for gender identity. Finally, the vital family of interdependence gives parents a way of demonstrating their caring for children without instilling a debilitating sense of guilt or indebtedness.

Parental authority is the foundation for successful parenting. The extensive authority of modern parenthood was beneficial for young people, although it was often a burden for parents. The diminished authority of postmodern parents has come at a time when the need for the exercise of this authority is greater than ever. As a result, although today's parents are less burdened with authority than in the past, this liberation is at the expense of the guilt and anxiety they feel in not providing the parental authority their children need in our contemporary society. Teachers and other social agents are too overburdened to assume the additional responsibility of parental authority. As a consequence, large numbers of our children and youth are in crises. It is hoped that the new vital family will help restore parental authority in ways that are healthy for both children and their parents.

REFERENCES

Bernard, J. (1981). "The Good Provider Role: Its Rise and Fall." *The American Psychologist* 36 (1): 1–12.

Blankenhorn, D. (1995). *Fatherless America.* New York: Basic Books.

Clarke-Stwernart, K. A. (1989). "Infant Daycare: Maligned or Malignant." *American Psychologist* 44: 266–73.

Connor, S. (1989). *Postmodern Culture.* Oxford: Basil Blackwell.

Cremin, L. (1961). *The Transformation of the School.* New York: Knopf.

——. (1990). *American Education: The Metropolitan Experience.* New York: Torchbook.

Dewey, J. (1916). *Democracy and Education.* New York: Free Press.

——. (1943). *The Child and the Curriculum: The School and Society.* Chicago: University of Chicago Press.

Elkind, D. (1987) *Miseducation.* New York: Knopf.

——. (1994). *Ties That Stress.* Cambridge, Mass.: Harvard University Press.

Friedan, B. (1963). *The Feminine Mystique.* New York: Norton.

Fromm, E. (1941). *Escape from Freedom.* New York: Rinehart & Co.

Hirsch, E. (1988). *Cultural Literacy.* New York: Vintage.

Lasch, C. (1977). *Haven in a Heartless World.* New York: Basic Books.

Mack, D. (1997). *The Assault on Parenthood.* New York: Simon & Schuster.

Matthews, G. (1987). *"Just a Housewife."* New York: Oxford University Press.

Rorty, R. (1989). *Contingency, Irony and Solidarity.* New York: Cambridge University Press.

Shorter, E. (1977). *The Making of the Modern Family.* New York: Basic Books.

NOTES

1. Postmodernism has become a kind of Rorschach card upon which people project their own worst fears and antipathies. As it is used here, however, it is merely descriptive of the many changes that have come about in our society since mid-century and that are not encompassed by the narrower terms "Postindustrial" or "Information Age."

3

From *Father Knows Best* to *The Simpsons*—On TV, Parenting Has Lost Its Halo

Bernice Kanner

When TV first burst into our collective consciousness in the 1950s, programming reflected a sanitized and idealized America and helped draw families together. Parents and their offspring gathered around what was likely their home's sole TV set to watch programs starring well-meaning parents with good children solving life's solvable problems. The family was emotionally connected and deferential to dad. It was a cheerful, innocent, genial picture of family life—the electronic equivalent to the popular "Home Sweet Home" embroidery of the time, a time when father knew best.

Father rarely knows best on prime-time TV any more. As the medium and society have evolved and programming choices exploded, the decent and happy families (caught up in Junior's development to the exclusion of outside social problems) disappeared. By the time color TV had become a fixture in American homes in the 1960s, many families owned multiple TVs and family members split off into their own rooms to watch. Programming began to cater to those diverse interests.

TV's spotlight today is on the individual more than the family. Television dads—and, to a lesser extent, moms—once portrayed as loving and wise are now depicted as neglectful, incompetent, abusive, or invisible. Parenthood, once presented as the source of supreme satisfaction on TV, is now largely ignored or debased.

Bernice Kanner wrote the "On Madison Avenue" column for *New York* magazine for many years and has been a marketing correspondent for CBS News, a marketing commentator for Bloomberg News, and a columnist for *Working Woman* magazine. She is the author of numerous articles and books, including *The 100 Best TV Commercials*.

WHY IT MATTERS

Television may be the most influential element in our lives. Jesse Jackson has called it "the third parent," and the Kaiser Family Foundation describes it as "the loudest voice in many American households." It has become an establishment whose visions we swallow whole and absorb into our "self."

It is especially influential among today's young "screen-agers." TV is on 60 hours a week in the average American household with kids. By the time high schoolers graduate, most will have spent more time with media than in school (on average, 3.5 hours a day on TV, or 18,000 hours in front of TV versus 13,000 in school).

That means ingesting a diet of sex, violence, and immorality. By sixth grade, the average student will have viewed 100,000 acts of violence, including 8,000 murders, on the tube. Watching just four videos, *Total Recall, Robocop 2, Rambo III,* and *Die Hard III,* he or she will have witnessed 525 deaths. And in one hour, on average, of MTV music videos, the young student will have observed 20 violent acts.

Popular music, with dark and hostile lyrics, also influences our children and society. The Parent's Music Resource Center reports that teens listen to an estimated 10,500 hours of rock music between the seventh and twelfth grades alone—just 500 hours less than the total time they spend in school over twelve years. Three out of four respondents to a Voter/Consumer Research panel said that the values promoted in music lyrics, as well as in movies and TV, do not represent their own values.

The conundrum has always been whether "art" leads life or reflects it. That question here is largely rhetorical, the point, moot, like chicken-egg. Whichever came first, the copy-cat copies in nanoseconds. Movies, popular music, and TV programming hold a mirror up to show us who and what we are—or perhaps secretly long to be, our idealized selves. The language of programming becomes our vernacular; their dress, our wardrobes; their mores, our customs, albeit sometimes exaggerated.

Many studies link violent, rude, or destructive behavior on TV with real-life behavior. A poll conducted for *Newsweek* in August 1999 found that 78 percent of Americans partially blamed the media for the recent mass shootings in Atlanta, California, and Colorado—just 3 percent less than those who pointed the finger at poor parental upbringing.

In 1996, according to the magazine *Headway,* 63 percent of eighteen- to thirty-year-olds blamed contemporary movies, music, and TV programs like *Melrose Place* and *Beverly Hills 90210* for fostering teenage sex. In the years since that poll was taken, TV's sexometer has only risen.

Similarly, Americans blame the cynical depiction of family on TV for contributing to the erosion of the nuclear family and of family values. A national survey commissioned by the Family Research Council found that four of every five parents believe that pop culture negatively affects children (as reported in *Headway*). "When a kid tells a teacher 'Eat my shorts,' we know he got it from Bart Simpson," noted Mary Larson, associate professor of communications at the University of Northern Illinois.

In a 1999 survey conducted for Shell Oil Co. by Peter D. Hart Research Associates, some 73 percent of Americans considered the portrayal of life and values by TV and the movies to be a major cause for kids' low values and standards. Eight percent even believe that TV has greater potential to positively shape children's moral development—more than peers and friends, more than teachers and religious officials, more even than parents. If it takes a village to raise a child, it seems the village walls need reinforcing.

A HALF CENTURY AGO

In the 1950s TV programs presented a kinder, gentler America than the loud and scary one outside their doors. David Robinson, in *The Scotsman* (March 19, 1999), described a land of "good white picket fences" where "everyone liked Ike and fought communism and had jobs and hated that new-fangled teen music and didn't worry about racism and where women knew their place." At a time (1954) when the top song was "Oh, My Papa" ("to me, he was so wonderful"), Americans embraced "the politics of the comfort blanket"—politics, according to Robinson, "whose appeal there was no denying."

One of the first shows to project this appeal was *The Adventures of Ozzie and Harriet,* which began on radio in the 1940s and migrated to TV in 1952. TV's longest-running sitcom was a case of life imitating art; members of the real-life Nelson family played themselves.

Soon afterward (1954) *Father Knows Best* starred super-dad Jim Anderson, adored and respected by his wife and children. Then came *I Love Lucy, The Donna Reed Show, The Life of Riley,* and *Good Times,* a show about a black family in an urban housing project, all with the same profamily bent.

Leave It to Beaver had it, too, although with a new twist. "The Beav," who smashes a car window and tries to keep the news from Dad and tries to give himself a haircut after losing the money earmarked for it, eschewed belly laughs for realistic humor and showed life through the eyes of a young, rambunctious boy whom trouble followed relentlessly. But it still glorified the paternalistic, middle-class life of its time.

These TV dads were strong, dependable, always available to their children, and deeply involved in their children's lives. They worked the strings to help their children choose right over wrong. The women were less prominent. Loyal and loving homemakers, they revered their husbands as more important than themselves; their advice was rarely solicited.

The TV mantra, that success and happiness hinged on dad's involvement, offered an ideological model for families to emulate. But it was also fictive propaganda. Most men were more likely away working long hours and the women, involuntarily stripped of power and marginalized, were probably inwardly seething. The shows aimed to reassert dad at the hub of the family, despite his wife's economic and social liberation during the war. Elevating him meant demoting and devaluing her, contends Nina Leibman in *The Fifties Family in Film* (1995). She points to the superfluous domestic tasks 1950s TV moms did—like arranging flowers, polishing silver, filling candy dishes—to underscore their relatively meaningless position in family life.

While magazines cautiously raised the equality issue, TV reassured mother "that housewife is the best job she can have, that she's loved for her attention to her family's needs and the ideal is invisibility," said Leibman. Women were duped into buying into this picture, Leibman theorized, because the shows were funny and, superficially, the TV moms seemed to have a stronger presence than analysis reveals.

THE 1960s AND 1970s

Even by the 1960s, the nuclear middle-class family was beginning to lose its place on center stage to supernatural situation comedies, as well as space, cop, and medical shows. Films were dominated by political thrillers, James Bond adventures, Broadway musicals translated to screen, romantic comedies, and corporate critiques. When families did appear, in addition to the nuclear ones there were often single-parent households or blends, like the *Brady Bunch*. Although they represented new demographics, they preached the same honest, upright family values. Carol Brady, a former widow, was the idealized mom, at day's end greeting her heroic husband, Mike, and three boys and three girls from merged families with a smile and eagerness to hear about their lives.

By the time *Mary Tyler Moore* debuted in the fall of 1970, new-type families were common. Mary Richards, a single woman and TV journalist, introduced another kind of family. Her boss, Lou Grant, acts as the crotchety father and news anchor Ted Baxter as the insufferable sibling, explained Robert

Thompson, a professor of film and TV at Syracuse University. The show endorsed the single life as a viable option and workplace colleagues as family. It also paved the way for *Murphy Brown,* about a journalist who juggled career and single motherhood, and *Ally McBeal,* a young Boston lawyer grappling with work, love, and co-ed bathrooms.

Conventional families—and their episodic moral lessons—still dominated. There were *The Waltons*—two parents, seven children, and a set of grandparents struggling to run a lumber mill in the rural South during the Depression. And the Ingalls—two parents and three daughters in the *Little House on the Prairie* in the American frontier of the 1870s. And the Huxtables on *The Cosby Show.*

The Huxtables were different because they were upper-middle-class blacks from Brooklyn, and mom had an outside job and was still a meaningful part in her five children's lives. But the show clung to the old mold, in that dad, played by comedian Bill Cosby, was still omnipotent and had the last word and right answer to guide and direct the children's moral well-being.

But conventions changed, as did "conventional" families, represented by the Bunkers in *All in the Family* (1971–1979). Bigoted, colorful blue-collar patriarch Archie Bunker, along with his wife, Edith; daughter, Gloria; and "meathead" son-in-law, Michael, were cruder and more realistic than their forebears. They were also more attuned to life beyond the Bunker home, including the socially divisive issues of the day.

A decade later, in *Roseanne* the blue-collar Connors clan picked up where the Bunkers left off. The characters bowled, pranced around in their undershirts, and belched; they also thought of themselves as much as of their children. Comedian Roseanne Barr goes beyond not venerating her husband; she derides him, and her two daughters and son as well. When one of them questions her meanness, she says it's "because I hate kids and I'm not your real mom." In another episode, she smirks, "They've left for school. Quick, change the locks." In still another show, when her pregnancy test is positive, hubby says, "We're not yuppies. We're supposed to have babies when we're young and stupid."

Roseanne (1989–1993) opened the gates to mean-spirited inner-directedness, epitomized by *Married with Children,* about a family of crude schemers whose aim in life seems to be to sabotage each other. And in marked contrast to the sentimental family of old, it presaged *The Simpsons,* which its creator, Matt Groening, called "the anti-Cosby show." Here, it's mother Marge who is the touchstone of reason and the moral pillar for bad boy Bart, his wise sister Lisa, baby Maggie, and bungling, screwball, but always endearing dad, Homer. Despite their political incorrectness, irreverence, and acting out of our basest impulses (or perhaps because of it), Americans have fallen for this animated clan and its muddled but sympathetic dad. A recent Yahoo poll found that we'd rather live without a bank cash card, coffee, chocolate, and even the Internet itself than without *The Simpsons.*

Even in *Home Improvement,* which some would have called an anachronistic morality tale, dad was a macho bumbler, far from the godlike creature of old, and mom, a rational and intelligent modern woman, was getting her degree in psychology. But for all the shift in power now conferred on mom, Tim-the-tool-man-Taylor was far closer to Cosby, and *Home Improvement* to its old-fashioned, familial-comedy predecessors than it was to most of the wisecracking shows of its time.

Steven Stark, in *Glued to the Set,* noted that *"Home Improvement* probed what it meant to be the best father and husband in an age of feminism and embattled male identity." It was a show about family issues. In *Friends, Beavis & Butthead, South Park,* or *Party of Five,* for example, there's no nuclear family in sight (in the latter they were killed by a drunk driver, leaving the five Salinger children to fend for themselves).

Although *Home Improvement,* which ended in 1999, was a TV star, even beating out *Seinfeld* and *Frasier* when up against them, the show's executive producer, Matt Williams, recently said he doubted that a network would buy it today. The show, which played to a mass audience, "was created to celebrate the American family, and I'm not sure you can do that in the same way now," he told the *New York Times* (May 6, 1999).

Indeed, Norman Lear, who created *All in the Family* and *The Jeffersons,* lamented the disappearance of the nuclear family from TV today. "The delight we once took in celebrating family seems to be vaporizing before us," he said. He called the plethora of shows about lone people coming together "a disease of our time," reflecting or perhaps encouraging the splintering of the family.

WHY

The networks agree that they no longer want traditional family sitcoms, but blame that on shifting viewer patterns. Cable and the Web have created so many options that parents and kids rarely watch TV together. Today, 74 percent of homes have more than one TV set, compared with 35 percent in 1970. Rather than programming to attract a wide demographic, the networks go after niches, individuals sitting alone before their individual TV sets.

In those solitary confines, solitary watchers tune in to shows that seem to glorify promiscuity, portray marriage negatively, and endorse childbearing outside marriage. Janeen Bjork, senior vice president and director of programming at Seltel Inc., a New York–based firm that advises stations on program choices, says it's hard to argue with the ratings success of these shows, which suggests "that people want something less tame and more outrageous."

Experts also say that the shows mirror socio-demographic changes sweeping the nation and consequently have replaced sitcoms of the hearth with those of the workplace. According to the Census Bureau, in 1997, for the first time in U.S. history, single-person households outnumbered households of married couples with children. For them and other Americans, work has become an increasingly prominent part of life, as the divorce rate, single parenthood, and women in the workforce have surged.

The nuclear family isn't what it used to be, says Melinda A. Blackman, a professor of industrial organizational psychology at California State University in Fullerton. Americans overall are now dedicating a third of their lives to work, which is slowly occluding family life, becoming a main priority for males and females, she says. Compare that to when the "father who knew best" came home at night, and viewers didn't even know what he did for a living. Now we rarely see TV characters at home.

Then, too, there's been a massive attitudinal shift. Nobel Laureate economist Gary Becker notes in his book *A Treatise on the Family* that women are no longer willing to subordinate themselves to men or to keep alive the fiction that men make the decisions.

Concurrently, the country is undergoing a backlash against both political correctness and sanitized, tentative, and self-conscious culture and values. Even while Hollywood studios try to avoid the death-knell NC-17 movie rating, Howard Stern tries to shock by satirizing political correctness and Beavis and Butthead pick their noses, torture pets, and play with matches—the things parents tell their kids not to do.

Then, too, Americans may simply have gotten bored with happy families. In *Anna Karenina,* Tolstoy noted the essential similarity of all happy families—resulting in dull shows about them. On the other hand, "every unhappy family is unhappy in its own fashion," the Russian novelist wrote.

TODAY

Unhappy families are as prevalent as loving ones on TV today—from the moms on Jerry Springer who admit to having affairs with their teenage daughter's boyfriends to Beavis telling Butthead that his mom is a slut. In TV land today, parent bashing is gratuitous.

Someone's called the whistle on the emperor's new clothes. Dad no longer reigns supreme. A 1999 survey sponsored by the National Fatherhood

Initiative found only four fathers out of 102 prime-time network series who are both loving and competent (*7th Heaven* on WB, *Promised Land* on CBS, *Smart Guy* on WB, and *Two of a Kind* on ABC). Dads were central, recurring figures on only 15, or 14.7 percent, of the shows. Instead, contemporary TV dads are largely either competent but uninvolved (i.e., CBS's *The Nanny* and Fox's *That '70s Show*), bumbling (Fox's Homer Simpson), or missing in action (i.e., *Buffy the Vampire Slayer, Sabrina,* and *Jessie*). Even the seemingly innocent movies *Home Alone,* where the parents leave for Paris and leave behind their eight-year-old son, and *Honey I Shrunk the Kids* (where dad turns the kids into thimble sizes) suggest that the father who once knew best now knows squat.

Traditional families are losing their perch. Not a single new NBC fall show has one; CBS has two among its six new shows, and the families on ABC's new shows are anything but conventional. In *Odd Man Out,* a fourteen-year-old boy lives with five women and must "fight his way through a sea of estrogen to find the man he will soon become," according to the network, and *Once and Again* is about "divorced parents who meet for the first time, but can't remember how to date.

TV's focus seems to be on teens and young singles in shows like *Seinfeld, Friends, The Drew Carey Show,* or *Ally McBeal* or older singles like *Frasier,* shows that, according to Brian Lowry in the *Los Angeles Times* (May 9, 1999), "wallowed in a kind of nasty self-absorption." TV today, Lowry says, exudes an "all about me" attitude "wallowing in neuroses and the unending quest for sex by urban singles" such as NBC's *Suddenly Susan, Caroline in the City,* and *The Naked Truth.*

ADLAND

Perhaps because its intent has been to sell products and ingratiate itself with potential purchasers, overall advertising has been more profamily than the programming it interrupts. *The 100 Best TV Commercials of All Time—And Why They Worked* is filled with examples of positive family life.

In 1981, AT&T's heart-tugging vignette of an aging mother moved to tears by her grown son Joey calling "just because I love you" reached out and touched us.

In 1990, Hallmark presented the 100th birthday of a spunky black grandma surrounded by her adoring family and friends. In an earlier spot grandma sifted through a lifetime of greeting cards, recalling her life as movers loaded her furniture on a truck. McDonald's ads have catered to America's hunger for family values. Its Super Bowl 1992 ode to peewee football honored dads—arms outstretched, posing as goal posts, for whom a good day wasn't determined by who won but by being with their sons. Steven Spielberg was so charmed by it that he created the movie *Little Giants,* based on it.

Family life has long been celebrated by Eastman Kodak. In its 1988 classic "Daddy's Little Girl" the father of the bride dances with his daughter on her wedding day, as he reminisces about her childhood. And Campbell has long equated serving soup with mother love. In one recent spot, a young child arrives at her new foster home, overwhelmed, withdrawn, and speechless, until her foster mother brings her a steaming bowl of Campbell's soup. That opens the door to a relationship.

Volvo has built a reputation as family-friendly, partly because of a 1976 spot in which worried parents only allow their daughter to go out in a storm if her date drives dad's Volvo. And John Hancock Financial Services carved a niche by showing dad cooing to his infant daughter about his hopes and dreams, suggesting that it understood people and their needs. More recently, an ad for the insurer asks a middle-ager to choose between educating her children and taking care of her parents. Narrator Sigourney Weaver asks, "Whose eyes can you look into and say you just can't help? For in both, you will surely see your own."

ADVERTISERS ACT

But it's not just the ads themselves but the actions of the advertisers that suggest a rebirth of family values. In 1996 Procter & Gamble Co. pulled its advertising from four popular talk shows because they feature "gratuitous sex, foul language, and references to violence." Last year P&G and other advertisers formed a coalition to do something about the problem. This year they acted.

Johnson & Johnson; P&G; along with AT&T; Coca-Cola; Ford Motor; General Motors; I.B.M.; McDonald's; Nestle; Pfizer; Sears, Roebuck; Warner-Lambert; and Wendy's International—which spend millions each year on TV—voted to foot the bill to develop creatively written family-friendly programming to run on the WB network. The advertisers also set up an awards show to honor family fare and have considered voluntarily paying premiums to run commercials during family programs.

Robert L. Wehling, corporate officer for global marketing at P&G, said the move wasn't about complaining, whining, or censorship, just "more choices we don't have to think twice about. We need to show this programming has a market and to show it can be financially successful for advertisers and networks. Some people are very clear they're after the teen-age and young adult urban audience that wants edgier programming, and that's O.K. We're not trying to take away choices. All we're asking for is an expansion of the choices available to us."

Andrea Alstrup, vice president for advertising at Johnson & Johnson, said that the group acted out of frustration in finding appropriate shows that families can watch together without embarrassment. That doesn't mean sanitized, she said, noting that programs such as *7th Heaven* often focus on issues like drug use, adultery, and sexual activity among teens, but they're in a context of the minister's teaching his children about right and wrong. And while most of these advertisers eschew violence, many would be very comfortable sponsoring, say, *Schindler's List* about the Holocaust, she said.

Advertisers are eager to buy shows labeled as family because "they don't have to worry about their image or protests or boycotts of their products," said John Camilleri, a media supervisor at Harmelin Media, Bala Cynwyd, Pa. And the shows can command higher rates because there are more potential advertisers for them. By contrast, when *NYPD Blue* debuted with much fanfare over the show's nudity, he said, "pricing of the show was lower than the ratings it would reflect" (*Electronic Media,* March 8, 1999).

OTHER HOPEFUL SIGNS

Other grassroots groups are also fed up with the current state of programming and are vowing not to take it anymore. A full-page ad in the Sunday, August 15, 1999, *New York Times* by the Accuracy in Media organization vowed to point a finger of shame at heads of TV, movie, and music companies guilty of "the unforgivable crime" of "destroying children's morals for profit." The ad charged that "they're knowingly letting people under their control flood America with filth, sex, vulgarity and violence while they look the other way and count the money."

Ironically, the cable explosion that fueled the problem is also offering some succor. New networks such as Fox Family Channel, Pax TV, and Odyssey now describe themselves as family-friendly shows and claim that running such fare differentiates them in a world of choice. Rich Cronin, president and CEO of the Fox Family Channel, says that "family" designation "is a way to break out from the nameless, brandless networks that offer a variety of programming."

New movies have also proclaimed the daddy prince. In *Jerry McGuire* selfish toads become father figures to little boys without dads of their own, and selfless heroes to daughters in *Fly Away Home, I'll Do Anything,* and the *Father of the Bride* series. *Three Men and a Baby* confirmed the importance of dads and the place of men in children's lives. And the father figure in *Life Is Beautiful* is anything but bad or bumbling.

Studios endorse the movie-rating systems, and national music distributors have vowed to improve the Parental Advisory Program that flags CDs with explicit lyrics. A recent Kaiser Family Foundation study shows that 54 percent of parents use the TV industry's voluntary program ratings system.

Despite the fact that their share of the dial has shrunk, there are still family-friendly shows on, like *Touched by an Angel* and *Promised Land,* as well as *7th Heaven, The Hughleys, Cosby,* and *Boy Meets World.* And although executive producer Phil Rosenthal said that the networks wanted "edgier, hipper, not so family," CBS bought his *Everybody Loves Raymond* and is still airing it.

They're also airing shows with different kinds of families in them—surrogates, says Dr. Jerry Herron, director of Wayne State University's American Studies program. *Buffy,* the vampire slayer, has a single mom and a substitute family of high school friends and a teacher and kids essentially parenting themselves, he says. That may be closer to the truth about the way youngsters really live, "for in many instances with two parents working long hours kids do end up turning to their peers for parenting."

Indeed, Margaret Loesch, president and CEO of the Odyssey channel, said research shows that the traditional family no longer exists. One recent study said there are 26 different types of moms and 18 different types of dads; another identified 200 different kinds of families. She now defines family as people taking care of each other. Loesch said that viewers claim they want the family values of the 1950s, as well as the freedom, independence, and choice of the 1960s and 1970s, the relevance of the 1990s, and help in being parents (*Chicago Tribune,* June 9, 1999, "Retro TV").

MORE TO BE DONE

There are other steps to take to make pop culture more family-friendly. Critics have called for a "family viewing hour" from 4 to 5 P.M., during which no objectionable material is shown or advertised. Others press for a stricter ratings system for movies and CDs, designed by parents for parents. Others urge more widespread use of the V-chip to help parents better control what their children see. Still others call for innovative ways to honor programming heroes like Jim Henson, who once gently rebuffed a suggestion to deal with drugs in a story by quietly insisting that TV "celebrate the good things . . . inspire kids to act and look and see, but in a positive way, and learn and be curious about the arts and about creativity. Once we celebrate that innocence,"

Henson said, "there's enough time for them to be introduced to the negative things, so let's celebrate the magic of life."

All of these are good suggestions and important steps. But no one actually believes that America will turn off its TV sets, as pediatricians recommend, or that TV will revert to the way it was in the 1950s.

For that matter, no one should really believe that TV in the glory days was as benign as it seems on first glance. Distance may have lent enchantment to the view. For family dramas of old were often motherless. Remember *Bonanza, Gidget, My Three Sons, Bachelor Father, The Courtship of Eddie's Father,* and *Family Affair?* And moms were dead or missing on such family-friendly fare as Disney's *Bambi, Aladdin, Beauty and the Beast,* and *The Little Mermaid.*

America survived that and it will survive Homer Simpson. But it is not easy to parent, transmit values, or foster the respect of children in a culture that makes fun of parents as nincompoops.

There is an opportunity to use media once again as a force in changing our view of parents and parenting to one that recognizes it as the most demanding job of all—but one that offers immeasurable joy and benefits.

We want to not just swing the pendulum back to support a fictive all-knowing parenthood, but to move it in a new direction—to present a new view of parenting as struggling against vast odds in dangerous, often uncharted terrain. We want to see parents presented as today's real heroes—and for TV to provide them with, if not a road map, then at least an outline.

PART TWO

THE ECONOMIC MARKETPLACE

4

The Economic Status of Parents in Postwar America

Edward N. Wolff

Almost all studies have confirmed a disturbing rise in the degree of inequality in U.S. society over the past quarter-century or so. This has been true for both income inequality and wealth inequality.

In the past twenty-five years, we have also seen some startling changes in the relative well-being of various groups in U.S. society. This chapter will look at the relative economic fortunes of parents from the early 1960s to the present. The findings reported in this chapter support the argument that the relative well-being of parents, especially in relation to that of the elderly, has been continuously eroding over the past three or four decades. Public policy, in particular, has favored the elderly population relative to families with children.

This chapter uses several indices to evaluate the relative fortunes of parents and nonparents in the U.S. population. These include family income, family wealth, poverty incidence, labor earnings, and time availability for children. Because of dramatic changes in family structure over the past few decades, particularly the rapid increase in single-parent households, separate statistics will be shown for two-parent and one-parent families. In addition, because of the persistence of racial disparities in income and wealth, tabulations will also be made separately for whites and nonwhites whenever possible. We then consider the role of government cash and noncash transfers, as well as federal taxes, on both the incomes and poverty incidence of families with children and the elderly population.

Edward N. Wolff is professor of economics at New York University, senior scholar at the Jerome Levy Economic Institute, and author of *Top Heavy: A Study of the Increasing Inequality of Wealth in America*.

DEMOGRAPHIC CHANGES

We first look into demographic changes in the U.S. population since the late 1950s. Table 4.1 documents the astonishing growth in the number of female-

Table 4.1.   Distribution of Families with Children by Family Structure, 1959–1998[a]

Year	All Families Number	All Families Percent	Married Couples Number	Married Couples Percent	Male Householders[b] Number	Male Householders[b] Percent	Female Householders[b] Number	Female Householders[b] Percent
1. All Races								
1959	27.0	100	24.1	89	0.3	1	2.5	9
1962	28.2	100	25.0	89	0.5	2	2.7	10
1974	31.3	100	25.9	83	0.5	2	4.9	16
1983	32.8	100	25.2	77	0.9	3	6.6	20
1989	34.3	100	25.5	74	1.4	4	7.4	22
1992	35.9	100	25.9	72	1.6	4	8.4	23
1995	36.7	100	26.0	71	1.9	5	8.8	24
1998	37.3	100	26.2	70	2.1	6	8.9	24
2. White Families								
1959	24.1	100	—	—	—	—	1.8	8
1963	25.1	100	—	—	—	—	2.0	8
1975	27.0	100	23.1	86	0.4	2	3.4	13
1983	27.3	100	22.4	82	0.7	3	4.2	15
1989	28.0	100	22.3	80	1.1	4	4.6	17
1992	28.8	100	22.4	78	1.3	4	5.1	18
1995	29.7	100	22.7	76	1.5	5	5.6	19
1998	30.0	100	22.6	75	1.7	6	5.7	19
3. Black Families								
1967	3.2	100	—	—	—	—	—	—
1975	3.9	100	2.1	55	0.1	3	1.7	43
1983	4.5	100	2.1	46	0.2	4	2.2	50
1989	5.0	100	2.2	43	0.2	5	2.6	52
1992	5.4	100	2.2	41	0.2	5	3.0	55
1995	5.3	100	2.1	40	0.3	6	2.9	54
1998	5.5	100	2.2	40	0.4	6	2.9	54
4. Hispanic Families[c]								
1975	1.9	100	—	—	—	—	—	—
1983	2.7	100	0.0	0	0.0	0	0.7	24
1989	3.3	100	2.3	70	0.2	5	0.8	26
1992	4.0	100	2.7	68	0.2	6	1.0	26
1995	4.4	100	2.9	66	0.2	5	1.3	29

[a] Only families with children under the age of 18 in the household are included. *Sources:* U.S. Bureau of the Census (1990); U.S. Bureau of the Census (1995); U.S. Bureau of the Census, "Detailed historical income and poverty tables from the March Current Population Survey, 1947–1998," available on the Internet.
[b] No spouse present.
[c] Hispanic families may be of any race.

headed families with children. In 1959, female-headed households comprised only 9 percent of families with children; by 1998, the proportion was 24 percent. In contrast, families with both spouses present fell from 89 percent of all families with children in 1959 to 70 percent in 1998.

This change has characterized both white and black families. Among white families, the proportion of families with children headed by a female grew from 8 percent in 1959 to 19 percent in 1998. Among black families, the corresponding figures are 43 percent in 1975 and 54 percent in 1998. Though the fraction of female-headed households increased for both blacks and whites, the proportion has been and remains considerably higher for the former than the latter—54 versus only 19 percent in 1998. Among Hispanic families, the proportion is 27 percent in 1998, which has increased somewhat from 24 percent in 1983.

POVERTY INCIDENCE

Among all persons, the poverty rate declined from a postwar peak of 22 percent in 1960 to 12 percent by 1979, rose to 15.1 percent in 1993, but has since fallen to 12.7 percent in 1998. Poverty rates among families with children have historically been higher than among those without children. However, as shown in table 4.2, the gap has widened considerably in the postwar period. In 1959, 20 percent of families with children were poor, compared to 16 percent of families without children. In 1998, the poverty rate among families with children stood at 15 percent, a 25 percent decline from its 1959 level, whereas the poverty rate among childless families had fallen to 4 percent, a 72 percent reduction.

The same pattern is evident among both married couple families and female-headed households. In 1974, the poverty rate among married couples with children was about 50 percent greater than among married couples without children (6.0 versus 4.3 percent); in 1998, the poverty rate was about double (6.9 versus 3.7 percent). Among female-headed families, the relative poverty rates increased from a three-fold difference in 1959 (60 versus 20 percent) to an almost fourfold difference in 1998 (39 versus 10 percent).

Similar patterns are also evident by racial and ethnic group. Among white families, poverty rates were roughly comparable between families with and without children in 1959. However, by 1998, the poverty rate among childless families was about 30 percent of the poverty rate among families that had children. For both married couples and female-headed families, the poverty rate has fallen faster for families without children than for those with children.

Poverty rates among black families have been much higher than among white families, two and a half to three times as great. However, as with white families, poverty rates have been greater among families with children than

Table 4.2.   Poverty Rates of Families with and without Children, 1959–1998[a]

Year	All Families With Children	All Families No Children	Married Couples With Children	Married Couples No Children	Female Householders[b] With Children	Female Householders[b] No Children
1. All Races						
1959	20.2	15.9	—	—	59.9	20.1
1962	19.4	13.9	—	—	59.7	20.6
1974	12.1	4.6	6.0	4.3	43.7	7.7
1983	17.9	6.1	10.1	5.1	47.1	13.5
1992	18.0	5.2	8.6	4.2	46.2	11.1
1995	16.3	4.7	7.5	3.7	41.5	11.2
1998	15.1	4.5	6.9	3.7	38.7	9.7
2. White Families						
1959	15.8	14.2	—	—	51.7	16.6
1963	13.3	12.1	—	—	45.0	16.8
1975	10.3	4.6	6.3	4.5	37.3	5.4
1983	14.1	5.1	9.2	4.6	39.8	9.7
1989	11.8	3.9	6.5	3.5	36.1	7.0
1992	14.0	4.3	7.8	3.7	39.6	8.1
1995	12.9	4.0	7.0	3.4	35.6	8.1
1998	12.2	3.9	6.6	3.5	33.8	6.9
3. Black Families						
1967	39.4	21.2	—	—	—	—
1975	33.9	11.7	16.5	10.5	57.5	15.6
1983	39.9	16.9	18.0	11.8	60.7	28.5
1989	35.4	12.1	13.4	9.7	53.9	16.7
1992	39.1	13.9	15.4	9.5	57.4	26.3
1995	34.1	11.3	9.9	6.6	53.2	19.0
1998	30.5	10.4	8.6	5.7	47.5	18.3
4. Hispanic Families[c]						
1975	29.1	12.7	—	—	—	—
1983	32.1	11.4	—	—	63.3	26.5
1989	29.8	9.6	19.6	8.8	57.9	14.6
1992	32.9	12.8	22.8	10.3	57.7	21.2
1995	33.2	12.1	22.6	10.9	57.3	17.8
1998	28.6	8.8	19.3	7.7	52.2	13.1

[a] Families are classified according to the presence of children under the age of 18 in the household. *Sources:* U.S. Bureau of the Census (1990, 1995); U.S. Bureau of the Census "Detailed historical income and poverty tables from the March Current Population Survey, 1947–1998," available on the Internet.
[b] No spouse present.
[c] Hispanic families may be of any race.

among those without children. Moreover, the gap has widened since 1967. Indeed, between 1967 and 1998, the poverty rate among families with children fell from 39 to 31 percent, whereas it had fallen by more than half among childless families (from 21.2 to 10.4 percent).

Poverty rates among Hispanic families have been about double the level of white families. For this group, poverty incidence has also been greater among families with children than among those who are childless, and the gap has widened over time. Between 1975 and 1998, the poverty rate fell by 31 percent among families without children, whereas it remained virtually unchanged (at 29 percent) among families with children.

In contrast, the elderly (persons sixty-five years of age or older) represent what is, perhaps, the greatest success story of the past thirty years. The poverty rate of elderly individuals fell from 35 percent in 1959, greater than the national average, to 10.5 percent in 1998, well below the overall average. Much of their improvement was due to substantial increases in Social Security coverage and benefit levels.

FAMILY INCOME

The picture is a little less bleak when we look at relative income levels. Median family income (the income of the average family, found in the middle of the distribution when families are ranked from lowest to highest in terms of income) among all families remained virtually constant in real terms between 1973 and 1989, declined by 7 percent between 1989 and 1993, but then rose by 12 percent by 1998. However, as shown in table 4.3, in 1974 the median income of families with children was a little higher (12 percent) than that of families without children. However, by 1998, families with children were making, on average, slightly lower incomes (6 percent less) than childless families. Indeed, between 1974 and 1998, the median income of families with children increased by 7 percent in real terms, whereas the median income of families without children rose by 27 percent. Among

Table 4.3. Median Income of Families with and without Children, 1974–1998[a] (income in 1992 dollars)

Year	All Families			Married Couples			Female Householders[b]		
	With Children	No Children	Ratio	With Children	No Children	Ratio	With Children	No Children	Ratio
1974	36,508	32,626	1.12	40,298	33,883	1.19	14,103	24,354	0.58
1983	34,264	34,992	0.98	39,674	37,110	1.07	12,893	23,312	0.55
1989	37,856	39,637	0.96	45,252	41,686	1.09	14,685	29,173	0.50
1992	35,872	37,819	0.95	44,483	39,768	1.12	13,445	27,495	0.49
1995	36,838	37,975	0.97	46,002	40,797	1.13	14,946	26,226	0.57
1998	39,113	41,511	0.94	49,081	44,175	1.11	15,845	27,776	0.57

[a] Families are classified according to the presence of children under the age of 18 in the household. *Sources:* U.S. Bureau of the Census "Detailed historical income and poverty tables from the March Current Population Survey, 1947–1998," available on the Internet.
[b] No spouse present.

married couples, the ratio of median incomes between families with and without children fell from 1.19 in 1974 to 1.11 in 1998, though median income increased for both groups in real terms. Among female-headed families, the ratio of median incomes, after declining from 0.58 in 1974 to 0.49 in 1992, recovered to 0.57 in 1998. Median income increased by 14 percent between 1974 and 1998 for female heads, both with children and without children.

An alternative way of comparing the well-being of families is on the basis of "equivalent incomes." These are derived from the poverty thresholds for families of different family sizes (for example, $9,414 for a two-person family and $14,763 for a family of four in 1993). It is assumed that larger families require greater income to achieve the same standard of living as a smaller one but that there are also economies of consumption as household size increases. In this case, $9,414 is believed to satisfy the same level of needs for a two-person family as $14,763 for a family of four. In this sense, the two incomes are equivalent in terms of the standard of living that can be attained. The full set of adjustment factors for different family sizes and types is referred to as an *equivalence scale*.

Table 4.4 shows equivalent income (expressed as a ratio to the poverty threshold) for different family types. In 1973, the average ratio of family in-

Table 4.4. Equivalent Family Income (as a Multiple of the Poverty Line), by Family Type, 1973–1994[a]

					Percentage Change	
Family Type	1973	1979	1989	1994	1973–89	1989–94
All Families	3.31	3.55	3.96	3.80	19.6	−4.3
All Families with Children	2.95	3.12	3.36	3.28	13.9	−2.9
Married Couples with Children	3.17	3.42	3.80	3.78	19.9	−0.7
Single Mothers with Children	1.42	1.60	1.61	1.64	13.4	−3.2
Nonelderly Childless Families	4.91	5.27	5.80	5.74	18.1	−2.6
Elderly Childless Families	3.32	3.58	4.36	3.85	31.3	−6.8
Ratio of Equivalent Family Income between All Families with Children and Nonelderly Childless Families	0.60	0.59	0.58	0.57	−3.6	−1.4
Average Number of Children per Family						
All Families with Children	2.33	1.97	1.86	1.86		
Married Couples with Children	2.28	1.92	1.86	1.87		
Single Mothers with Children	2.18	1.83	1.70	1.71		

[a] Families are classified according to the presence of children under the age of 18 in the household. Equivalent family income is computed by dividing pre-tax cash income by the poverty line for the appropriate family size and type. *Source:* U.S. House of Representatives (1996)

come to the poverty threshold among all families was 3.31. This ratio increased by almost 20 percent between 1973 and 1989 (to 3.96), before declining by 4 percent from 1989 to 1994. Among families with children, equivalent family income increased by 14 percent from 1973 to 1989, less than for all families, and then fell by 3 percent from 1989 to 1994, about the same degree as for all families. Married couples with children saw their equivalent income rise by 20 percent from 1973 to 1989, while single mothers with children enjoyed only a 13 percent increase. Nonelderly childless families did better than families with children, with their average equivalent income rising by 18 percent from 1973 to 1989 and falling by only 3 percent from 1989 to 1994. Finally, elderly families (without children) saw a very large increase in their equivalent income from 1973 to 1989—31 percent—though it fell by 7 percent from 1989 to 1994.

However, by and large, families with children performed better in terms of equivalent income than ordinary income. The reason is that the average number of children fell over this period, from 2.33 in 1973 to 1.86 in 1994. As a result, equivalent income among families with children actually rose over the period 1973 to 1994 (by 11 percent), whereas their ordinary income fell. Moreover, the ratio of equivalent family income between families with children and nonelderly families without children slipped by only 5 percent from 1973 to 1994 (from 0.60 to 0.57), whereas their ratio of ordinary income fell by 15 percent over the same period.

EARNINGS, LABOR FORCE PARTICIPATION, AND TIME AVAILABILITY

Another piece of grim news is that the real wage (average wages and salaries adjusted for inflation) has fallen since 1973. Between 1973 and 1998, the real wage fell overall by 5 percent, although in the past few years real wages are finally creeping up (see table 4.5). This contrasts with the preceding years, 1950 to 1973, when real wages grew by 58 percent.

However, the pattern of wage growth was quite different for male and female workers. For men, median annual earnings among full-year, full-time (FY-FT) workers grew at an annual rate of 2.7 percent from 1960 to 1973, but then declined at 0.4 percent per year from 1973 to 1998. In contrast, female earnings grew at only 2.2 percent between 1960 and 1973, slower than male wages, but enjoyed positive growth from 1973 to 1998, at 0.7 percent per year. As a result, the ratio of earnings between males and females, after falling from 0.61 in 1960 to 0.57 in 1973, jumped to 0.73 by 1998.

Another telling trend is the declining value of the minimum wage. As shown in table 4.6, the minimum wage was set at $0.25 per hour in 1938,

Table 4.5.   Mean Hourly Earnings and Median Annual Earnings by Gender, 1950–1998

Year	Mean Hourly Earnings (1993$)[a]	Median Annual Earnings FY-FT Workers (1992$)[b]		
		Male	*Female*	*Ratio*
1950	7.74	—	—	—
1960	9.84	23,389	14,191	0.61
1967	11.14	27,759	16,040	0.58
1973	12.22	33,250	18,831	0.57
1989	11.20	30,924	21,236	0.69
1992	11.10	30,197	21,375	0.71
1995	11.07	28,996	20,711	0.71
1998	11.60	30,423	22,260	0.73
Average Annual Growth Rates (in percent)				
1950–73	2.0	—	—	
1960–73	—	2.7	2.2	
1973–98	−0.4	−0.4	0.7	

[a] Hourly earnings are for total private nonagricultural production and non-supervisory workers. The figures are adjusted for overtime in manufacturing and interindustry employment shifts. *Source:* Council of Economic Advisers (2000).
[b] Statistics are for full-year, full-time (FY-FT) workers. *Source:* U.S. Bureau of the Census (1993); U.S. Bureau of the Census, "Detailed historical income and poverty tables from the March Current Population Survey, 1947–1998," available on the Internet.

which was 40 percent of the average hourly earnings of production workers in that year. The federal law covered only workers engaged in interstate commerce or in the production of goods for interstate commerce. In essence, the law applied mainly to manufacturing and mining at its inception and covered less than half of all nonsupervisory workers.

Over time, the minimum wage has been gradually increased, and the coverage of the law extended to more and more workers. Table 4.6 shows the years in which the minimum was changed (1993 is also shown for comparative reasons). The minimum wage has been raised over time on a rather sporadic basis. In real terms, the minimum increased between 1938 and 1968, when it peaked at $6.67 in 1993 dollars, almost three times its original level in 1938. However, since that time, the minimum wage has eroded in real terms, particularly since 1981. In 1991 it was raised again to $4.25, but this was almost identical to the 1987 level in real terms. By 1995, the real minimum wage was at its lowest point since the late 1940s. The recent increase to $5.15 per hour in 1997 brings it back only to the level of 1986 in real terms. The "collapse" of the minimum wage is one factor often cited in explaining the decline in the average real wage and the rise in poverty among working families.

Table 4.6. Minimum Wage in Current and Constant Prices and the Ratio of Minimum Wage to Average Hourly Earnings and the Poverty Line for a Family of Four, 1938–1998[a]

	Minimum Wage (Current $)	Minimum Wage (1993$)	Ratio of Minimum Wage to Average Hourly Earnings[b]	Ratio of Annual Earnings of FT-FY Worker at the Minimum Wage to Poverty Line for Family of Four[c]
1938	0.25	2.57	0.40	0.35
1939	0.30	3.13	0.48	0.43
1945	0.40	3.22	0.39	0.44
1950	0.75	4.51	0.52	0.62
1956	1.00	5.34	0.51	0.73
1961	1.15	5.59	0.50	0.76
1963	1.25	5.92	0.51	0.81
1967	1.40	6.08	0.49	0.83
1968	1.60	6.67	0.53	0.91
1974	2.00	5.89	0.45	0.80
1975	2.10	5.66	0.43	0.77
1976	2.30	5.86	0.44	0.80
1978	2.65	5.89	0.43	0.80
1979	2.90	5.79	0.43	0.79
1980	3.10	5.46	0.43	0.74
1981	3.55	5.67	0.44	0.77
1987	3.55	4.54	0.36	0.62
1991	4.25	4.53	0.38	0.62
1993	4.25	4.25	0.36	0.58
1995	4.25	4.04	0.36	0.55
1997	5.15	4.64	0.41	0.63
1998	5.15	4.57	0.39	0.62

[a] *Sources: Social Security Bulletin,* Annual Statistical Supplement, 1999; Internet <www.bls.gov>.
[b] Earnings are for production workers in manufacturing.
[c] This assumes that the workers works 2,000 hours per year. The poverty threshold for a family of four in 1993 was $14,763.

Another way of looking at the minimum wage is in relation to the average hourly earnings of production workers. In 1938, it was set at 40 percent of average hourly earnings, and this gradually increased over time to 53 percent by 1968. Since that time, this ratio has also fallen, particularly since 1981. In 1987, the minimum wage stood at 36 percent of average earnings. In 1991, the ratio rose slightly to 38 percent, in 1995 it had fallen back to 34 percent, but by 1998 it had recovered slightly to 39 percent, about the same ratio as in 1991. A single family member working full year and full time (at 2,000 hours per year) at the minimum wage has never been able to support a family of four above the poverty line. However, in 1968, the annual earnings of such a worker would have reached 91 percent of the poverty threshold for a family of four, up considerably from a 35 percent ratio in 1938. However, with the erosion of the minimum wage, the degree to which a single earner at the minimum wage could meet the poverty threshold has likewise diminished, so that by 1995 the annual earnings of such a worker reached only 55 percent of the poverty line, though by 1998 it was back to 62 percent of the poverty line.

Because of the falling real wages of men, particularly at the low end of the scale, the labor force participation of wives has risen dramatically since the early 1970s in order to maintain living standards. The percentage of wives with a job increased from 41 percent in 1970 to 61 percent in 1998 (see table 4.7). Among mothers with children ages six to seventeen, the percentage at work grew from 55 percent in 1975 to 78 percent in 1998, and for mothers with children under the age of six, the proportion at work increased from 39 to a staggering 65 percent over the same period. Another interesting trend is that the percentage of female employees who work full time and full year increased from 37 percent in 1950 to 41 percent in 1970 and then jumped to 56 percent in 1998.

Table 4.8, which shows the number of families with two or more wage earners, provides another cut at the same issue. Between 1954 and 1998, the number of such families grew two and a half times, whereas the total number

Table 4.7.   Labor Force Participation Rates for Females by Marital Status, 1947–1998[a]

Year	All Males	All Females	Never Married	Married Spouse, Present	Widowed, Divorced, Separated	Females with Children in Age Group 6–17	Under 6	Percent of Female Employees Who Work FT-FY[b]
1947	86.4	20.0	37.4					
1950	86.4	33.9	50.5	23.8	37.8			36.8
1955	85.4	35.7	46.4	27.7	39.6			37.9
1960	83.3	38.1	44.1	30.5	40.0			36.9
1965	80.7	40.3	40.5	34.7	38.9			38.8
1970	79.7	43.4	53.0	40.8	39.1			40.7
1975	77.9	46.3	57.0	44.4	40.8	54.9	39.0	41.4
1980	77.4	51.5	61.5	50.1	44.0	64.3	46.8	44.7
1985	76.3	54.5	65.2	54.2	45.6	69.9	53.5	48.9
1988	76.2	56.6	65.2	56.5	46.1	73.3	56.1	50.7
1992	75.6	57.9	66.2	59.3	47.1	75.9	58.1	53.5
1995	75.0	58.9	66.8	61.0	47.4	76.6	62.3	54.1
1998	74.9	59.8	68.5	61.2	48.8	77.6	64.9	56.3

[a] Statistics refer to population age 16 and over. *Sources:* U.S. Department of Labor (1990); U.S. Bureau of the Census (1994); U.S. Bureau of the Census, "Detailed historical income and poverty tables from the March Current Population Survey, 1947–1998," available on the Internet.
[b] FT-FY: full time (35 hours or more per week), full-year (50 or more weeks per year).

Table 4.8.   Number of Families with Two or More Wage Earners, 1954–1998

Year	All Two-Earner Families		Husband-Wife Earners	
	Number (1,000s)	Percent of Total Families	Number (1,000s)	Percent of Married Couple Families
1954	16,872	43.6	—	—
1958	19,742	47.9	—	—
1962	22,143	49.6	—	—
1967	26,380	52.9	18,888	43.6
1972	28,706	53.0	21,279	45.7
1976	30,171	52.5	23,104	48.0
1979	32,949	55.0	25,595	52.1
1983	33,473	53.5	26,119	52.1
1987	37,085	56.5	29,369	56.6
1993	38,659	56.4	31,419	59.1
1995	39,523	56.8	32,118	60.0
1998	40,638	56.8	32,873	60.0

Sources: U.S. Bureau of the Census, Current Population Reports, various years; U.S. Department of Labor (1990); U.S. Bureau of the Census (1995); and U.S. Bureau of the Census, "Detailed historical income and poverty tables from the March Current Population Survey, 1947–1998," available on the Internet.

of families grew by 71 percent. As a result, the proportion of families with two or more earners increased from 44 to 57 percent.

Results are also shown for the number of families in which both the husband and wife worked. Between 1967 and 1987, their number grew by 74 percent, and the proportion of married couple families in which both husband and wife worked increased from 44 to 60 percent. By the 1980s, the "typical" married family was one in which both spouses were at work.

The growth in two-earner families helps to explain the apparent anomaly that while real wages have been declining since 1973, median family income has increased somewhat. The increased labor force participation of wives has helped compensate for the falling income of their husbands. Moreover, the increasing presence of working wives in the labor force is one factor explaining the widening disparities in family income since the 1970s, particularly between married couples and single men and women. According to data from the U.S. Census Bureau (provided on Internet), the median income of families with two earners was almost twice as great as those with only one earner in 1998 ($58,397 versus $31,483).

One unfortunate consequence of the increased labor force participation of wives is that the time available for child care has fallen. The time available for child care—or "parental time," for short—is another indicator of child well-being. To the extent that parents spend time with their children, they can be considered as investing in their children's current and future well-being. I treat parental time in two ways here—(1) as a "public good," assuming that the total parental time is available to all children in a family, and (2) as a private good, equally divided among the children. Parental time is estimated indirectly, according to the time actually spent at work, as 16 (assuming 8 hours for sleep) times 365 hours minus hours worked per year, summed over one or two parents, depending on family structure.

Table 4.9 documents trends in the parental time available for child care. Among all families with children, average parental available time fell from 8,700 hours per year in 1962 to 7,900 hours in 1983, or by 9 percent, and then to 7,600 hours in 1992, or by another 4 percent. Over the thirty years, average parental time declined by 13 percent. The change over time in parental time availability primarily reflects two factors: (1) the increased work time of mothers; and (2) changing family structure—in particular, the increasing proportion of single-mother families.

A breakdown by race and family structure in the same table provides details on these changes. Overall, white families fared better than nonwhite families, with total parental time declining by only 4 percent between 1962 and 1992 for the former and 17 percent for the latter. The difference is due primarily to the much larger increase in the proportion of female-headed families in the nonwhite community. Among white families, there are interesting differences between two-parent and single-parent families. Among two-parent families in which the wife stays at home, there was a slight increase in total parental time available over the years 1962 to 1992 (due to a modest decline in hours worked by fathers). However, in two-parent families in which the wife works, parental time declined by 9 percent over this period, reflecting the greater number of hours worked by working wives. Among single-mother families, parental time declined by 12 percent between 1962 and 1983 and by another 5 percent between 1983 and 1992, because of the increasing labor force participation of this group.

Patterns were similar in the nonwhite community, and the reasons are the same. Parental time increased slightly between 1962 and 1992 in two-parent families where the wife stayed at home, fell sharply in two-parent families in which the wife worked, and declined even more sharply in single-mother families.

A contrasting picture is presented by the other indicator of time availability— parental time per child. This indicator increased for all groups over the thirty-year period from 1962 to 1992. The increases were rather large—38 percent among white two-parent families where the wife did not work, 15 percent among white two-parent families where wife works, and 13 percent among white single-parent families. Increases were even more dramatic among nonwhite families. The difference in results between parental time per child and total parental time reflects the sharp drop in the average number of children per family in all groups—both whites and nonwhite, both two-parent and one-

Table 4.9. Mean Parental Time Availability for Families with Children, 1962, 1983, and 1992[a] (in 1,000s of Hours per Year)

	1962	1983	1992	Percentage Change 1962–1983	1983–1992
1. All Families with Children					
Total Parental Time	8.7	7.9	7.6	−9	−4
2. White Families with Children					
Total Parental Time	9.0	9.0	8.6	0	−4
A. Two Parents, Wife Home					
Total Parental Time	9.6	9.6	9.8	0	2
Per Child Parental Time	3.7	4.8	5.1	30	5
Children per Family	2.18	1.83	1.77	−16	−3
B. Two Parents, Wife Works					
Total Parental Time	8.5	7.9	7.7	−7	−2
Per Child Parental Time	4.0	4.5	4.6	13	1
Children per Family	2.11	1.96	1.90	−7	−3
C. Single Mothers					
Total Parental Time	5.0	4.4	4.2	−12	−5
Per Child Parental Time	2.3	2.7	2.6	17	−2
Children per Family	2.13	1.62	1.50	−24	−7
3. Non-White Families with Children					
Total Parental Time	7.6	7.3	6.4	−4	−13
A. Two Parents, Wife Home					
Total Parental Time	9.7	10.1	9.9	4	−2
Per Child Parental Time	3.0	4.4	4.4	47	1
Children per Family	3.22	2.30	2.23	−29	−3
B. Two Parents, Wife Works					
Total Parental Time	8.8	7.9	7.8	−10	−1
Per Child Parental Time	3.1	4.1	4.2	32	2
Children per Family	2.75	1.93	1.87	−30	−3
C. Single Mothers					
Total Parental Time	5.2	5.0	4.5	−4	−11
Per Child Parental Time	1.5	2.2	2.0	47	−8
Children per Family	3.69	2.17	2.02	−41	−7

[a] Households are classified according to the presence of children under the age of 18 in the households and by age group according to the age of the head of household. Parental time is estimated as follows: It is assumed that total time available to adults is 16 hours times 365 (days in the year). On the basis of information provided in each of the surveys, I compute the total hours worked per year by each parent (or a single parent in the case of single-parent families). In the case of two-parent families, total work time is summed over the two parents. Parental time availability is then estimated as the difference between 16 times 365 hours and total time worked by the parent(s), depending on family structure. *Sources:* Author's computations from the 1962 Survey of Financial Characteristics of Consumers and 1983 and 1992 Surveys of Consumer Finances.

parent families, and in families in which the wife works and those in which the wife does not work.

Another dimension is afforded by comparing household consumption expenditure patterns for the average family over time—in the case of table 4.10, between 1950 and 1993. In 1950, 31 percent of the outlays of the average

Table 4.10. Consumption Expenditures of the Average Family, 1950 and 1993ᵃ (in percent)

	1950	1993
Food and Alcohol	30.8	13.9
Tobacco	1.8	0.8
Clothing	10.9	5.0
Shelter	10.3	16.1
Utilities	3.5	6.3
House Furnishings	6.5	3.7
Household Operation	3.9	2.6
Automobile Purchase and Operation	10.5	14.4
Other Transportation	1.9	1.8
Medical Care	4.9	5.3
Personal Care	2.1	1.1
Recreation	4.4	4.8
Reading	0.8	0.5
Education	0.4	1.4
Miscellaneous Goods and Services	1.1	3.3
Cash Contributions	—	2.9
Pensions	—	1.4
Taxes Paid	6.0	14.9
Total Expenditures	100.0	100.0

ᵃ Out-of-pocket outlays only. *Sources:* U.S. Bureau of the Census, *Historical Statistics of the United States Colonial Times to 1957,* 1960; and U.S. Bureau of the Census, Statistical Abstract, 1995.

family were spent on food and alcohol; 11 percent on clothing; 10 percent on shelter; 11 percent on automobiles, including vehicle operations; and 6 percent on taxes. There have been some notable changes since 1950. With regard to necessities, outlays on food and alcohol fell from 31 percent in 1950 to 14 percent in 1993 and outlays on clothing from 11 to 5 percent, but expenditures on housing increased from 10 to 16 percent and those on utilities from 3.5 to 6.3 percent. Expenditures on household furnishings and operations also fell off from 10.4 to 6.3 percent, while outlays on automobiles, including their operation, rose from 10.5 to 14.4 percent. The taxes paid by the average family also rose sharply, from 6 to 15 percent, mainly due to the large increase in the Social Security tax.

On net, it appears that average families, particularly those with children, are almost as hard pressed in the 1990s as they were in 1950, despite the apparent increase in the standard of living. The proportion of income spent on the basic necessities of life—food, clothing, shelter (including utilities), transportation, and medical care—has declined over this period, from 83 to 69 percent (mainly due to the sharp decrease in food expenditures). However, when taxes are added in, then the share falls by only 5 percentage points, from 89 to 84 percent. Of these 5 percentage points, 1.4 percentage points are absorbed in pension contributions, leaving only a net gain of 3.6 percentage points for discretionary expenditures. Indeed, the share spent on the most discretionary of activities—recreation—has risen from 4.4 percent of total outlays to only 4.8 percent.

HOUSEHOLD WEALTH

Another dimension is afforded by looking at differences in household wealth between families with and without children. Household wealth is defined as the total assets owned by a family minus its household debts. Assets included in this calculation are (1) the gross value of owner-occupied housing; (2) other real estate owned by the household; (3) cash and demand deposits; (4) time and savings deposits, certificates of deposit, and money market accounts; (5) government bonds, corporate bonds, foreign bonds, and other financial securities; (6) the cash surrender value of life insurance plans; (7) the cash value of defined contribution pension plans, including IRAs, Keogh plans, and 401(k) plans; (8) corporate stock, including mutual funds; (9) net equity in unincorporated businesses; and (10) equity in trust funds. Total liabilities are the sum of: (1) mortgage debt, (2) consumer debt, and (3) other debt. Savings are another important indicator of household well-being since they provide economic security (in case of loss of job or change in family structure from death or divorce) and are therefore a source of potential consumption.

According to the calculations shown in table 4.11, the relative position of families with children has improved in terms of wealth since the early 1960s. From 1962 to 1998, average net worth (in real terms) grew by 139 percent among married couples with children, by 93 percent among nonelderly married couples without children, and by 161 percent among elderly families. Among female heads under the age of 65, the corresponding figures are 62 percent for those with children and 22 percent among those without children. However, even by 1998, families with children had lower net worth than those without children—a ratio of 61 percent among married couples and 58 percent among female heads.

An alternative concept of wealth is financial reserves, which are defined here as net worth less equity in owner-occupied housing. Financial reserves are a better indicator of the financial resources a family has immediately on hand to meet emergencies of the type occasioned by loss of job, family separation, and other types of income loss. Results here are very similar to those

Table 4.11. Mean Household Wealth for Households with and without Children, 1962, 1983, and 1998[a] (wealth in thousands of 1992 dollars)

Age Group	1962	1983	1998	Percentage Change		
				1962–1983	1983–1998	1962–1998
A. Net Worth						
All Households	124.9	195.1	232.6	56	19	86
Married Couples, Under 65						
With Children	91.4	139.9	218.4	53	56	139
Without Children	184.7	303.1	357.3	64	18	93
Female Heads, Under 65						
With Children	33.4	54.8	54.2	64	−1	62
Without Children	77.1	106.2	93.9	38	−12	22
Families, 65 and over	185.1	295.2	483.7	59	64	161
B. Financial reserves						
All Households	99.3	143.3	182.7	44	28	84
Married Couples, Under 65						
With Children	69.6	92.0	172.9	32	88	148
Without Children	148.8	231.9	291.5	56	26	96
Female Heads, Under 65						
With Children	21.2	28.1	43.9	33	56	107
Without Children	59.0	74.6	66.8	26	−10	13
Families, 65 and over	154.5	234.0	370.3	51	58	140

C. Debt/Equity Ratio [percent]

All Households	16.4	15.3	17.6	-7	16	7
Married Couples, Under 65						
With Children	32.9	28.5	31.3	-13	12	-5
Without Children	11.8	13.4	15.6	14	14	32
Female Heads, Under 65						
With Children	18.6	30.1	29.3	62	-13	57
Without Children	12.7	22.4	26.5	77	12	109
Families, 65 and over	3.7	3.0	4.4	-19	87	18

D. Home Ownership Rate [percent]

All Households	57.0	63.4	66.3	11	4	16
Married Couples, Under 65						
With Children	54.7	66.9	76.5	22	4	40
Without Children	66.8	74.2	74.6	11	-1	12
Female Heads, Under 65						
With Children	34.7	40.1	30.8	16	-22	-11
Without Children	32.5	40.4	49.7	24	20	53
Families, 65 and over	55.3	84.1	92.7	52	10	68

[a] Households are classified according to the presence of children in the households under the age of 18 and by age group according to the age of the head of household. *Sources:* own computations from the 1962 Survey of Financial Characteristics of Consumers and 1983 and 1992, and 1998 Surveys of Consumer Finances.

for net worth. The financial reserves of married couples with children increased by 148 percent between 1962 and 1998, compared to 96 percent for nonelderly married couples without children, and 140 percent for elderly families. Among female heads, the corresponding figures are 107 percent for those with children and 13 percent for those without children. However, as with net worth, the financial reserves of families with children were still considerably less than those of childless families and elderly families in 1998.

Another important dimension of wealth is the degree of indebtedness (relative to net worth) of a family. Families with children have had much larger indebtedness than families without children. In 1998, for example, the debt/equity ratio of married couples with children was almost twice as great as that of nonelderly families without children (31 versus 16 percent) and more than seven times as great as that of elderly families (31 versus 4 percent). Among married couples, families with children have made progress relative to childless families in this dimension as well. Between 1962 and 1998, the debt/equity ratio remained virtually unchanged for married couples with children, whereas it increased by 32 percent among nonelderly married couples without children and 18 percent among elderly families. However, among female heads, the debt/equity ratio more than doubled among those with children, while it increased by 57 percent for those without children.

Home ownership rates (the percentage of families that own their own homes) are more nearly comparable between families with and without children—in 1998, 77 percent for married couples with children, 75 percent for nonelderly married couples without children, and 93 percent for elderly families. However, female-headed households with children have seen their home ownership rate fall by 11 percent over this period, compared to a 53 percent increase among female heads without children.

One may speculate on why families with children have done better (in both relative and absolute terms) with regard to their wealth holdings than their income. The likely reason is that such families have received financial help from their parents. Elderly families, as is evident, have considerably greater financial resources than the nonelderly, and it is quite likely that they have transferred wealth to their (grown) children, particularly those with children of their own, in the form of gifts and through bequests.

THE ROLE OF GOVERNMENT TRANSFERS AND TAXES

How has the government fiscal system affected the well-being of families with children? There are two major ways this takes place. First, the government provides income transfers to families, particularly needy ones with children, through a variety of government programs, though most notably through Aid to Families with Dependent Children (AFDC) and, since the passage of welfare reform in 1996, Temporary Assistance for Needy Families (TANF). Second, the government taxes different families at different rates, depending principally on family income and family size.

A summary of the effects of government transfers and (federal) taxes is provided in table 4.12. Among female-headed families with children in 1979, the poverty rate based on income before taxes and transfers is 50.1 percent. The addition of social insurance such as unemployment compensation (but excluding Social Security) reduces the poverty rate by 1.0 percentage point. The further addition of Social Security results in a 3.9 percentage point reduction and that from means-tested cash transfers, such as AFDC, another 4.9

Table 4.12. The Effect of Government Transfers on the Poverty Rate for Families with Children, 1979 and 1992[a] (figures are in percentage points)

	Female-Headed Families with Children		Married Couples with Children		Elderly Families	
	1979	1992	1979	1992	1979	1992
Poverty Rate Based on Cash Income before Transfers	50.1	51.5	9.4	12.2	59.9	57.0
Reduction in Poverty Rate due to:						
Social Insurance (other than Social Security)	1.0	1.0	0.7	1.0	1.2	1.2
Social Security	3.9	2.3	1.0	0.9	39.6	40.5
Means-Tested Cash Transfers	4.9	3.0	0.0	0.7	2.0	1.2
Food Stamps and Housing Assistance	10.1	6.1	1.8	1.1	2.1	2.3
Federal Taxes[b]	−0.1	0.6	−0.3	0.0	0.0	0.0
Total Reduction in Poverty Rate	19.8	13.0	3.2	3.7	44.9	45.2
Poverty Rate Based on Cash Income after Transfers and Taxes	30.3	38.5	6.2	8.5	15.0	11.8

[a] Families are classified according to the presence of children under the age of 18 in the household. *Source:* U.S. House of Representatives (1994).
[b] Includes federal payroll taxes.

percentage point decrease. The biggest effect comes from food stamps and housing assistance, which further decreases the poverty rate by 10.1 percentage points. In 1979, the poor paid federal income taxes, which actually increases the measured poverty rate by 0.1 percentage point. All told, the addition of transfers and taxes results in a 19.8 percentage point reduction in this group's poverty rate in 1979, to 30.3 percent.

In contrast, the addition of government transfers and taxes reduces the poverty rate of this group by only 13.0 percentage points in 1992. The biggest change occurs in the effect of food stamps and housing assistance, which decreases the poverty rate by only 6.1 percentage points in 1992, compared to 10.1 percentage points in 1979. The antipoverty effectiveness of means-tested cash transfers, such as AFDC, also drops from 4.9 to 3.0 percentage points, as does Social Security, from 3.9 to 2.3 percentage points. One piece of good news is that federal taxes now reduce the poverty rate, in this case, by 0.6 percentage point, due to the implementation of the Earned Income Tax Credit (EITC).

The antipoverty effectiveness of government programs actually increased somewhat for married couples with children, from 3.2 percentage points in 1979 to 3.7 percentage points in 1992. Most of the gain is due to increases in the poverty-reduction effect of means-tested cash transfers, though this is offset to some extent by decreases in the level of food stamps and housing assistance.

Among elderly families, the government transfer system reduced their effective poverty rate in 1979 from 59.9 percent to 15.0 percent, or by almost 45 percentage points. The lion's share of this gain comes from Social Security, which by itself reduces the poverty rate of elderly persons by almost 40 percentage points. Between 1979 and 1992, the antipoverty effectiveness of government transfer programs increases slightly among the elderly, from 44.9 to 45.2 percentage points, mainly due to increased Social Security benefits (from a 39.6 to a 40.5 percentage point reduction).

Table 4.13 shows a comparison of the antipoverty effectiveness of government programs on the poverty rates of children for seventeen advanced industrialized countries, including the United States. The results dramatically underline the feebleness of the U.S. effort, in comparison to countries at similar levels of development. Before including the effects of government transfer programs, the United States ranked as one of the highest countries in terms of child poverty, at 25.9 percent, but not the highest. Ireland, at 30.2 percent, and the U.K., at 29.6 percent, outranked the United States, and France, at 25.4 percent, was very close. However, after the effects of government programs are accounted for, the United States is by far the highest in terms of child poverty incidence—at 21.5 percent. Australia is in a distant second place, at 14.0 percent, and Canada in third place, at 13.5 percent.

Table 4.13. The Effect of Government Programs in Selected OECD Countries on the Poverty Rate of Children, various years[a] (figures are in percentage points)

Country and Year	Poverty Rate before Government Programs	Poverty Rate after Government Programs	Difference in Poverty Rates
Australia, 1989	19.6	14.0	5.6
Belgium, 1992	16.2	3.8	12.4
Canada, 1991	22.5	13.5	9.0
Denmark, 1992	16.0	3.3	12.7
Finland, 1991	11.5	2.5	9.0
France, 1984	25.4	6.5	18.9
Germany, 1989	9.0	6.8	2.2
Ireland, 1987	30.2	12.0	18.2
Israel, 1986	23.9	11.1	12.8
Italy, 1991	11.5	9.6	1.9
Luxembourg, 1985	11.7	4.1	7.6
Netherlands, 1991	13.7	6.2	7.5
Norway, 1991	12.9	4.6	8.3
Sweden, 1992	19.1	2.7	16.4
Switzerland, 1982	5.1	3.3	1.8
United Kingdom, 1986	29.6	9.9	19.7
United States, 1991	25.9	21.5	4.4

[a] The figures are based on the Luxembourg Income Study and were graciously supplied to me by Timothy Smeeding.

The third column measures the poverty-reducing effect of government programs. Government programs in the United States reduced the child poverty rate by 4.4 percentage points. This compares to a poverty-reduction effect from government transfers of 19.7 percentage points in the U.K., 18.9 percentage points in France, 18.2 percentage points in Ireland, 12.8 percentage points in Israel, and 12.7 percentage points in Denmark. The United States does not have the lowest antipoverty effectiveness of government programs—Switzerland, Italy, and Germany rank lower. However, in these three cases, the initial poverty rates are also a lot lower than in the United States.

SUMMARY AND CONCLUSION

The most dramatic demographic change over the past three decades or so has been the rise in the number of female-headed families with children. The proportion of white families with children headed by a female grew from 8 percent in 1959 to 19 percent in 1998; whereas among black families, the corresponding figures are 43 percent in 1975 and 54 percent in 1998.

One consequence of this demographic shift has been that poverty incidence among families with children has risen relative to that of families without children and, in particular, relative to that of elderly families. The poverty rate among families with children was about one-fourth lower in 1998 compared to 1959—15 versus 20 percent—whereas it had fallen from 16 percent to 4 percent among all childless families and from 35 to 10 percent for elderly persons. Increases in relative poverty occurred among both married couple families and female householders. The increasing poverty rate among families with children (in both relative and absolute terms) since the early 1970s is partly a result of declining real wages and also the fraying of the safety net for families with children. Another reason is that the minimum wage has fallen in real terms, by 31 percent between 1968, its peak year, and 1998.

Families with children also saw their incomes slip relative to those of childless families. Between 1974 and 1998, the median income of the former increased by 7 percent in real terms, whereas the median income of the latter increased by 27 percent. Relative losses occurred among both married couples and female-headed households. The situation is a little less bleak when we consider equivalent income (that is, adjusted for family size). Between 1973 and 1994, equivalent income increased by 11 percent among all families with children, 19 percent among nonelderly childless families, and 16 percent among elderly families. The reason for the better relative and absolute performance of families with children in terms of equivalent income in comparison to terms of ordinary income is that the average number of children in each family with children also fell over this period, from 2.33 to 1.86. Moreover, in terms of actual consumption expenditures made by families in 1950 and 1993, there has been very little increase in the share spent on discretionary activities such as recreation and entertainment.

One disturbing piece of news is that the real wage has fallen by 5 percent between 1973 and 1998. However, whereas the earnings of male workers fell over this period, the earnings of female workers actually increased over this period. One consequence of the falling real wages of men, particularly at the low end of the scale, is that more wives went into the labor market in order to maintain family incomes. The percentage of wives with a job increased from 41 percent in 1970 to 61 percent in 1998. Increases have occurred for women with children, both school-age and preschool.

This, in turn, has meant less time availability for children. Over the thirty years from 1962 to 1992, average parental time declined by 13 percent. Reductions in parental time were particularly acute for nonwhite families—reflecting to a large extent the greater increase in the proportion of single-mother families. On the other hand, parental time per child did increase among all family types, particularly nonwhite families. The difference in results between parental time per child and total parental time reflects the sharp drop in the average number of children per family in all family types.

Families with children have also had lower wealth holdings than those without children. In 1998, the net worth of married couples with children averaged 61 percent that of nonelderly married couples without children and 45 percent that of elderly families. However, families with children have seen their wealth grow relative to that of families without children over the period from 1962 to 1998. The average net worth of married couples with children increased by 139 percent over this period, compared to a 93 percent increase for nonelderly married couples without children (though a 161 percent increase for elderly families). The likely reason why their relative wealth position has improved over these years, while their relative income position has deteriorated, is that families with children have benefited from transfers of wealth from their parents.

The effectiveness of government transfer programs and taxes has also suffered a sharp reduction among female-headed families with children. The antipoverty effectiveness of government programs fell from a 20 percentage point reduction in the poverty rate in 1979 to a 13 percentage point reduction in 1992, mainly from cuts in welfare, food stamps, and housing assistance. The change over to TANF in 1996 may have further lessened the poverty reduction effect of welfare because of its more stringent eligibility requirements, though it is still too early to say for sure. In contrast, the antipoverty effectiveness of government transfers has increased slightly for married couples with children and for elderly individuals over this period. Moreover, in comparison with other advanced economies, the United States has by far the highest poverty incidence among children after the effects of government transfer programs are accounted for.

All in all, over the past quarter century, families with children have suffered a modest decline in income relative to families without children, though an even less pronounced decline in income adjusted for family size, because of the reduction in the average number of children in families. Total parental time available for child care has also fallen, but parental time per child has risen, again due to smaller family size. The wealth holdings of families with children, on the other hand, have risen relative to those of families without children—probably because of increased intergenerational transfers. The biggest problem is that poverty rates among families with children have increased relative to those of other families, particularly the elderly. This is true for both married couples and, particularly, for female-headed households. For the former, the predominant reason seems to be declining real wages. For the latter, the main reason is cuts in welfare, food stamps, and housing assistance.

SOURCES

Council of Economic Advisers, *Economic Report of the President, 2000* (Washington, D.C.: U.S. Government Printing Office, 2000).

U.S. Bureau of the Census, *Money Income and Poverty Status in the United States, 1989,* Series P-60, no. 168 (Washington, D.C.: U.S. Government Printing Office, 1990).

U.S. Bureau of the Census, *Money Income of Households, Families, and Persons in the United States: 1992,* Series P60-184 (Washington, DC: U.S. Government Printing Office, 1993).

U.S. Bureau of the Census, *Statistical Abstract of the United States, 1994* (Washington, D.C.: U.S. Government Printing Office, 1994).

U.S. Bureau of the Census, *Income, Poverty, and Valuation of Noncash Benefits: 1993,* Series P60-188 (Washington, D.C.: U.S. Government Printing Office, 1995).

U.S. Department of Labor, Bureau of Labor Statistics, *Handbook of Labor Statistics 1989,* Bulletin 2340 (Washington, D.C.: U.S. Government Printing Office, 1990).

U.S. House of Representatives, Committee on Ways and Means, U.S. House of Representatives, *Overview of Entitlement Programs: 1996 Green Book* (Washington, D.C.: U.S. Government Printing Office), July 15, 1996.

5

Time Crunch among American Parents

Juliet B. Schor

In the late 1980s and early 1990s, the topic of working hours was thrust into the public spotlight. The consensus view—that hours of work were a "solved problem"—unraveled. On one side, two Harvard economists presented estimates from the Current Population Survey showing that annual hours had risen appreciably (Leete and Schor 1992, 1994; Schor 1992). "Working harder for less" became a popular mantra in the public discourse. On the other side, researchers from the Universities of Michigan and Maryland challenged this view. Relying on time diary data, they claimed that Americans were enjoying more leisure time than ever before (Robinson 1989a, 1989b; Robinson and Bostrom 1994; Juster and Stafford 1991). Subsequent studies ensued, but disagreement about trends in worktime persists.

Although much of this debate has concerned estimates for the general population, the trends in parental hours are an important subtheme. Leete and Schor found that hours of work for parents, and in particular, for single and young parents, rose more substantially than hours for other groups. Other data support the view that large numbers of parents experience significant time pressures.

If correct, the finding that a significant fraction of American parents is working longer hours, working at more demanding jobs, and experiencing high levels of stress and time pressure is worthy of serious attention. Do trends in time use affect the quality of parental interactions with children? Are they relevant to outcomes such as the well-being of children, the quality of

Juliet B. Schor is professor of sociology at Boston College and the author of *The Overworked American: The Unexpected Decline of Leisure* and *The Overspent American: Upscaling, Downshifting and the New Consumer*.

school education, or the transmission of values? Certainly, we can expect that rising work hours for parents will affect their availability for participation in the larger unpaid domestic and civic economies. How that affects parental time with children is another question. In this chapter, I first discuss trends in work time, as well as the controversies that have arisen over those trends. I then present some data on trends in parental work hours, time pressure, and job characteristics.

GENERAL TRENDS IN HOURS OF PAID WORK

Types of Data on Hours of Paid Work

There are three major sources of data on hours of work. The first is provided by business establishments to the government. These data, which are less prominent in the public debates, measure hours per job rather than per person. Although establishment data are preferable for some issues (i.e., measurements of productivity per hour), they are less well-suited to trends in individual or household time use, because of the growth in multiple jobholding and the underground economy. The second type of data is derived from household surveys such as the Current Population Survey (CPS), the census, and the Panel Study of Income Dynamics (PSID). These large data sets provide representative samples of the population and use recall questions such as "How many hours did you work last week?" The third type of data is time diaries.[1] In these surveys respondents are asked to record, at fifteen-minute intervals, how they are using their time over a twenty-four-hour period. The U.S. diary studies vary in methodology (some are recorded at the time of activity; others use recall methods). The diary surveys have been carried out by university survey research centers at various points in time. They typically use small samples, because of the cost and difficulty of such a detailed and rich approach. Here I will discuss only the evidence from the household surveys and the diary studies.

Findings from the Household Surveys

A number of estimates from the household surveys, such as the CPS and the PSID, show clear evidence of rising hours in paid work. My own estimates with Laura Leete for the period 1969–1989 (Leete and Schor 1992, 1994; also reported in Schor 1992 for the period 1969–87) show an average increase of 53 hours, composed of a 208-hour rise for women and a 20-hour decline for men[2] (table 5.1). However, once underemployment is accounted for, a different picture emerges. To control for underemployment, we con-

Table 5.1. Annual Hours, Labor Force Participants Only, 1969–1989

	1969	1973	1979	1989	Change 1969–1989
Market Hours	1751	1737	1731	1804	53
Men	2007	1987	1962	1987	−20
Women	1385	1392	1451	1593	208
Non-Market Hours	893	897	974	938	45
Men	628	637	756	725	97
Women	1271	1255	1239	1182	−89

Source: Leete and Schor (1994).

structed a sample we called the "unconstrained labor force," which consists of employed persons who have not reported that they are involuntarily un- deremployed (i.e., working part time or part year when they would prefer full time or full year work). (See tables 5.2 and 5.3.) Annual hours of mar- ket work among the unconstrained labor force increased for both men and women, by 72 and 287 hours, respectively.

An important and generally overlooked feature of the data is that annual hours among the constrained labor force (i.e., those who are involuntarily part time or part year) fell dramatically over this period, from 1,312 to 1,066 (table 5.3). Thus, not only were more people underemployed, but their extent of un- deremployment rose substantially. There is also controversy about trends in unpaid household work, hereafter termed "nonmarket hours." This includes all child care, housework, shopping, and so forth. For a discussion and de- fense of our methods, see the accompanying note. For a list of included ac- tivities, see Leete and Schor 1994.[3]

A longer series from the CPS, which omits some of the corrections of Leete and Schor's estimates (including by labor market constraint), is provided by Mishel et al. (2001). They find an increase of 140 hours between 1967 and

Table 5.2. Percent of Labor Force Experiencing Labor Market Constraint, 1969–1989

	1969	1973	1979	1989
In Labor Force, Constrained	7.2	9.8	16.2	14.5
No Work All Year	0.4	0.7	0.8	0.6
Part Year/Part-Time	1.0	1.8	4.0	3.9
Full Year/Part-Time	0.2	0.3	0.9	1.3
Part Year/Full-Time	5.6	7.0	10.5	8.7
In Labor Force, Unconstrained	92.8	90.2	83.8	85.5
Full Year/Full-Time	59.0	58.8	57.4	61.6

Source: Leete and Schor (1994).

Table 5.3.   Annual Hours by Labor Market Constraint, 1969–1989

	1969	1973	1979	1989	Change 1969–1989
Unconstrained LF					
Market Hours	1786	1798	1855	1924	138
Men	2054	2060	2093	2126	72
Women	1406	1436	1558	1693	287
Non-Market Hours	889	888	939	900	11
Men	621	626	727	688	67
Women	1268	1248	1204	1142	−126
Constrained LF					
Market Hours	1312	1163	1075	1066	−246

Source: Leete and Schor (1994).

1998. Because working hours fell in this series between 1967 and 1973, the increase since 1973 is even greater—178 hours per year. Notably, they find that hours have continued to rise substantially in the 1990s, by 75 hours between 1989 and 1998 (see table 5.4).[4]

Bluestone and Rose (1997), using the Panel Study of Income Dynamics (PSID), find similar trends. In response to Robinson's criticisms that the CPS weekly hours series is plagued by overestimation bias (i.e., people overstating the amount they work [Robinson and Bostrom 1994]), Bluestone and Rose have argued that the PSID is a more accurate measure because respondents are asked to provide more detail about vacation days, leaves, and primary and second jobs. After controlling for the cyclical effects and looking at prime-age workers (ages twenty-five to fifty-four), they find that annual hours have increased 3.3 hours per year, for a total rise of 66 hours between 1969 and 1989. (This is similar to Leete and Schor's finding of a 2.75 yearly increase for those years for all labor force participants. The .65 hour difference is likely attributable to the exclusion of the fifty-five-plus age group from Bluestone and Rose's sample, figure 5.1.)[5] Dual-earner families have

Table 5.4.   Trends in Average Hours, 1969–1998

Year	Annual Hours	Weeks per Year	Hours per Year
1969	1,758	43.5	39.3
1973	1,720	43.4	38.6
1979	1,745	43.8	38.8
1989	1,823	45.4	39.3
1995	1,868	45.9	39.7
1998	1,898	46.6	39.9

Source: Mishel et al. 2001, Table 2.1, p. 115. Authors' analysis of CPS data and Murphy and Welch (1989).

Figure 5.1.   PSID Data, 1967–1989

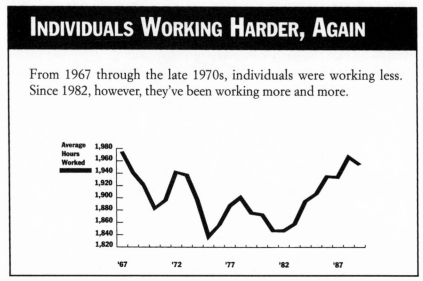

INDIVIDUALS WORKING HARDER, AGAIN

From 1967 through the late 1970s, individuals were working less. Since 1982, however, they've been working more and more.

been a special focus of debate in the time-squeeze discussion. Bluestone and Rose find particularly large increases in hours for families where both husbands and wives are employed—husbands' plus wives' annual hours increased from 2,850 to 3,450. Because there is frequent misinterpretation of this point (including by Bluestone and Rose in their discussion of my estimates), it is worth noting that this rise is not due to rising participation among married women. These estimates show that the average dual-earner family worked 600 fewer hours in 1967 than it did in 1989. Furthermore, once business cycle effects are controlled for, the total increase is even larger, at 640. A later set of estimates by Bluestone and Rose (2000) similarly finds increases in hours from 1982 to 1996, although in this work they find a decline between 1967 and 1982.[6] Perhaps most strikingly, they find that the combined annual hours of prime-aged dual-earner couples rose from 2,850 in 1971 to 3,450 in 1988, an increase of 684 hours per year.

Another household survey, the 1997 National Study of the Changing Workforce (hereafter NSCW), carried out by the Families and Work Institute, similarly finds a substantial rise in worktime. For comparability with the 1977 Quality of Employment Survey, this sample includes only employees who worked 20 or more hours per week and were interviewed in English. It found that employees were working 47.1 hours per week in 1997, as compared to only 43.6 hours in 1977 (Bond et al. 1998, pp. 72–73).

One set of estimates from household surveys provides a more ambiguous picture. Coleman and Pencavel (1993a, 1993b), using census data from 1940 to 1980, and the CPS for 1988, find no aggregate trends in hours. (Because Coleman and Pencavel do not provide aggregate estimates but only data broken down by race and gender, direct comparisons with the foregoing studies are not possible.) Coleman and Pencavel find that among those with college degrees, hours of work have risen across the board. White males' hours have risen since 1940 by 89 hours, black males' by 55; white females' by 177; and black females' by 391 hours. By contrast, hours of work for everyone with fewer than 12 years of schooling have fallen. Bluestone and Rose (1997) find a similar pattern. The likely explanation for differences between these data and those of Leete and Schor is that the decline for those with low educational attainment is due to their disproportionate rise in underemployment.

Findings from the Time Diaries

Results from the household surveys are disputed by researchers who rely on time diaries. Thomas Juster and Frank Stafford of the University of Michigan (Juster and Stafford 1991) have claimed that Americans' free time has risen, on the basis of data covering the period 1965–1981. John Robinson, from the University of Maryland, using the Michigan data for 1965 and 1975 and his own diary surveys for 1985 and 1992–95, also argued against the finding that hours of work were increasing. (See Robinson 1988, 1989a, 1989b; Robinson and Bostrom 1994; and Robinson and Godbey 1999.)

Robinson and Godbey (1999) have argued strongly that work time is declining, not rising, on the basis of their findings from time diary data (table 2, p. 95). For example, they find that hours of work have fallen for both employed men and women between 1965 and 1985 (see table 5.5). Women's weekly hours declined from 36.8 to 30.8, while men's declined from 46.5 to 39.7. An update with a combination of surveys taken over the years 1992–95 finds some alteration in trends. Hours for employed women increased between 1985 and 1992–95, from 34.3 to 37.3. Hours for employed men declined from 42.6 to 42.3. (See figure 5.2.) The updated estimates contain an unexplained discrepancy for women in 1985—in table 2 women's hours are reported as 30.8 per week; in Robinson and Godbey's figure 16, reproduced here as figure 5.2, the 1985 hours are reported as 34.3. If the table 2 estimate is correct, the increase between 1985 and 1992–95 is a very substantial 6.5 hours per week.

Who's right? Has free time increased, as the diaries show, or are hours of work rising, the picture we get from the household surveys? As is usual in debates of this kind, some of the differences are due to the fact that we are not dealing with uniform time periods, uniform measures of work, labor force coverage, and the like. But such large discrepancies indicate there are other

Table 5.5.   Time Diary Estimates, 1965–1985

Trends in Average Hours Spent at Paid Work:
Diary vs. Workweek Estimates (in hours per week)

	1965		1975		1985	
A. Diary Worksheet Figures						
Women						
Employed	36.8	(306)	35.8	(489)	30.8	(1,234)
Nonemployed	2.0	(382)	3.0	(618)	3.8	(814)
Total women	17.5		17.8		20.3	
Men						
Employed	46.5	(507)	42.9	(865)	39.7	(1,327)
Nonemployed	10.5	(54)	8.7	(124)	10.6	(354)
Total men	43.0		37.8		33.6	
Total diary paid work	28.9		26.8		26.1	
B. Workweek Estimate Questions						
Women						
Employed	40.4		40.2		41.6	
Nonemployed	1.2		1.9		2.9	
Total women	18.4		19.0		22.7	
Men						
Employed	47.1		46.8		46.4	
Nonemployed	3.9		2.6		3.1	
Total men	42.6		40.3		35.1	
Total estimated paid work	29.4		28.5		28.3	

Source: Americans' Use of Time Project. Robinson and Godbey (1997).

differences. The major disagreements center on the quality of recall data (Robinson and Godbey's critique of the household surveys), the importance of underemployment and the unrepresentativeness of the 1965 sample (Leete and Schor's critique), differences between weekly and annual hours, and the importance of business cycle trends (Leete and Schor, Mishel, and Rose and Bluestone). For a fuller discussion of these disagreements, I refer the reader to Schor 2000 and the accompanying note.[7] Robinson and Bostrom (1994) argue that the extent of bias is not constant, but is growing over time. That is because higher-hours individuals engage in more overestimation than those who work less. (There is relatively little overestimation bias in the 20–44 hour range, but high exaggeration in the 55+ category.) But if the size of the bias is growing, it is most likely due to precisely the trend Robinson contests—the rise in working hours. Because more people are working longer hours, there is more overestimation. Overestimation may well inflate the magnitude of the increase, but does not account for the basic upward trend itself. However, even given these differences, there are two points of substantial agreement. First, the large decline in worktime found in the diary surveys

Figure 5.2. Trends in Paid Work Time, Estimated vs. Diaries, 1965–1995 (aged 18–64, employed only, hours per week)

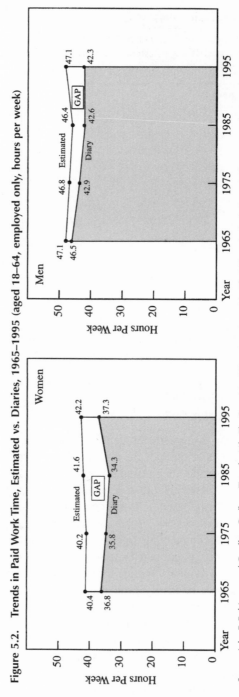

Source: John P. Robinson and Geoffrey Godbey, *Time for Life: The Surprising Ways Americans Use Their Time,* 2nd ed. (State College: Pennsylvania State University Press, 1999, figure 16), p 326. Americans' Use of Time Project.

until 1985 has been arrested—employed women's hours increased by 3 per week after 1985,[8] and men's hours fell by only a very small amount (0.3 hours). Second, everyone agrees that certain groups—including parents—are experiencing greater time pressure. For example, Robinson and Godbey find that the "gain" in free time is much smaller (and in some cases, nonexistent) for those with higher educational attainment, higher incomes, for those aged 25–44, as well as for married persons, for parents, and for parents with children under five. We turn now to the latter groups.[9]

PARENTS AND WORK

Working Hours of Parents

In their estimates of trends from 1969–1989, Leete and Schor (1992) found that parents experienced particularly rapid increases in hours of work. Excluding the underemployed and unemployed, we found that market hours for parents have risen by 72 hours. Disaggregated by sex, we found that mothers' hours rose by 346, fathers' hours by 14. Accounting for trends in nonmarket hours, the total change in hours was 139, on average—comprised of a 165-hour increase for women and a 142-hour increase for men (table 5.6). For women, nonmarket hours have declined; for men, they have risen.

For younger parents (defined as ages 18–39), the total rise is even larger. This group went from an average of 2,920 total hours (market plus nonmarket) in 1969 to 3,089 in 1989, an increase of 169. For young mothers, the net increase in hours (rising market hours minus declining nonmarket hours) was 241 hours. For younger fathers, the increase was 189. Among single parents, the increase in hours was 222. (See table 5.6.)

Table 5.6. Changes in Working Hours of Parents, 1969–1989

	Market	Nonmarket	Total Net Increase
All parents	72	67	139
Mothers	346	−181	165
Fathers	14	128	142
Young parents (ages 18–39)			169
Young mothers			241
Young fathers			189
Single parents			222

Source: Leete and Schor (1992), p. 14.

Mishel et al. (2001) provide estimates for parental hours through the 1990s. Annual market hours for married couples aged 25–54 with children under 18 rose from 3,331 in 1979 to 3,685 in 1998, an increase of 10.6 percent (Mishel et al. 2001, table 1.29, p. 98). The increase in wives' hours was much greater—from 870 to 1,235, 42 percent. But husbands' hours also rose, from 2,120 to 2,205, or 4 percent (Mishel et al. 2001, table 1.31, p. 103). Disaggregated by income, race, and educational status, the data show increases across all these categories, with smaller growth among the top income quintile, whites, and those of lower educational attainment (Mishel et al. 2001, tables 1.29 and 1.30, pp. 98–103).[10]

An unpublished 1999 report by the Council of Economic Advisers entitled "Families and the Labor Market, 1969–1999: Analyzing the 'Time Crunch'" looks specifically at parental work hours. Again, using CPS data, this study finds very large increases in hours of market work for families with children. Among two-parent families, annual hours increased by 497 hours (or 18 percent) between 1969 and 1997; for single-parent households the increase was 297 (28 percent) (CEA 1999, pp. 3–4). These estimates are higher than those listed previously because they count only market hours, and they include the effects of changes in labor force participation, as well as longer weekly hours and more weeks' work per year. In this study all of the increase in hours was concentrated in mothers' hours, which rose by 576 (93 percent); fathers' annual hours declined slightly. The growth in hours was general across many types of families, although the extent of the increase varied by subgroup. Families whose heads had attended college experienced more than twice the increase of families whose heads had a high school diploma or less. Families with a young child increased their hours more than those with only school-age children (CEA 1999, pp. 4–5). The CEA report notes that for both married-couple and single-parent families, time available to devote to unpaid activities has declined, although this statistic does not correct for the substantial fall in the number of children per household.

The NSCW data also show a substantial increase in paid work hours of parents. Between 1977 and 1997, mothers' hours rose 5.2 hours per week, and now stand at 41.4; while fathers' hours increased 3.1 hours, to 50.9. (See table 5.7.)

Parental Time with Children

While growing hours of market work reduce the time potentially available for child care, the effect on actual time spent with children is more complex. It is well worth recognizing that one should not overstate the extent to which even full-time homemakers have historically engaged in child care as a pri-

Table 5.7. Working Hours Data on Married Parents from the NSCW, 1977 and 1997[a]

Weekly Hours of Paid Work

	1977	1997
Mothers with children under 18	36.2	41.4
Mothers with children under 6	—	40.8
Fathers with children under 18	48.5	50.9
Fathers with children under 6	—	51.6

Daily Hours of Child Care

	Working Days		Nonworking Days	
	1977	1997	1977	1997
Mothers	3.3	3.0	7.3	8.3
Fathers	1.8	2.3	5.2	6.4

Preferred and Actual Hours of Employed Parents, 1997

	Preferred Hours	Actual Hours	Difference
Mothers	30.6	41.4	10.8
Fathers	38.8	50.9	12.1

[a] Sample is for employees with children, working 20 hours or more.
Source: Bond et al. (1998) and Galinsky and Swanberg (1998).

mary activity. This is a point I made in Schor (1992, chap. 4) and which Suzanne Bianchi addresses in her presidential address to the Population Association of America (2000). Mothers have historically been able to substitute out of other kinds of activities (housework, informal economic activity) rather than reduce child-care hours. Such a perspective is consistent with the research on the difference in employed versus nonemployed mothers' hours of care.[11]

Indeed, both the time diary evidence and the NSCW indicate that parents have maintained their hours with children.[12] Robinson and Godbey (1999) find that parental care hours have risen. Employed mothers' weekly hours of child care as a primary activity rose from 6.3 to 6.7 between 1965 and 1985, while fathers' hours remained exactly equal (2.6 hours) in 1965, 1975, and 1985[13] (table 3, p. 105). Bianchi reports similar findings for mothers, on the basis of updates of the time diary data (see figure 5.3; see also Bianchi and Robinson 1998–99). From 1965 to 1998, child care as a primary activity rose from 1.5 to 1.7 hours per day and total time with children (including child care as a secondary activity) from 5.3 to 5.5. (These data are for all mothers, however, not only those who are employed.) Bianchi and Robinson also find rising care hours for fathers. (See figure 5.3.)

Figure 5.3a.   Change in Mothers' Hours of Child Care and Time with Children

Figure 5.3b.   Change in Married Fathers' Hours of Child Care and Time with Children

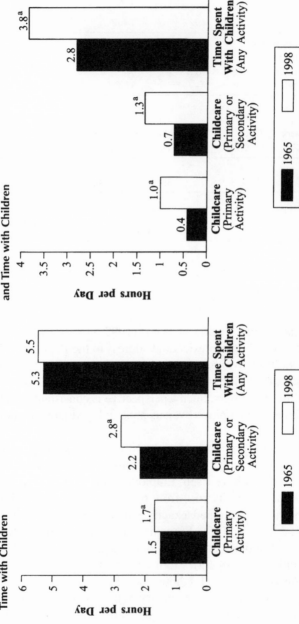

Sources: "Americans' Use of Time" (1965–1966); Bianchi and Robinson (1998–1999). Bianchi (2000), Figures 1 and 7.

Notes: Estimates are base on one-day "yesterday" time diaries collected from 417 mothers in 1965–1966 and 273 mothers in 1998–1999, all with children under age 18 at the time of the interview. Child care includes child and baby care, helping/teaching children, talking/reading to children, indoor/outdoor play with children, medical/travel/other child-related care.

[a] Test of 1965–1998 difference in means is statistically significant, *p* < .05.

Sources: "Americans' Use of Time" (1965–1966); Bianchi and Robinson (1998–1999). Bianchi (2000), Figures 1 and 7.

Notes: Estimates are base on one-day "yesterday" time diaries collected from 326 married fathers in 1965–1966 and 194 married fathers in 1998–1999, all with children under age 18 at the time of the interview. Child care includes child and baby care, helping/teaching children, talking/reading to children, indoor/outdoor play with children, medical/travel/other child-related care.

[a] Test of 1965–1998 difference in means is statistically significant, *p* < .05.

The NSCW estimates are considerably higher because they measure contact time, rather than child care as a primary activity. (The time diary estimates suggest that contact time is about four times as high as child care as a primary activity.) According to the NSCW, between 1977 and 1997, employed married mothers' contact hours with children on workdays went from 3.3 to 3.0, a change that is not statistically significant. (See table 5.7.) On non-working days, mothers' contact hours have risen from 7.3 to 8.3. Among married fathers, working-day contact hours have risen from 1.8 to 2.3, and non-workday hours from 5.2 to 6.4 (Bond et al. 1998, pp. 40–41). Furthermore, because these estimates are for total time with children, and the number of children per married couple has fallen, it seems that the contact time per child has most likely risen.

While these data are comforting, I would suggest that we need more evidence before becoming complacent about parental contact with children. Both case study (for example, Hochschild 1997) and anecdotal evidence (such as the long hours of child-care facilities) suggest that a subset of children may be experiencing high levels of parental absence, which is masked by the stability of averages. This is consistent with the growing polarity in the distribution of time use, reflecting disproportionate increases in worktime among certain subgroups (professionals and managers in long-hours jobs and low-wage workers who need to work many hours to survive economically). Jacobs and Gerson, using CPS data, note the substantial rise in the fraction of men and women working more than 50 hours per week. For men, the increase between 1970 and 1997 was from 21.0 percent to 25.2 percent; for women from 5.2 percent to 10.8 percent. In 1997, 34.5 percent of men and 17.0 percent of women professional, managerial, and technical employees were working more than 50 hours per week. A next step for research should be to look at contact time among long-hours workers.

Similarly, there has been a rise in the fraction working fewer than 30 hours per week (Jacobs and Gerson 2000, table 6.1, p. 90). This partly reflects the emergence of "downshifting" in the 1990s. (See Schor 1998.) It is not possible from the published studies to determine whether a rise in contact hours among "short-hours" employees is offsetting a decline in contact hours among "long-hours" types. Similarly, these sources have not looked much at single-parent families, a group that has grown substantially and whose working hours, Leete and Schor found, grew disproportionately.

There are also methodological issues. On the one hand, there are major drawbacks associated with using existing time diaries to reflect trends over time, especially with respect to comparisons back to 1965. (See Schor 2000.) Second, the question of whether survey respondents overestimate their worktime, which Robinson has argued they do, may be more serious in the area of child care than paid work. This is on account of social desirability bias—that is, the tendency of respondents to give socially desirable answers. (See Schor 2000 for a discussion of overestimation in recall data.)

Finally, we might also want to ask about the quality of parenting and not merely hours of contact. If parents are in fact more time stressed (see the next section), then it is possible that any given contact hour yields less parent–child interaction.

IS THERE A WORKTIME PROBLEM FOR PARENTS?

Personal Stress and Time Pressure among Parents

If the foregoing data on parental working hours and child contact time are correct, does this mean that there is no problem of "time crunch" or "work-family" conflict for parents? Not necessarily. Indeed, whatever the trends in actual time-use, attitudinal data suggest that employed parents feel strongly that they do not have enough time to spend with their children. In the NSCW, 70 percent of married parents said they personally did not have enough time to spend with their children. Strikingly, 43 percent of fathers said they wish their partners would spend more time with their children (as did 56 percent of mothers) (Bond et al. 1998, p. 42).

Furthermore, the trends on worktime and child contact cited previously suggest that parents must be cutting back substantially on some other activities. This appears to be the case. In the NSCW, "time for self" declined substantially for both mothers and fathers. Mothers' time for self declined from 1.6 to 0.9 hours on working days and 3.3 to 2.5 on nonwork days. Fathers' time for self declined from 2.1 to 1.2 and 5.1 to 3.3, respectively (Bond et al. 1998, pp. 47–48). (Again, these data are for married parents only.)

This substantial loss of uncommitted time is most likely implicated in the dramatic rise in feelings of time pressure, stress, and hurry that has occurred over this period and about which all participants in the debates about worktime trends agree. For example, Robinson and Godbey have found substantial increases in the fraction of the population aged 18–64 that always feels rushed, from 24 percent in 1965 to a peak of 38 percent in 1992, with a reduction to 33 percent in 1995 (Robinson and Godbey 1999, table 22, p. 232).[14] More generally, they found that rates of "always feeling rushed" were higher among parents than nonparents, and that rates rise by the number of children (Robinson 1990, p. 33). Similarly, Robinson and Godbey find that parents are a particularly high-stress group, compared to the population as a whole. Mothers especially rate high on their "time crunch" scale (Robinson and Godbey 1999, table 24, p. 237).

The Desire to Work Less

Given these high levels of time crunch and pressure, it is not surprising that the proportion of Americans, and parents, who are working more hours than they would like to has risen dramatically since the 1970s and even the mid-1980s. The percentage of people who say they would prefer to work less and earn less has increased steadily since 1985, from about 5 percent, to 15 percent in 1994, and 17 percent in 1995.[15] (Before 1985 it had been roughly steady for at least twenty years.) And in some formulations of the question, the fraction wanting to work less is substantially higher. For example, a Gallup poll from August 1994 found that one-third of all respondents said they would prefer that either they or their spouse reduce hours and income up to 20 percent in order to gain more time for family (*Health Magazine* 1994, p. 48). In 1991, John Robinson found nearly half the working population reporting that they would prefer a four-day workweek with the loss of the fifth day's pay (Hilton Hotels Values Survey, reported in Hymowitz 1991).

The NSCW also found that people are working more hours than they would prefer, although in their formulation of the question, respondents were not asked about willingness to trade income for shorter hours. Asked whether they work more than they would like, nearly two-third of respondents (63 percent) reported that they would prefer to work fewer hours, on average 11 per week (table 5.7).

Job Demands, "Burnout," and Work-Family Spillover among Parents

In addition to the temporal demands of jobs, stress and pressure are created by particular aspects of scheduling and the spatial demands of work. For example, in the NSCW, 18 percent of parents reported that they work overtime with little or no notice every week. Increasing numbers of parents bring work home or are away from home overnight on business. Furthermore, other aspects of job pressure such as workload have risen dramatically (table 5.8).

In an analysis of the NSCW data on the impact of high "job demands" (a combination of hours of work and other aspects of the job, such as nights away from home, job pressures, etc.), Galinsky and Swanberg (1998) find that job demands are *the* key factor explaining job "burnout" and what is referred to in the literature as "job-to-home spillover." (The job burnout measure is composed of questions about emotional drain, stress, and fatigue in the past three months. Job-to-home spillover is composed of questions about time scarcity, including with family; inadequate energy for family, moods, etc. Both burnout and job-to-home spillover are strongly correlated with personal well-being.) Among parents, rates of burnout and spillover are higher

Table 5.8. Selected Data on Job Characteristics among Married Parents from the NSCW, 1977 and 1997[a]

	1977	1997
Job Pressure on Parents	*(percentage agreeing)*	
My job requires that I work very fast	58	68
My job requires that I work very hard	71	88
I never seem to have enough time to get everything done on my job	41	62
Selected Job Demands on Parents		
Work overtime with little notice once a week		18
Six or more nights away from home in the past three months		9
Bring job-related work home once a week or more	21	31
Never bring work home		49

[a] Sample is for married employees with children.
Source: Galinsky and Swanberg (1998).

than they are for employees as a whole. For example, 32 percent of parents, versus 26 percent of nonparents, report that they "do not have the energy to do things with their families or other important people in their lives" often or very often. And 39 percent of parents report that within the past three months, they have "sacrificed personal time because of their jobs" very often or often. The authors conclude that "employed mothers and fathers today are working longer, faster and harder on the job and at home than they were 20 years ago . . . [and] they are feeling the squeeze" (p. 19).

CONCLUSION

Estimates of working hours for American parents suggest a dramatic rise between 1969 and the present, with most of the increase concentrated in the 1980s and 1990s. The available estimates suggest that parents have compensated, not by reducing their contact hours with children, but by cutting back on time for themselves and other chores. As a result, they have experienced high levels of stress and time pressure. This strategy raises at least two questions. First, what has been the impact on the quality of parent–child interaction? And second, if working hours trends continue, can parents continue to protect their time with children? These would seem to be important questions for further research. Finally, this chapter does not address an extremely important issue that relates to parental stress and pressure—namely, the behavior of absolute and relative earnings over the period in question. To the extent that they have fallen for most American parents, and they have, this is a related and important source of pressure. (See Mishel et al. 2001 for extensive analysis of income trends, and Schor 1998 for the argument that relative incomes have fallen for all but the top 20 percent.)

REFERENCES

Bianchi, Suzanne M. (2000). "Maternal Employment and Time with Children: Dramatic Change or Surprising Continuity?" *Demography* 37 (4) (November): 401–14.

Bianchi, Suzanne M., and John Robinson (1998–99). "Family Interaction, Social Capital, and Trends in Time Use." Time diary data, University of Maryland.

Bluestone, Barry, and Stephen Rose (2000). "The Enigma of Working Time Trends." In Lonnie Golden and Deborah M. Figart, *Working Time: International Trends, Theory and Policy Perspectives* (London: Routledge), 21–37.

—— (1997). "Overworked and Underemployed: Unraveling an Economic Enigma." *The American Prospect* 31 (March–April): 58–69.

Bond, James T., Ellen Galinsky, and Jennifer E. Swanberg (1998). *The 1997 National Study of the Changing Workforce* (New York: Families and Work Institute).

Burtless, Gary (2000). "Squeezed for Time? American Inequality and the Shortage of Leisure." *Brookings Review* (Fall): 18–22.

Coleman, Mary T., and John Pencavel (1993a). "Changes in Hours of Work of Male Employees since 1940." *Industrial and Labor Relations Review* 46 (2): 262–83.

—— (1993b). "Trends in Market Work Behavior of Women since 1940." *Industrial and Labor Relations Review* 46 (4): 653–76.

Council of Economic Advisers (1999). "Families and the Labor Market, 1969–1999: Analyzing the 'Time Crunch,'" mimeo, May.

Fuchs, Victor (1986). "His and Hers: Differences in Work and Income, 1959–1979." *Journal of Labor Economics* 4: S245–72.

Galinsky, Ellen, and Jennifer E. Swanberg (1998). "Employed Mothers and Fathers in the United States: Understanding How Work and Family Life Fit Together." Unpublished paper, Families and Work Institute.

Health Magazine (1994). "A Nation Out of Balance" (October): 44–48.

Hochschild, Arlie (1997). *The Time Bind: When Work Becomes Home and Home Becomes Work* (New York: Metropolitan).

Hymowitz, Carol (1991). "Trading Fat Paychecks for Free Time." *Wall Street Journal,* August 5, 1991, B1.

Jacobs, Jerry A., and Kathleen Gerson (2000). "Who Are the Overworked Americans?" In Lonnie Golden and Deborah M. Figart, *Working Time: International Trends, Theory and Policy Perspectives* (London: Routledge), 89–105.

Juster, F. Thomas, and Frank P. Stafford (1991). "The Allocation of Time: Empirical Findings, Behavioral Models, and Problems of Measurement." *Journal of Economic Literature* 29 (2): 471–522.

—— (1985). *Time, Goods and Well-Being* (Ann Arbor, Mich.: Survey Research Center, Institute for Social Research, University of Michigan).

Leete, Laura, and Juliet B. Schor (1994). "Assessing the Time Squeeze Hypothesis: Esti-
mates of Market and Non-Market Hours in the United States, 1969–1989." *Industrial
Relations* 33 (l): 25–43.
—— (1992). "The Great American Time Squeeze." *Economic Policy Institute* (Febru-
ary).
Merck Family Fund (1995). Yearning for Balance Poll (Takoma Park, Md.)
Mishel, Lawrence, et al. (2001). *The State of Working America 2000–01*. An Economic
Policy Institute Book (Ithaca, N.Y.: Cornell University Press).
PEW Global Stewardship Initiative Survey (February 1994). Washington, D.C., mimeo.
Robinson, John P. (1990). "The Time Squeeze." *American Demographics* (February): 30–33.
—— (1989a). "Time for Work." *American Demographics* (April): 68.
—— (1989b). "Time's Up." *American Demographics* (July): 33–35.
—— (1988). "Technology and the American Economic Transition: Choices for the Fu-
ture" (Washington, D.C.: Congress of the United States, Office of Technology Assessment).
Robinson, John P., and Ann Bostrom (1994). "The Overestimated Workweek? What Time
Diary Measures Suggest," *Monthly Labor Review* (August): 11–23.
Robinson, John P., and Geoffrey Godbey, (1999). *Time for Life: The Surprising Ways
Americans Use Their Time*. 2nd ed. (State College: Pennsylvania State University
Press).
—— (1997). *Time for Life: The Surprising Ways Americans Use Their Time*. (State College: Pennsylvania State University Press).
—— (1996). "The Great American Slowdown." *American Demographics* (June): 42–48.
Schor, Juliet B. (2000). "Working Hours and Time Pressure: The Controversy about
Trends in Time Use." In Lonnie Golden and Deborah M. Figart, *Working Time: International Trends, Theory and Policy Perspectives* (London: Routledge), 73–86.
—— (1998). *The Overspent American: Upscaling, Downshifting and the New Consumer*
(New York: Basic Books).
—— (1994). "Short of Time: American Families and the Structure of Jobs." Unpublished
paper, Harvard University.
—— (1992). *The Overworked American: The Unexpected Decline of Leisure* (New York:
Basic Books).
Shank, Susan E. (1986). "Preferred Hours of Work and Corresponding Earnings." *Monthly
Labor Review* (November): 40–44.

NOTES

1. In the time diary studies, respondents are asked to record, for every fifteen-minute
interval, how they spent their time. Analysts then choose a particular definition of "work,"
or "leisure," in order to produce the kinds of measures that are used in debates on time allocation. Time budgets are always weekly, either because the diaries are filled out for an
entire week, or because a synthetic week is created from daily diaries. In a classic diary
study, respondents receive the diary before it is to be filled out. In Robinson's 1985 and
later surveys, respondents are asked about yesterday and asked to recall in fifteen-minute
intervals how they used their time.

2. Our estimates are derived by combining respondents' estimates of their actual hours the past week and the number of weeks they worked in the previous year. We found similar trends using the "usual weekly hours" question, which has been available since 1979.

3. Our basic methodology, following that of Victor Fuchs (1986), was the following. To avoid the shortcomings we were concerned about in the time diary data, we used CPS data to construct annual hours of paid work. One controversy about these estimates concerns the accuracy with which respondents estimate their own hours of work. Robinson and Godbey's comments (1997, p. 50) concern the way we calculated household hours. For household hours we created predicted estimates from the 1975 Michigan Time Diary Survey and the CPS. (Time diaries provide the only existing estimates of household hours.) Using the 1975 survey, we constructed an econometric model to predict average amounts of weekly housework for various demographic and socioeconomic groups. Taking the coefficients from that model, we applied them to the CPS in order to construct trends in household work. We reasoned that because trends in housework are largely driven by demographic and socioeconomic trends, and because the CPS is the more accurate reflector of demographic and socioeconomic trends, this was the preferable method. On this point it may be worth noting that like Robinson and Godbey, we, too, find significant declines in women's hours of housework and increases in men's hours, so that their suggestion to the contrary is somewhat puzzling.

4. For additional estimates using the CPS, see Burtless (2000), who looks at weekly hours between 1968 and 1998 by sex, income, and age. While he finds an average increase in hours among prime-aged workers, men in all but the top income quintile have had declining weekly hours. However, his figures are not strictly comparable to Mishel's because they include the unemployed. Furthermore, the weekly hours miss the large increases in weeks worked per year found by Leete and Schor and Mishel. Burtless finds that hours have increased on average for those in the under-fifty-five age group.

5. There are differences in the trends once they are broken down by gender, however. Bluestone and Rose report (but do not present) that in their estimates, male hours declined slightly, after controlling for the business cycle. This may be partly due to the large declines in hours (7.7 per year) registered for black men, a finding that accords with that of Coleman and Pencavel (see further on). But note also that Leete and Schor find a twenty-hour decline in market hours for men before underemployment and unemployment are taken into account. By contrast, Bluestone and Rose find even larger increases in women's hours than Leete and Schor, recording a rise of 18.8 hours per year, or 376 over the period.

6. The difference is likely due to the fact that in the later paper, Bluestone and Rose only use the PSID for the period 1967–74; they then switch to the CPS.

7. There are a series of disagreements between Robinson and me. A major one is the usefulness of the 1965 survey that forms his benchmark year. The 1965 survey was not representative of the U.S. population, and its sample characteristics resulted in a bias toward individuals with above-average hours of work. By then comparing to representative samples (in 1975 and 1985), the finding of declining hours was partly a statistical artifact. A second difference is in whether the trends are controlled for the substantial business cycle effects on working hours. (It is well-known among economists that average hours of work fluctuate with the business cycle, rising in expansions, as firms increase production more rapidly than employment, and falling in recessions as production shrinks.) Leete and Schor 1994 and subsequent studies look at comparable business cycle points, but time

diary studies ignore this issue. A second macroeconomic effect concerns unemployment or underemployment, which is discussed in the text.

Other differences include time at work versus time actually working, annual versus weekly hours, and time periods covered. Finally, the core of Robinson's critique of the CPS is that individuals overestimate their working hours when asked about them in the standard recall format but give true estimates when they fill out a time diary. While plausible, it is important to remember that this conclusion is not necessarily relevant to trends in working hours, which are the focus of the debate. If the extent of overestimation bias is constant over time, overestimation will have no impact on measured trends.

8. Or by 6.5, depending on which of the two reported figures is correct.

9. Burtless (2000) and Jacobs and Gerson (2000) discuss differences in working hours and time pressure among subsets of the employed population.

10. Data on weeks per year for married couples with children, aged 25–54, are available back to 1969 and show an average increase of 10.7 weeks (from 80.4 to 91.1 total weeks worked 1969–1998) (Mishel et al. 2001, table 1.28, p. 97).

11. See Bianchi (2000) for a discussion of this literature. She does not discuss the subset of mothers who work long hours. This is discussed later.

12. Leete and Schor did not publish hours of child care separately from other nonmarket activities, so their estimates are not discussed here.

13. Trends in total contact hours, which include child care as a secondary or lesser activity, are not provided. Estimates for parents only are not given in the 1992–95 update; however, Robinson and Godbey note that overall child-care hours remained constant and number of children per household fell, so that hours spent per child must have risen (Robinson and Godbey 1999, p. 331).

14. The "always feel rushed" measure peaked in 1992 and dropped 6 points by 1995. Robinson and Godbey (1997) report other measures of a possible slowdown in time pressure, which is consistent with the downshifting trend reported by Schor (1998). Robinson and Godbey's 1992–1995 "trend" is not statistically significant, however.

15. The 1985 figure is from Shank (1986); 1994 figure from PEW Global Stewardship Initiative Survey, February 1994 (data provided to author); 1995 figure from Merck Family Fund Yearning for Balance Poll, February 1995 (data provided to author).

6

Low-Income Parents and the Time Famine

S. Jody Heymann

The political rhetoric of the 1980s and 1990s often dichotomized individuals' responsibility and society's. In no area has this dichotomy been greater than in debates regarding the lives of those living in poverty in the United States. In August 1996, the United States Congress repealed the federal promise of income for parents and children living in poverty. They replaced welfare guarantees that had been in place for over sixty years with work mandates and block grants to states. Training and education for welfare recipients decreased and work requirements increased. The overall notion of the legislation, entitled "The Personal Responsibility and Work Opportunity Reconciliation Act of 1996," was that at the root of persistent poverty was a lack of personal responsibility.

This chapter is based on a different paradigm: one that argues that while, ultimately, social responsibility may lie in the hands of individuals, societal actions lay the groundwork that can make it either a straightforward or a nearly Olympian feat for individuals to exercise that responsibility.

BACKGROUND

Needing to Meet Caretaking Responsibilities While Working

Demographic and policy changes have contributed to the increased caretaking responsibilities of the employed. The overall percentage of women with

S. Jody Heymann, M.D., Ph.D., is director of policy at the Harvard Center for Society and Health and associate professor at the Harvard School of Public Health and Harvard Medical School. Her books include *Equal Partners: A Physician's Call for a New Spirit of Medicine* and *The Widening Gap: Why America's Working Families Are in Jeopardy and What Can Be Done About It*.

preschool children who work rose more than fivefold over a half century, from 12 percent in 1947 to 64 percent in 1999. The percentage of women with school-aged children who are in the paid workforce has almost tripled over the same period of time, from 27 percent to 79 percent.[1] While the percentage of mothers working has risen sharply, the percentage of fathers working has not fallen. Over 95 percent of married men aged twenty to forty-four are in the labor force.[2] For many low-skilled workers, two incomes are now necessary in order to have a standard of living that was possible on a single income in the past.

In addition, over the past twenty-five years, the number of children living in single-parent homes has risen markedly. In 1970, 13 percent of families with children under eighteen years old were headed by one parent. By 1998, that number had risen to 27 percent of families.[3] It has been estimated that one out of two children will live in a one-parent home before they turn eighteen.[4] Changes in family structure and the availability of parental time are important in themselves[5] and in their effect on the ability of working parents to succeed at filling multiple roles. Previous studies have shown that both the resident and nonresident parents spend less time with children in single-parent families.[6] The custodial parent in one-parent families has to balance more responsibilities and thus often has less time for child care. While married mothers spend on average ten hours a week in primary child-care activities, single mothers spend only seven. Fifty-six percent of parents who live apart from their children see their children less than once a month and 36 percent less than once a year.[7]

Finally, elder care has become an increasingly important problem. Low-skilled workers who receive low wages are often less able to afford to pay for others to care for sick and elderly relatives. Americans who have only a high-school education are significantly more likely than Americans with a college education or higher to be caring for elderly and disabled relatives.[8]

Work and Family Roles across Social Class

By 1996, when the United States Congress passed "The Personal Responsibility and Work Opportunity Reconciliation Act of 1996" and repealed the federal guarantee of income support for mothers and children living in poverty, the country had made an about-face.

In 1935, when Aid to Dependent Children (ADC) was passed as part of the sweeping reforms of the New Deal, the country had decided that it was impossible for single mothers, most of whom were single because of the death of or abandonment by a spouse, to support themselves economically and still provide adequate care for their children.

By 1996, a fundamental shift in the public debate over single parents living in poverty had taken place. The public had changed from believing it was impossible for most single women to care for their children while earning enough money to subsist to buying the idea that there was nothing other than willpower stopping single parents living in poverty from working full-time and caring for their children.

The argument seemed simple. Middle-class mothers were seemingly able to work and care for their children well, so why weren't poor mothers? It hadn't hurt middle-class children, so why should it hurt poor children? Little was said about the fact that there were two parts of the bargain: what parents contributed to the workforce and to their families, and what private and public policies were laid down as the foundation on which parents were carrying out their multiple roles.

This chapter looks at how society has shaped the different conditions faced by parents across social class as they try to meet their family and work responsibilities.

Current Policy

Adults working in the labor force who have caretaking responsibilities need to find ways to meet the many unpredictable time demands of children, disabled family members, and elderly parents. These demands include, among others, caring for sick children who are unable to go to child care or school, caring for elderly parents who are too sick to care for themselves, meeting with child-care providers and teachers when children are having difficulties, meeting with elder-care providers when parents are having difficulties, caring for children when child-care providers are sick or schools are closed, caring for parents when elder-care providers aren't available, arranging for special services when children have learning disabilities or behavioral problems, and arranging for new care when child- and elder-care arrangements fall through.[9] Just caring for family illness involves work disruptions or finding substitute care for three weeks or more every year for one out of four families.[10]

Only one benefit is guaranteed federally to employees with respect to caretaking roles and that benefit is guaranteed to only half of all employed parents. The Family and Medical Leave Act (FMLA) of 1993 requires that employers provide up to twelve weeks unpaid leave to employees who have a major illness themselves or whose immediate family members have a major illness, as well as providing for unpaid leave around the birth or adoption of a new child. The FMLA was an important step toward allowing employees to care for their elderly parents, ill spouses, and, less commonly, children during major illnesses. However, the coverage offered by the FMLA is limited to those who have been employed for at least 1,250 hours over the previous 12 months, in a firm that has at least 50 employees. Furthermore, it is unpaid.

Box 6.1   A Father's Story

Luis Marquez

A single, low-income parent with few extended family members he could call on, Luis Marquez was raising two children on an inadequate hourly wage that forced him to work overtime and nights to get by.

He was barely able to pay his family's living costs on his wages as a security guard. He wanted to visit his children's school regularly because he was worried about what they were facing. He described one time when he visited and watched children playing outside. "This bunch of kids, young boys, had this little girl . . . in the corner, and they were all spitting on her: spit, all over. And . . . if you see the look on this girl, she was humiliated." But Luis couldn't afford to visit the school often when he worked days, since each visit meant taking unpaid leave from work and having more trouble paying the bills.

During the year before we spoke with Luis, he changed from a daytime shift to a nighttime one. If he went without sleep, he could be at the school in an emergency during the day—if he didn't have to work overtime. But working at night made finding child care extremely difficult. To continue working nights, he needed to find someone both to care for his children at night and to get them to school in the morning. Eventually, he was able to pull things together, to make a patchwork quilt that would cover child care temporarily. He kept the night shift because it paid an extra dollar an hour, and he worked overtime when the family needed more money. Otherwise, his pay didn't even cover the rent in public housing after he paid for the car he needed to get to work and for his children's child care, food, and clothing. Even with the overtime, he could afford child care only because the child-care provider, who received income from welfare, accepted well below the minimum wage. Luis's situation was the same one faced by many poor working parents who rely on the only child care they can afford—child care that was indirectly subsidized through welfare payments and is vanishing under welfare reform.

Box 6.2   Two Mothers' Stories

Elizabeth Carter

A thirty-six-year-old mother of three, Elizabeth Carter had a daughter with asthma. Elizabeth struggled to hold onto a job, while meeting Lucy's needs, but Lucy was sick frequently. Elizabeth explained, "There were nights when sometimes I would go into emergency, stay with her all night, rock her in the rocking chair, and come home. My mother would watch her and [I would] go to work. How I did it, I don't know. I was half asleep. Going to the store to get the medicine . . . Lucy, she was in the hospital . . . every two weeks."

Whenever possible, Elizabeth stayed at the hospital during Lucy's critical times while continuing to work; she did this by not sleeping and by having her mother's assistance. But sometimes Elizabeth had to miss work in order to be with Lucy. She described one time: "When I had rushed her in [to the hospital] one night and it was a work night, I had stayed in. Went through emergency and I stayed in with her, just holding her and oxygen and all that. . . . I just called my boss and said I wouldn't be in, and that's when everything started going down."

From that point on, her boss gave her "a lot of static." Every time Elizabeth was out, she had to bring a doctor's note to work, and her boss did everything possible to make it harder for her to continue to work. Eventually, Elizabeth said, "it was a choice—either the job or my child, and I picked my child."

Agnes Charles

Agnes Charles was a single mom whose daughter also had asthma. She knew of stories like Elizabeth Carter's so she sent her own two-year-old daughter to child care with her medicine when she was getting sick and asked the child-care provider to call her if she grew sicker. But the provider never called and failed to give the medicine. As soon as Agnes came to pick her up at the end of the day, she knew her daughter was having serious difficulty breathing. Agnes took her straight to the emergency room, where she was admitted to the hospital. For a week Agnes spent each night in the hospital with her daughter and each day at work. It was clear how committed she was to both her daughter and her work. But commitment wasn't enough to prevent the hospitalization in the first place when her poor working conditions and the inadequate child care available had made it impossible for Agnes to adequately care for her daughter's health while employed.

From *The Widening Gap: Why America's Working Families Are in Jeopardy and What Can Be Done about It* (New York: Basic Books, 2000). Copyright © 2000 by Jody Heymann. By permission of Basic Books, a member of Perseus Books, L.L.C.

Although the FMLA addresses major illnesses for those working parents who are covered and can afford unpaid leave, it does nothing to address the many routine illnesses and caretaking demands of children, elderly parents, or other sick family members. Nor does it help families that cannot afford unpaid leave. More relevant to the ability of those who cannot afford unpaid leave to address major illnesses and to the ability of all employees to meet routine family needs while working is the availability of such job benefits as paid sick leave, paid vacation leave, paid personal days, and job flexibility. When employees work at jobs where they have flexible schedules, where they have autonomy over when and where to get their work done, they are more likely to be able to take leave to care for their children, elderly parents, or other family members when necessary. When employees have paid sick leave that they can take for family members, they can more readily meet the needs of caring for children during frequent common illnesses or assisting elderly parents when meeting routine health needs. When employees have paid vacation or paid personal days, they are more likely to be able to take time off to arrange for child or elder care and to fill in when care arrangements fall through.

METHODS

Analyses Conducted

Being responsible for children, working parents need to find ways to meet the many unpredictable time demands of children. Employers often see as most responsible those workers who have no unexplained absences, do not take more than the sick leave or vacation leave allowed, and who, when they need to take time off for "personal" reasons, make up the time that is missed.

In jobs where parents receive paid sick leave, receive paid vacation leave, and have job flexibility, the conflict between meeting these two sets of goals is greatly reduced. Parents may take sick leave to care for children who are ill. They may take vacation leave when their child-care facility or children's school is closed. Flexibility in the workplace may be used to meet unpredictable demands at home while making up for the missed time at work. In jobs with no paid sick leave, no paid vacation leave, and no flexibility, meeting the demands of the workplace and responsibilities of a family may be untenable for low-income parents.

Analyses were conducted to examine the extent to which low-income parents face working conditions and have the social supports that make it possible for them to meet both work and family responsibilities.

The National Longitudinal Survey of Youth (NLSY) was used to examine the "concrete working conditions" faced by mothers who leave welfare for work, including the availability of paid sick leave, paid vacation leave, and flexible work schedules. The benefits and flexibility available to mothers who had received welfare for a lifetime total of five or more years before their current job and women who had received welfare less than five years were compared with the benefits and flexibility available to working mothers who had never received welfare. Because the overwhelming majority of working parents who had received welfare were women and because women may receive different benefits than men, women were used as the control group.

Sampling weights were used; a Pearson chi-square test was used to test for significant differences in proportions. Tests of significance were adjusted for the use of weights and design effects resulting from the NLSY survey sampling methods.

Parents with more say in decisions about their work have greater flexibility in meeting work demands while caring for their children. Therefore, this study also examined the extent to which decision-making latitude at work differed for low-income and middle- and upper-income parents. Data from the Survey of Midlife Development in the United States (MIDUS) were analyzed to take this detailed look at how flexibility varied in low-wage jobs.

Parents who are unable to take time from work to meet their children's needs must rely on substitute child care; otherwise, their children's needs go unmet. The principle source of substitute care for low-income working parents is *unpaid* substitute care. The availability of members of a parent's support network—of family, friends, and neighbors to provide unpaid help—determines the extent to which individual parents can rely on unpaid substitute care. Data were collected in MIDUS on the extent to which working parents could rely on family, friends, and neighbors for help.

Pearson chi-square statistics were used to test for significant differences in the support reported by working parents with low family incomes. Sampling weights from MIDUS were used; tests of significance were adjusted for the use of weights.

Data Sources

The NLSY consists of a nationally representative probability sample of 11,406 civilian men and women ages 14 to 21 when they were first surveyed in 1979.[11] Respondents are currently aged 35 to 42. Poor and minority populations were oversampled in the NLSY. The working conditions faced by the 2,261 mothers in the sample who worked at least 20 hours per week and who were not self-employed were examined. Of the 2,261 working mothers, 736 have at some time been on welfare and 1,525 have never been on welfare. Total years of welfare receipt were calculated between January 1978 and December 1993. Our analyses included 215 women who had received welfare for over five years. Only mothers who worked at least 20 hours per week were examined because only these workers were asked about employer-provided benefits in the NLSY. Since many employees who work less than half-time are ineligible for many employer-provided benefits, our estimates of the proportion of employed parents who have benefits will be an overestimate.

The MIDUS survey, conducted in 1995, involved a national probability sample of 3,485 respondents aged 25 to 75, selected using random digit telephone dialing. Respondents included 908 working parents, aged 25 to 66 (mean 39.0, SD 7.3), who had children under 18 years old. MIDUS does not contain information on the history of welfare receipt among respondents, so the experiences of low-income working parents were compared with those of middle- and high-income working parents. The majority of parents who leave welfare for work land jobs with wages that leave their family income near or below 150 percent of the federal poverty level.[12] A respondent was considered to be low-income if his or her total family income was less than or equal to 150 percent of the federal poverty threshold for 1995 for his or her family size. MIDUS surveyed 743 working parents with family incomes above and 146 working parents with family incomes at or below 150 percent of the federal poverty threshold. (Nineteen working parents did not report their income.)

RESULTS

Concrete Working Conditions Faced by Parents Who Have Left Welfare

Working mothers who have received welfare income support in the past are significantly more likely than working mothers who have never received welfare to lack paid vacation leave ($p < 0.001$), lack paid sick leave ($p < 0.001$), and lack flexibility in their work schedule ($p = 0.03$). Those working mothers who received welfare for more than five years in the past are significantly more likely than those who received welfare for less than five years to lack paid sick leave ($p < 0.001$), lack paid vacation leave ($p < 0.001$), and lack flexibility in their work schedule ($p < 0.02$). Twice as many working mothers who have received welfare for more than five years in the past lack paid sick leave and paid vacation leave, as do working mothers who have never been on welfare (see figure 6.1).

Among those who do receive paid sick or vacation leave, mothers who have received welfare are significantly more likely than working mothers who have never received welfare to have one week or less of paid leave ($p < 0.005$); among mothers who have received welfare for five years, 39 percent have neither paid sick leave nor paid vacation leave; among those who do re-

Figure 6.1.   Parents Who Lack Paid Leave

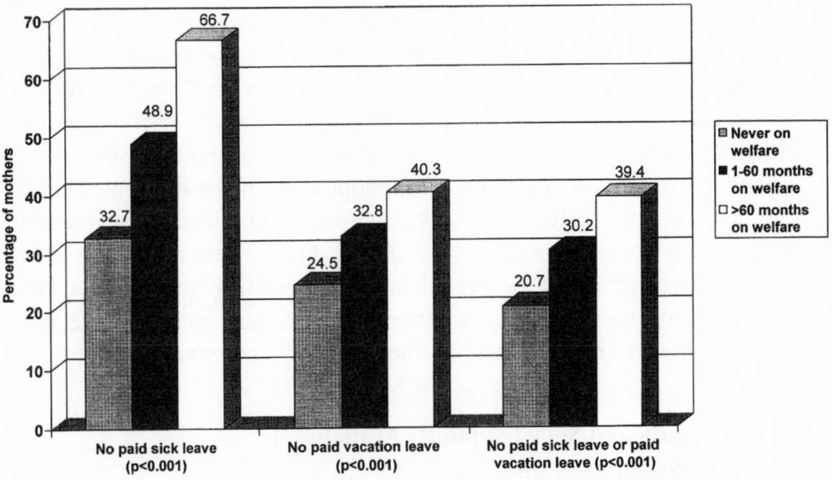

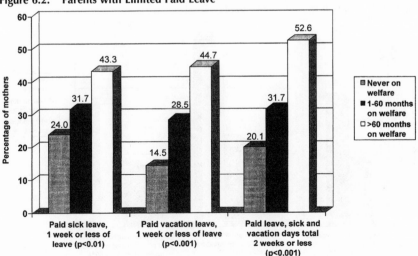

ceive either paid sick or paid vacation leave, more than half receive less than two weeks of total paid leave (see figure 6.2).

Paid leave and flexible work schedules can be used as partial substitutes for each other when it comes to meeting children's needs. However, mothers who have left welfare for work have little chance to use either. They are significantly more likely to be at multiple jeopardy and lack flexibility and paid leave than working mothers who have never received welfare (p < 0.001). In fact, mothers who have received welfare for more than five years were three

Figure 6.2.   Parents with Limited Paid Leave

times as likely to be at multiple jeopardy and lack flexibility and paid leave as mothers who have never received welfare (see figure 6.3).

Parents with few benefits and little flexibility in the workplace may rely on other adults in the household to help meet children's needs while working. However, mothers with a history of receiving welfare were significantly more likely than mothers who had never received welfare to find themselves, even after leaving welfare, single, with no grandparents in the household, at the same time as having neither paid sick leave nor paid vacation leave and no flexibility in their work schedules ($p < 0.001$). One in four mothers who had received welfare in the past for more than five years finds herself in the workplace single, with no grandparents in the household and no paid leave, compared to one in forty mothers who has never received welfare.

Decision Latitude and Social Supports Available to Low-Income Working Parents

Low-income working parents were significantly more likely than middle- and upper-income parents to be unable to decide how their job was done ($p = 0.02$), to be unable to decide what jobs were done ($p = 0.01$), to lack say in decisions about their work in general ($p = 0.004$), and to lack say in planning their work environment ($p < 0.001$) than middle- and upper-income parents were. One in four working parents whose family income was below 150 percent of the poverty threshold lack say in general decisions about his or her work or in deciding what jobs are done. Nearly one in three lack say in planning his or her work environment (see table 6.1).

Figure 6.3.   Parents at Multiple Jeopardy

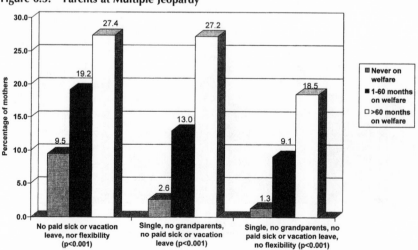

Table 6.1.   Working Conditions and Social Supports: Do They Differ for Low-Income Parents?

	Income ≤150% of the poverty line	Income >150% of the poverty line	P
*Lack Decision Latitude**			
Do not decide how job is done	11.0	6.4	0.024
Do not decide what jobs are done	25.9	17.4	0.014
Do not have a say in decisions about their work	23.2	13.0	0.004
Do not have a say in planning their work environment	30.4	17.9	<0.001
*Lack Social Support at Work**			
Do not get help and support from their coworkers	13.0	9.3	0.008
Do not get help and support from their immediate supervisor	17.9	16.6	0.738
*Lack Social Support Outside of Work**			
Do not feel they can rely on family for help	19.8	10.9	0.005
Do not feel they can rely on a friend for help	23.6	19.5	0.054
Do not feel they can rely on a neighbor for help	28.9	13.1	<0.001
*Multiple Jeopardy**			
Have no decision latitude and no workplace support	8.9	4.8	0.067
Have no decision latitude and no support	7.9	2.3	<0.001

*Figures given are percent of working parents.

There were no significant differences in the amount of contact that low-income and higher-income working parents had with their neighbors, family members, and friends. However, low-income working parents were significantly less likely to state that they could rely on a neighbor ($p < 0.001$) or on family for help ($p = 0.005$). Their families and neighbors were more likely to be overburdened themselves. Twice as many low-income working parents as higher-income parents stated that they could not rely on family or neighbors for help. Low-income parents were also significantly less likely to get help and support from co-workers ($p = 0.008$). One and a half times as many reported that they could not get help and support from co-workers (see table 6.1).

To some extent, social support from family, friends, and neighbors can serve as a partial substitute for job autonomy and flexibility when parents are seeking to meet work demands at the same time as caring for their children. However, low-income working parents were significantly more likely than higher-income parents to lack both latitude in the workplace and social supports ($p < 0.001$). Nearly twice as many low-income working parents found themselves both in the lowest quartile of respondents in terms of workplace support and in the lowest quartile of respondents in terms of decision latitude as higher-income parents. More than three times as many low-income working parents found themselves in the lowest quartile of respondents both in terms of decision latitude and in terms of outside support as did higher-income parents (see table 6.1).

DISCUSSION

It is understandable to ask people to take responsibility for themselves and to ask parents to take responsibility for their children. It is reasonable to ask people to carry their own weight, if they are given a reasonable chance.

However, right now, too many families in the United States face circumstances that make it difficult—and some families face conditions that make it nearly impossible—to succeed at meeting their responsibilities at work while caring well for their children's health and development.

Low-income workers face significantly worse working conditions and significantly greater barriers to balancing work and caring for their families. In effect, we ask all parents in our country to jump high—to clear a ten-foot bar. Yet middle-income families start at ground level, while low-income families are asked to jump just as high but are placed in a hole twenty feet deep in the ground.

If as a society we are going to expect that parents be responsible for paid work in the labor force and the unpaid work of caretaking, then society must take responsibility for making it feasible. As a nation, we must ensure that all parents face conditions in their workplaces, children's schools, neighborhoods, and communities that make it possible to care for their children's health and development while working.

Employees need paid leave to care for children, partners, elderly parents, and disabled relatives when they become sick. They need the flexibility to take time from work to arrange for child care and elder care, to address problems that arise in school.

There are a wide range of ways to achieve this that span the political spectrum and include both primarily public initiatives, primarily private initiatives, and public-private collaborations.

We can afford to debate the best way to address society's responsibilities. What we can't afford is to do nothing.

NOTES

I am indebted to Alison Earle for her research assistance; to Cara Bergstrom, Bora Lee, and Jennifer Eckerman for their staff and research assistance; and to colleagues in the Canadian Institute for Advanced Research and the MacArthur Foundation Research Networks for their thoughtful suggestions. This work would not have been possible without the help of after-school child-care providers and the help and patience of my family.

This research was supported by the National Institute of Child Health and Development, the William T. Grant Foundation, the Canadian Institute for Advanced Research, and the John D. and Catherine T. MacArthur Foundation Research Network on Successful Midlife Development.

1. Committee on Ways and Means, U. S. House of Representatives, *1993 Green Book: Overview of Entitlement Programs* (Washington, D.C.: U.S. Government Printing Office, July 7, 1993); U.S. Bureau of the Census, unpublished tabulations from the Current Population Survey, March 1999, Marital and Family Supplement.

2. U.S. Bureau of the Census, *Statistical Abstract of the United States: 1993,* 113th edition (Washington, D.C.: U.S. Bureau of the Census, 1993).

3. U.S. Bureau of the Census, *Statistical Abstract of the United States: 1997,* 117th edition (Washington, D.C.: U.S. Bureau of the Census, 1997); U.S. Bureau of the Census, *Statistical Abstract of the United States: 1999* (Washington, D.C.: U.S. Bureau of the Census, 1999).

4. Bumpass, L., "Children and Marital Disruption: A Replication and Update," *Demography* 21 (1984): 71–82.

5. Presser, B. B., "Can We Make Time for Children: The Economy, Work Schedules and Child Care," *Demography* 26 (1989): 523–44; Earls, F., and M. Carlson, "Towards Sustainable Development for American Families," *Daedalus* 122 (1) (1993): 93–122; Dawson, D. A., "Family Structure and Children's Health: United States, 1988," *Vital Health Statistics* 10 (1991); McLanahan, S., and G. Sandefur, *Growing up with a Single Parent* (Cambridge, Mass.: Harvard University Press, 1994).

6. Hamburg, D. A., *Today's Children: Creating a Future for a Generation in Crisis* (New York: Random House, Inc., 1992).

7. Goldstein, N., *Are Changes in Work and Family Harming Children?* Report to the Carnegie Corporation Task Force on Meeting the Needs of Young Children, 1993.

8. Marks, N. F., "Caregiving across the Lifespan: National Prevalence in Predictors," *Family Relations* 45 (1996): 27–36.

9. Heymann, S. J., "Labor Policy: Its Influence on Women's Reproductive Lives," in *Power and Decision: The Social Control of Reproduction,* ed. G. Sen, and R. Snow (Boston: Harvard University Press, 1994), 43–57.

10. Heymann, S. J., A. Earle, B. Egleston, "Parental Availability for the Care of Sick Children," *Pediatrics* 98 (1996): 228–30.

11. Center for Human Resource Research, *NLS Handbook 1995* (Columbus: Center for Human Resource Research, Ohio State University, 1995).

12. Harris, K. M., "Life after Welfare: Women, Work and Repeat Dependency," *American Sociological Review* 61 (1996): 407–26; Nightingale, D. S., D. A. Wissoker, L. C. Burbridge, D. L. Bawden, N. Jeffries, *Evaluation of the Massachusetts Employment and*

Training (ET) Program (Washington, D.C.: Urban Institute, 1991); United States Department of Labor, *Work Incentive (WIN) Program Data Summary: Fiscal Years 1981 and 1984–1988* (Washington, D.C.: United States Department of Labor, August 19, 1989), table 1.

PART THREE

THE POLITICAL MARKETPLACE

7

Political Trends among American Parents: The 1950s to 1996

Ruy Teixeira

In the political campaigns of the late 1990s, the problems of America's parents (particularly the iconic "soccer mom") were ostentatiously recognized and lamented by politicians of all persuasions. It was widely observed that the always difficult task of raising children has become progressively more difficult: economic stress has been heightened by twenty years of declining wages and stagnating incomes; partially reflecting this struggle to maintain living standards, two-earner families have become the norm; and, partially reflecting the development of this norm, the time pressures on America's families have become extraordinary. And, in the midst of all these pressures, the values upon which stable family life rests have appeared to be unstable themselves and in decline.

It is certainly to be applauded that these problems have been publicly recognized. But what has been lacking is a match between the acknowledged magnitude of parents' problems and a political agenda of sufficient scope to address those problems. As Winn and Carlson show (see chapters 8 and 10 of this volume), policy in the immediate post–World War II period, through a combination of tax, education, and housing measures, played a huge role in encouraging family formation and making American society "family-friendly." Nothing of this scale is on the current agenda of either political party.

Why? One possibility is that parents, despite their difficulties, don't have much of an agenda themselves. Thus politicians are simply responding to parents' own lack of interest in an activist approach to solving their problems. But a 1996 poll of parents conducted for the National Parenting Association

Ruy Teixeira is a senior fellow at the Century Foundation in Washington, D.C., a nonpartisan research organization. He is the author of *The Disappearing American Voter* and (with Joel Rogers) of *America's Forgotten Majority: Why the White Working Class Still Matters*.

(NPA) by Penn + Schoen Associates shows that parents both endorse a wide range of bold measures to ease their time and economic pressures and are unconvinced that government and business are doing what they can to help meet parents' needs.[1]

So the origins of this disconnect between parental needs and the current political agenda must lie elsewhere. This chapter investigates three key possibilities: (1) demographic shifts, both within families and between families and the rest of the population, that may have reduced the political power of parents; (2) voter turnout differentials between parents and nonparents that may reduce the relative political power of parents below their demographic weight in the population; and (3) shifts in political attitudes among both parents and nonparents that may undercut support for an activist proparent agenda.

DEMOGRAPHIC SHIFTS AND PARENTAL POWER

One important set of demographic changes has been noted by Wolff. These are changes that have taken place within the distribution of America's parents over time. As Wolff shows, in 1959 only about 10 percent of families with children were headed by a single parent. By 1998, that figure had reached 30 percent, primarily through dramatic growth in the number of single female–headed households with children.

Related to this, the relative incidence of poverty among parents increased in this period, from about 4 percentage points higher among families with children in 1959 to about 10.6 points higher in 1998. Moreover, in the twenty-year period of 1974–1993, the absolute incidence of poverty among parents increased from 12 to 19 percent, although more recently, in 1998, it has dropped to 15 percent.

Finally, in roughly the same period (1974–1998), the relationship between median family income of parents and nonparents reversed. In 1974, median income of families with children was 12 percent *higher* than that of childless families, while in 1998, it was 6 percent lower.

All else being equal, these changes within the distribution of families with children should have produced some diminution in the political power of parents, since poorer individuals, for a variety of reasons, exert less influence on politicians than richer individuals (Verba, Schlozman, and Brady 1995). But I believe a more significant demographic shift has occurred *between* parents and nonparents in the adult population. Specifically, the relative weight of parents[2] among the eligible electorate[3] has declined dramatically between 1956 and the present day.

For example, according to the National Election Studies (NES), a biennial survey of the American electorate conducted by the University of Michigan,

Table 7.1. Proportion of Parents and Nonparents in the
Eligible Electorate, 1956–1996

	Parents	Nonparents
1956	55	45
1958	55	45
1960	54	46
1962	51	49
1964	53	47
1966	48	52
1968	48	52
1978	45	55
1980	41	59
1982	38	62
1984	42	58
1986	43	57
1988	40	60
1990	40	60
1992	38	62
1996	36	64

Source: Calculated by author using survey data from National Election Studies.

the proportion of parents in the eligible electorate declined from 55 percent in 1956 to 36 percent in 1996, a drop of 19 percentage points (table 7.1). In other words, parents have gone from a solid majority of potential voters in the mid-1950s to a distinct minority among today's electorate.

There are a number of reasons for this, including: (1) the increasing weight of the elderly in the population, few of whom are currently raising children; (2) the increasing weight of single nonelderly individuals due to the increased incidence of divorce and the postponement of child rearing to later ages; and (3) the introduction of eighteen- to twenty-year-olds into the electorate in 1972, few of whom have had children. But whatever the reasons, this is obviously a change of no small significance. Nonparents now strongly outnumber parents among the eligible electorate, and this has probably commensurately reduced the political power of parents.

TURNOUT PATTERNS AND TRENDS AND PARENTAL POWER

A related source of problematic political influence of parents may be underrepresentation of parents in the voting electorate. That is, whatever the weight of parents in the *potential* electorate, that weight may be less among actual voters, due to relatively poor turnout among parents. The data in table 7.2 suggest that there is at least some problem along these lines.

Table 7.2.   Turnout Rates of Parents and Nonparents, 1956–1996

	Parents	Nonparents	Difference
1956	69	78	−8
1960	78	81	−3
1964	77	78	−1
1968	75	76	−1
1978	52	57	−5
1980	67	74	−7
1982	57	63	−6
1984	70	76	−6
1986	45	58	−13
1988	64	74	−10
1990	37	53	−16
1992	75	78	−3
1996	64	76	−12

Source: Calculated by author using survey data from National Election Studies.

As the table shows, in every year for which data is available, from 1956 through 1996, the National Election Studies[4] recorded poorer turnout[5] among parents than nonparents. The parent/nonparent turnout gap ranged from lows of 1 point less in 1960 and 1964 to highs of 13 points less in 1986 and 16 points less in the 1990 elections. And note that the turnout gap was also fairly high in the 1996 presidential election (12 points).[6]

Why do parents vote less? One reason is that parents tend disproportionately to be noncitizens, who, of course, do not vote at all. But the main reason is that they are younger (for example, 71 percent of parents are ages twenty-five to forty-four, compared to just 29 percent of nonparents) and younger individuals vote less often. Indeed, once the factor of age is controlled for, statistical models[7] suggest that parents are slightly *more* likely to vote than nonparents. But their relative youth results in underrepresentation, rather than overrepresentation.

Some sense of the scale of the parental underrepresentation problem can be gained by comparing the representation of parents among potential voters to their representation among actual voters and computing an underrepresentation index[8] (table 7.3). Generally, these data show a pattern of moderate underrepresentation of parents, with most values of the index over .9 and some very close to 1 (perfect representation). Note, however, that all the elections where parental underrepresentation dipped below .9 are fairly recent: 1986, 1990, and 1996.

Note also that, at least in presidential elections, the NES data suggest that parental turnout may have been declining faster than nonparental turnout over time.[9] For example, compared to 1956, parental turnout has declined 5 points,

Table 7.3. **Parental Representation among Voters and Eligible Electorate, 1956–1996**

	Among Voters	Among Eligible Electorate	Underrepresentation
1956	52.1	54.8	.951
1960	53.3	54.3	.982
1964	53.8	54.0	.996
1968	48.5	48.8	.994
1978	42.8	45.3	.945
1980	38.6	41.2	.937
1982	36.2	38.5	.940
1984	41.2	43.1	.956
1986	36.2	42.6	.850
1988	35.7	39.1	.913
1990	31.6	39.6	.798
1992	38.0	39.0	.974
1996	32.8	36.7	.894

Source: Calculated by author using survey data from National Election Studies.
Note: Figures in the second column differ slightly from corresponding figures in table 7.1 since data in this table are restricted to those respondents who had a valid answer to the question on whether they voted in the November election.

while nonparental turnout has declined only 2 points. Similarly, parental turnout has declined 14 points since 1960, compared to 5 points among nonparents. These figures suggest that declining parental turnout—in addition to a consistent parent/nonparent turnout gap—may play a role in parents' current political problems.

So far, this analysis suggests that a long-standing gap in turnout between parents and nonparents, accentuated by a relatively large decline in parental turnout, may contribute to the current weakness in parents' political influence, though not to the same extent as their declining weight in the overall electorate. However, combined with the diminution of parents' raw numbers, it undoubtedly further undermines parents' ability to influence public policy.

It may also be the case that the turnout figures used previously, because they lump all parents together, cloak more serious underrepresentation problems among different groups of parents. The data in table 7.4, based on census data[10] on parental turnout,[11] allow this possibility to be evaluated.

These data show that parental turnout is sharply lower than among comparable nonparents at the lower ends of the education and income distribution and among minorities. For example, high school dropout parents vote at a 22 percentage-point lower rate than high school dropout nonparents do, and high school graduate parents' turnout is 8 points below that of high school graduate nonparents. Similarly, turnout among parents with less than $15,000 in household income is 18 points below that of nonparents with the

Table 7.4. Turnout Rates of Parents and Nonparents, by Key Demographics, 1992

	Parents	Nonparents	Difference
All	58	63	−5
Education			
high school dropout	23	45	−22
high school graduate	52	60	−8
some college	68	69	−1
college graduate	81	79	2
postgraduate study	84	82	2
Income			
less than $15,000	32	50	−18
$15,000–$29,999	50	62	−12
$30,000–$49,999	66	69	−3
$50,000–$74,999	75	76	−1
$75,000 and over	81	79	2
Race			
Hispanic	25	33	−8
white	66	67	−1
black	51	56	−5
other	30	32	−2
Gender			
male	59	61	−2
female	58	65	−7
Marital Status			
unmarried	50	59	−9
married	63	72	−9

Source: Calculated by author using survey data from census voter supplement.

same economic status, and turnout among parents with $15,000 to $30,000 in household income is 12 points below that of similarly situated nonparents. Finally, turnout among black and Hispanic parents is, respectively, 5 and 8 points lower than that among black and Hispanic nonparents.

On the other end of the education and income spectrums and among whites, however, this turnout gap essentially disappears. Indeed, parents with a four-year college degree or postgraduate education show turnout rates slightly *higher* than among comparable nonparents, as do parents with over $75,000 in household income.

The reasons for such poor relative turnout among low-education and low-income parents have a great deal to with their relative youth. That is, nonparents with these low education and income levels tend to include a disproportionate number of elderly voters, who, despite their low socioeconomic status (SES), vote relatively frequently. This helps elevate the turnout rate of low SES nonparents over that of low SES parents.

Whatever the reason, the fact remains that low SES and minority parents, by virtue of their relatively low turnout rates, will tend to get less attention from politicians than corresponding nonparents. Indeed, since low SES and minority nonparents themselves will tend to get less attention than more affluent and white voters (whose turnout rates are generally higher), this puts low SES/minority parents at the bottom of the political totem pole.

POLITICAL ATTITUDES AND BEHAVIOR AND PARENTAL POWER

The previous sections suggest that parents are at a political disadvantage. Their relative numbers in the eligible electorate have dropped precipitously over time, while their (possibly increasing) tendency to vote less than nonparents exacerbates their political difficulties. And this does not even begin to take into account changes in political attitudes and voting proclivities that may have contributed to the current lack of interest in a substantive proparent political agenda.

Historical Changes in Political Attitudes and Behavior, 1952–1992

One such change that should be considered is changes in partisanship. Since Republicans have traditionally favored other means to help voters, including parents, than the active use of government, a long-term trend toward Republican partisanship would tend to tilt the political agenda away from the activist measures endorsed in the Penn + Schoen/NPA poll.

The NES data suggest that the trend toward Republican partisanship overall was only modest and indirect in the 1956–92 period, generated by a decline of just 4 points in the percentage of Democrats and Democratic leaners[12] and a concomitant rise in the proportion of pure independents. However, as table 7.5 shows, the trends were quite different among parents and nonparents, leading to a perhaps surprising result.

In 1956, parents were markedly more Democratic than nonparents, by a 55 to 49 percent margin. However, by 1992, that relationship had reversed.[13] The Democratic leanings of parents trailed nonparents by 44 to 50 percent. Thus, the Democratic partisanship of parents sank 11 points over the period, while that of nonparents actually rose 1 point.

A similar story is told by the time trend in ideology, albeit over a shorter period (table 7.6). In the first year for which data are available, 1978, parents

Table 7.5.   Democratic Partisanship among Parents and Nonparents, 1956–1996

	Parents	Nonparents	Difference
1956	55	49	6
1958	60	56	4
1960	52	54	−2
1962	58	54	4
1964	63	60	3
1966	55	55	0
1968	58	54	4
1978	54	56	−2
1980	52	54	−2
1982	58	55	3
1984	47	50	−3
1986	48	54	−6
1988	46	49	−3
1990	50	54	−4
1992	44	50	−6
1996	60	55	5

Source: Calculated by author using survey data from National Election Studies.

were slightly less conservative than nonparents by 36 to 38 percent. However, by 1992, parents had become substantially more conservative by a 45- to 36-percent margin, reflecting a shift of 9 percentage points by parents toward conservatism.[14]

Thus, part of the reason why the political environment has not been friendly to an activist, proparent agenda lies in a long-term trend away from Democratic partisanship and toward conservatism, *a trend that was strongest among parents themselves.* While, as we shall see, there are signs this is changing, the trend obviously had some important political effects.

Table 7.6.   Conservative Ideology among Parents and Nonparents, 1978–1996

	Parents	Nonparents	Difference
1978	36	38	−2
1980	45	43	2
1982	46	40	6
1984	41	41	0
1986	38	41	−3
1988	47	45	2
1990	40	38	2
1992	45	36	9
1996	43	39	4

Source: Calculated by author using survey data from National Election Studies.

The data in table 7.7 illustrate some of these effects. They show that the partisan and ideological trends just described did indeed have their counterparts in the voting booth. For example, in terms of the Congressional House vote, parents were somewhat more Democratic than nonparents in 1956 (55 to 51 percent), while, by 1992, they were much *less* Democratic (51 to 60 percent). Similarly, the presidential vote among parents was more Democratic than among nonparents in 1956 (42 to 39 percent), but had switched to substantially less Democratic by 1992 (43 to 49 percent).

Table 7.7. Democratic Vote among Parents and Nonparents, 1956–1996

	Parents	*Nonparents*	*Difference*
1956			
House	55	51	4
Presidential	42	39	3
1958	62	60	2
1960			
House	57	55	2
Presidential	51	47	4
1962	59	58	1
1964			
House	66	63	3
Presidential	69	66	3
1966	59	56	3
1968			
House	52	52	0
Presidential	44	39	5
1978	56	61	−5
1980			
House	51	57	−6
Presidential	35	42	−7
1982	61	56	5
1984			
House	58	53	5
Presidential	39	43	−4
1986	57	62	−5
1988			
House	59	59	0
Presidential	44	48	−4
1990	60	66	−6
1992			
House	51	60	−9
Presidential	43	49	−6
1996			
House	56	51	5
Presidential	59	54	5

Source: Calculated by author using survey data from National Election Studies.

Table 7.8.   Views about Government among Parents and Nonparents, 1958–1996

	Parents	Nonparents	Difference
1958			
can't be trusted	21	28	−7
wastes tax money	42	49	−7
1964			
can't be trusted	20	26	−6
wastes tax money	45	52	−7
run for big interests	28	35	−7
1966			
can't be trusted	28	36	−8
run for big interests	35	42	−7
1968			
can't be trusted	32	42	−10
wastes tax money	57	64	−7
run for big interests	41	46	−5
1978			
can't be trusted	69	71	−2
wastes tax money	78	80	−2
run for big interests	71	75	−4
1980			
can't be trusted	74	75	−1
wastes tax money	79	81	−2
run for big interests	74	79	−5
1982			
can't be trusted	71	63	8
wastes tax money	68	68	0
run for big interests	71	66	5
1984			
can't be trusted	54	56	−2
wastes tax money	63	69	−6
run for big interests	56	60	−4
1986			
can't be trusted	60	62	−2
1988			
can't be trusted	60	58	2
wastes tax money	59	67	−8
run for big interests	69	66	3
1990			
can't be trusted	70	72	−2
wastes tax money	65	69	−4
run for big interests	70	78	−8
1992			
can't be trusted	70	71	−1
wastes tax money	64	72	−8
run for big interests	76	81	−5
1996			
can't be trusted	70	65	5
wastes tax money	60	62	−2
run for big interests	75	71	4

Source: Calculated by author using survey data from National Election Studies.
Note: Actual question wording for items is contained in Teixeira (1992), appendix C.

Another key long-term political trend in the 1952–1992 period was the dramatic increase in political cynicism.[15] But here, parents and nonparents appear to have participated about equally in the huge increases in the number of people who believe the government can't be trusted, who believe the government wastes a lot of tax money, and who believe the government is run for the benefit of a few big interests (table 7.8). For example, in 1958, 49 percent of nonparents and 42 percent of parents thought the government wasted a lot of tax money, compared to 72 percent of nonparents and 64 percent of parents in 1992—increases of, respectively, 23 and 22 percentage points. Similarly, in 1964, 35 percent of nonparents and 28 percent of parents thought government was run for the benefit of a few big interests, compared to 81 percent of nonparents and 76 percent of parents in 1992—huge increases of, respectively, 46 and 48 points.

Thus the public, parents and nonparents alike, became sharply more cynical about government in the 1952–1992 period. Combined with increased conservatism, both in ideology and voting behavior, and particularly among parents themselves, this helped produce a political environment where politicians could afford to ignore the need for an activist approach to parents' problems.

RECENT CHANGES IN POLITICAL
ATTITUDES AND BEHAVIOR, 1992–1996

That was then. This is now. If we examine data that are closer to the present day, the picture that emerges of parents is of a group that, while retaining some suspicion of government and government efficacy, has been moving in a direction that is quite supportive of an activist agenda. Indeed, parents may be poised to take the lead in moving the country back toward an activist approach to solving problems, just as they apparently did in moving the country away from that approach in the past.

First, consider the 1996 NES data included in tables 7.5 through 7.8. These data show a remarkable turnaround in parents' partisanship and voting behavior. For example, parents' Democratic partisanship went from 6 points lower than nonparents in 1992 to 5 points *higher* in 1996 (table 7.5). Similarly, parents' support for Democratic House and presidential candidates went from 9 points and 6 points less than nonparents' in 1992 to 5 points higher in each category in 1996[16] (table 7.7).

In addition, there was even a narrowing, by 5 points, of the difference between parents and nonparents in self-reported conservatism (table 7.6). But parents' conservatism did continue to be 4 points higher than nonparents' in 1996. And furthermore, parents became *relatively* more cynical about government in the 1992–1996 period (table 7.8). For example, the proportion of parents that thought the government couldn't be trusted held steady at 70 percent, while nonparents with similar views dipped from 71 to 65 percent. Similarly, the proportion of parents that thought government was run by a few big interests hardly changed, while nonparents with the same assessment fell by 10 percentage points. In both cases, the end result was that parents are now apparently more cynical about government than nonparents, reversing a long-standing pattern of being less cynical.

There was also a negative relative trend in parents' sense of political efficacy[17] (efficacy is essentially a belief in one's ability to influence the actions of the government). In 1992 the proportion of parents with low political efficacy was 34 percent, 3 points lower than among nonparents. But in 1996, that relationship had reversed: parents with low efficacy rose sharply to 51 percent, 8 points *higher* than the comparable figure for nonparents.[18]

However, when we turn to parents' views on the responsibilities of government and its spending priorities, results more in line with the observed changes in partisanship and voting behavior emerge. For example, a long-standing NES question asks whether "the government should see to it that every person has a job and a good standard of living." In 1978, the first year when the NES both asked this question and collected information on children in the household, the average rating for parents and nonparents was the same: 4.7 (out of 7 points, where 1 is highest agreement with the statement and 7 is agreement with the opposite statement ["government should let each person get ahead on their own"]). By 1992, the parental rating had moved down to 4.2, while nonparents had only gone down to 4.4. And by 1996, parents had moved all the way down to 3.8, while nonparents moved only slightly down to 4.3. This means that both parents and nonparents have been moving toward the position that government should guarantee jobs and a good standard of living, but parents have been moving in that direction much faster.

In terms of spending priorities, the noteworthy finding from the NES is that, between 1992 and 1996, support for increased federal spending on a series of budget items generally went up, but far more among parents than nonparents. For example, the proportion of nonparents supporting increased spending on the public schools went up from 64 to 67 percent between 1992 and 1996, while the proportion of parents with similar views increased from 70 to 82 percent. Similarly, the proportion of nonparents favoring increased child-care spending rose modestly from 49 to 53 percent over the period, while among parents, pro-spending views increased substantially, from 57 to 70 percent.

The 1996 Voter News Service (VNS) exit poll data, with its far superior sample size,[19] allow the NES results concerning the key role of parents in the 1996 election to be confirmed and examined in more detail. As shown in table 7.9, parents were indeed a crucial source of Bill Clinton's growing support,

Table 7.9. Democratic Vote for President among Parents and Nonparents, by Key
Demographics, 1992 and 1996

	1992	1996	Change
All			
nonparents	45	49	4
parents	39	48	9
Whites			
nonparents	42	44	2
parents	34	40	6
Blacks			
nonparents	84	83	−1
parents	84	85	1
Hispanic			
nonparents	61	75	14
parents	43	70	27
Women			
nonparents	48	54	6
parents	41	53	12
college parents	43	50	7
noncollege parents	39	57	18
working noncollege parents	39	60	21
Men			
nonparents	42	44	2
parents	38	42	4
college parents	36	37	1
noncollege parents	39	45	6
working noncollege parents	34	46	12

Source: Calculated by author using survey data from 1992 VRS and 1996 VNS exit polls.
Note: Noncollege includes all those without a 4-year college degree; college refers to those with a 4-year
college degree.

increasing their support of Clinton by 9 percentage points, compared to only
a 4 point increase among nonparents. (For comments on Bush–Gore election,
see note.)[20]

The table also shows the 1992–96 change for parents and nonparents
broken down by race. The data suggests that black parents, whose levels of
Democratic presidential support remained stable at an extremely high level,
played little role in the shift toward Clinton in 1996.[21] Instead, the pro-
Clinton shift among parents was driven by a shift among white parents (significant due to the large relative size of the white parent voting pool) and a
shift among Hispanic parents (significant due to the huge size of the shift).

Breaking the data down further by gender, we can see that mothers increased their support more than fathers, reflecting the widely documented "gender gap" in the 1996 election. But note that not only did women parents increase their support of Clinton by much more than women nonparents (12 points to 6 points), so did men parents compared to men nonparents (4 points to 2).

The data also show that there was a class component to the increase in parental Clinton support. Mothers without a four-year college degree increased their support by 18 points, compared to just 7 points among college-educated mothers. Similarly, non–college-educated fathers increased their Clinton support by 6 points, compared to only 1 point among college-educated fathers.

The increase in support among noncollege mothers is particularly striking. And the swing toward Clinton among *working* noncollege mothers is even more striking: an astonishing increase of 21 percentage points. Clearly, there was something about the 1996 campaign that really galvanized parents, in general, and these mothers, in particular.

One possibility is the Clinton campaign emphasis on values issues and small-bore parent-oriented programs such as school uniforms. In light of results from the 1996 Penn + Schoen/NPA poll cited earlier, this seems implausible. As the poll convincingly shows, parents are substantially more enthusiastic about policies that provide concrete help for parents like flextime, higher wages for low-income parents, and tax deductions for parents than they are about moral stands on issues like divorce, same-sex marriage, and welfare and mini-programs like school uniforms. So it is hard to see how the Clinton campaign's "values" approach could have been really responsible for parents' increased support.

A more plausible reason is the relative health of the economy—which produced rising family incomes in the period leading up to the election[22]—and Clinton's protection of social spending programs that parents perceived as supportive. This interpretation is supported by data both from the exit polls and from a postelection survey conducted by Stanley Greenberg for the Campaign for America's Future (CAF). Both surveys show that parents—as well as nonparents—were overwhelmingly motivated to support Clinton by the economy, Medicare/Social Security, and education, rather than values-laden issues like crime and welfare.

But there is an important difference between parents and nonparents within this cluster of pro-Clinton motivations. Whereas nonparents were much more likely to be motivated by Medicare and Social Security than education, with parents it was the reverse: education was far more important than Medicare/Social Security in motivating their support for Clinton.

Nor is it the case that parents' concern for the education issue reflected enthusiasm for small-scale, values-linked reforms like school uniforms or curfews. On the contrary, the Greenberg/CAF poll shows that parents' policy priorities in the education area are for large-scale programs that provide significant resources and concrete support for parents. For example, 47 percent of parents said that a "100 billion dollar investment program to improve and expand education at all levels" should be one of the top few priorities of the incoming administration, and 45 percent expressed the same level of support for a $10,000 a year tax deduction for college expenses. This compares to just 16 percent of parents who believed curfews and school uniforms should be one of the top priorities.

Indeed, in general, parents' policy priorities were notable for their commitment to substantial public spending and an active role for government, rather than spending cutbacks, punitive welfare reform, and minimalist government programs. These priorities included (in addition to the education priorities just named): preventing Medicare cuts, comprehensive healthcare reform, guaranteeing health insurance to every child under eighteen, and changing the welfare law to guarantee able-bodied welfare recipients a job.

Of course, the political agendas since 1996 of neither political party seem truly responsive to the kind of bold agenda suggested by either this poll or the 1996 Penn + Schoen/NPA poll. The main exception is tax breaks: the budget deals in Congress have included parental tax breaks both for having children in the household and for children's college education. Secondarily, healthcare coverage has been extended to some uncovered children through expansion of the CHIPS program. But, by and large, a debt reduction–oriented— and now tax cut–oriented—fiscal regime has left little room for aggressive efforts to attack the problems of America's parents.

Partial explanations for this disconnect may lie, as discussed earlier, in the relatively small weight of parents in the eligible electorate and their relatively poor turnout rates, particularly among parents most in need of government support. But a more important explanation lies in parents' continuing doubts about the efficacy of government, in general, and government spending, in particular—doubts shared by nonparents as well.

This means that even though parents have been shifting in a political direction suggestive of support for greater activism and spending, and even though parents are enthusiastic about an agenda that calls for such activism and spending, they are still sending signals (recall the data from the 1996 NES about high cynicism and low efficacy among parents) that allow politicians to be only lightly responsive to the parental agenda and to provide tax cuts in lieu of any other actions.

There are signs, however, that parental commitment to fiscal austerity is soft and that, in time, parental commitment to key priorities like education could override suspicion of government spending and activism. For example, in the Greenberg/CAF poll, 66 percent of parents said they favored increased investment in domestic programs, like education, paid for by taxes on the wealthy and corporations.

One particular reason why parents may take the lead in moving away from fiscal austerity and deregulation is simply that they feel the time and economic squeeze more severely and need relief. For example, in the 1996 CAF/Greenberg poll, parents, by 52 to 36 percent, said they have less time than four years ago to spend with their family, rather than more time, while nonparents have the reverse view by 48 to 36 percent. Also, in an April 1996 poll conducted by Peter Hart and Mark Mellman for the AFL-CIO, 61 percent of parents, compared to 53 percent of nonparents, felt that "many families are under stress, because both parents have to work in order to make ends meet" was a perfect description (10 on a 10-point scale) of today's economy.

Given the level of stress parents feel, it is also not surprising that they are developing a jaundiced view of the proximate source of much of that stress: America's employers. For example, in the Hart/Mellman/AFL-CIO poll just cited, over three-fifths (62 percent) of parents agreed that downsizing "American companies are choosing to boost short-term profits, stock prices and executives' salaries at the expense of their employees," rather than (28 percent) downsizing "American corporations are doing what they need to compete and survive in the global economy." Similarly, 54 percent of parents thought that "working hard often isn't enough anymore, because employers aren't loyal to their employees," rather than (38 percent) "if you get a good education and work hard today, you can really do well and get ahead." This level of cynicism about corporate motives may lead parents to be bolder in their demands for improved workplace policies like flexible hours and affordable day care (endorsed by 81 percent as "very effective" in improving employees' situations), since there is clearly little faith that corporations will choose to improve their employees' situations on their own.

CONCLUSION

The data presented here suggest that political trends among parents since the 1950s have created a number of obstacles to an activist proparent agenda. First, and of critical importance, the political power of parents has been diminished by a very substantial drop in their weight in the active electorate. Second, their consistently low relative turnout further disadvantages them politically. Third, there has been a long-term trend among parents themselves, just recently reversed, toward partisan and ideological positions associated with less government activism. Finally, and perhaps most important, there has been a dramatic increase (not yet reversed) among both parents and nonparents in cynicism about government and government spending. The latter development makes it relatively easy for politicians to evade engagement with a substantive proparent agenda.

There are signs, however, that parents may be regaining their political voice. Indeed, they may be poised to take the lead in moving the country back toward a more activist approach to solving problems, just as they did in leading the country away from such an approach in the past. In the 1996 election, for example, parents swung heavily toward Clinton, apparently motivated by Clinton's protection of social spending programs, particularly education.[23] Postelection polls revealed a parental policy agenda notable for its boldness and some softness in commitment to fiscal austerity. And parents, of course, continue to be acutely aware of the time and economic squeeze that bedevils today's families. The questions are: Will parents' commitment to easing this problem overcome their still-existing suspicion of government? And will politicians respond to the signals coming from parents about their plight? It is too early to tell, but it seems fair to say that the more focused and organized the signals coming from parents, the better.

REFERENCES AND DATA SOURCES

Carlson, Allan (1996). "Taxes and the Family: A Conservative Perspective." See chapter 8 in this volume.

Frisby, Michael K. (1997). "Both Parties Take Stock of Jump in Black Male Turnout." *Wall Street Journal,* February 13, A20.

Greenberg, Stanley (1996). Survey for Campaign for America's Future. November 5–8.

Hart, Peter, and Mark Mellman (1996). Survey for AFL-CIO. April 19–22.

National Election Studies (1952–1996). University of Michigan Center for Political Studies.

Penn + Schoen Associates (1996). *What Will Parents Vote For?* Survey for National Parenting Association. September 15–17.

Teixeira, Ruy (1992). *The Disappearing Voter.* Washington, D.C.: Brookings Institution.

——— (1997). "Finding the Real Center: Lessons of the 1996 Election." *Dissent* (Spring).

U.S. Bureau of the Census (1992). November Current Population Survey Voter Supplement.

Verba, Sidney, Key Lehman Schlozman, and Henry Brady (1995). *Voice and Equality: Civic Voluntarism in American Politics.* Cambridge, Mass.: Harvard University Press.

Winn, Peter (1996). "Back to the Future: A GI Bill for the Twenty-First Century." See chapter 10 in this volume.

Wolff, Edward N. (1996). "The Economic Status of Parents in Postwar America." See chapter 4 in this volume.

NOTES

1. National Parenting Association, *What Will Parents Vote For?* (New York: National Parenting Association, 1996). The 2000 survey update found that this is still true. See chapter 14 by Nancy Rankin in this volume.

2. Defined as adults, married or unmarried, living in a household with dependent children. Note that this definition excludes biological parents who are not living with their children (e.g., divorced or unmarried fathers who do not have custody of their children).

3. Defined as age-eligible citizens.

4. The NES is the only data source on turnout that allows parental turnout to be tracked back very far in time. The census voter supplement data, a generally far superior source for voting demographics, only began including information on the presence of children in the household in 1984, making its utility for parental turnout time trends fairly limited. It is, however, the best source for detailed consideration of contemporary parental turnout patterns and is utilized further on for such purposes.

5. Note that the turnout levels displayed in table 7.2 for both parents and nonparents are probably considerably overstated from their actual levels. This reflects the endemic problem of vote overreporting in the NES (and all other political surveys). For example, in 1992, the overall turnout rate of the NES sample was 77 percent. A reasonable estimate for the actual turnout level of age- and citizen-eligible citizens is around 57 percent—a difference of 20 percentage points.

6. This figure should be treated with caution, however. For various technical reasons, the NES collected data on children in the household from less than one-fourth of its sample—around 400 individuals. The small sample size means that turnout estimates (and other estimates) based on this sample (and, even more, the subsamples of parents and nonparents) are subject to relatively large sampling errors.

7. Based on the 1992 census voter supplement data.

8. The index is simply the proportion of parents among voters divided by the proportion among the eligible electorate. A value of 1 indicates perfect representation, while a value of 0 represents perfect underrepresentation.

9. There are problems with the NES time trend, however, that suggest this finding should be treated with caution. In addition to the small sample size in 1996, the 1956 figures are particularly suspect. The NES shows overall turnout *increasing* 4 points between 1956 and 1992, while data based on actual voting records indicate a decline of 5 percentage points over the same period.

10. 1992 census voter supplement data.

11. Note once again that these survey data overstate turnout. However, the overstatement is much less severe than in the NES. The 1992 census data show a turnout level of 61 percent of the VAP (voting age population), compared to 55 percent based on official voting records—a difference of only 6 percentage points. The census data can also be adjusted to estimate true parental turnout in 1992: I estimate that turnout as about 53 percent, compared to the unadjusted estimate shown in table 7.4 (58 percent).

12. "Independents" who said they leaned Democratic in a follow-up question. The political source literature suggests that these independent leaners are not much different than weak partisans in their political behavior and are therefore more usefully lumped with other partisans than with "pure" independents.

13. Note that this story does not change if independent leaners are classified with independents, as in most newspaper polls and in the exit polls.

14. Exactly why parents became more conservative over time is an interesting—and important—question. One hypothesis is that parents were particularly likely to be affected by the negative economic trends of the past twenty years and particularly likely to lose faith in the efficacy of government intervention and spending as a result. But the literature affords no definitive judgment on this question or the larger issue of the overall rise in antigovernment sentiment since the 1960s.

15. See Teixeira (1992), chapter 2, for a detailed discussion of this trend.

16. The 1996 VNS (Voter News Service) exit poll data generally confirm this turnaround, though the magnitude of the turnaround in the exit poll data is less. Given the larger sample size of the exit poll, as well as some technical problems with the NES data, there are reasons to suspect that the NES change estimates are too large.

17. This variable is a scale constructed from two NES items about whether "public officials care much what people like me think" and whether "people like me . . . have any say about what the government does."

18. It is also true, among both parents and nonparents, that individuals with low education and income levels are more likely to exhibit low levels of political efficacy. However, the sample sizes are too small to determine whether this relationship is stronger among parents than nonparents or whether the trend toward low efficacy among parents has been particularly strong among those with low education and income.

19. The 1996 VNS dataset includes 11,617 cases where information about children in the household was collected.

20. Preliminary data from the 2000 VNS exit poll, however, indicate this pattern of support was reversed in the 2000 election: parental support for the Democratic candidate declined by several percentage points, while nonparental support actually increased by one point.

21. Another possibility is that black parents played a role due to increased turnout, rather than due to any change in levels of support. The NES data, however, do not support this proposition, showing a *decrease* in the turnout of black parents in 1996. The NES sample size for black parents, though, is extremely small, so a reliable judgment on this issue will have to wait until release of the 1996 census voter supplement data.

22. Though note that these rising family incomes were attributable to increased work hours and more family members working, rather than rising wages (see Teixeira 1997).

23. Preliminary data from the 2000 election indicate that education continues to be a top priority for parents, if not *the* priority, outdistancing rival fiscal priorities like tax cuts.

8

Taxes and the Family: A Conservative Perspective

Allan C. Carlson

While high levels of taxation have been common for most of the twentieth century, relatively little attention has focused on the influence of taxes on family behavior. Instead, decisions regarding marriage, divorce, and the birth and spacing of children have usually been viewed as exogenous to fiscal policy.

Gary Becker's seminal work on the economics of an individual's use of time[1] opened the way for a fresh understanding of choices regarding marriage and fertility.[2] This new approach, often called the *new home economics,* soon generated theoretical attempts to identify the specific effects of taxation on family behavior.[3] Actual effects have also been measured. For example, recent work led by Leslie Whittington has shown a "robust," almost stunning, relationship between fertility and the real value of the *personal exemption* provided by the U.S. income tax code. Where earlier researchers dismissed the personal exemption as too insubstantial to have any fertility effects, Whittington calculated that its value (in 1982–83) ranged between 4 and 14 percent of the annual estimated cost of raising a child, a figure she labeled significant. Moreover, it is ongoing in nature and would be available each year a child could be claimed as a dependent, increasing its perceived value. In one investigation, using Panel Study on Income Dynamics (PSID) data for 1979–1983, Whittington found an elasticity of birth probability with respect to the exemption of between .839 and 1.31. Using just the lower figure, this would mean that a 1 percent increase in the exemption value would cause a

Allan C. Carlson is the president of the Howard Center for Family, Religion and Society in Rockford, Illinois, and editor of *The Family in America*. In 1988 he was appointed to the National Commission on Children, which produced *Final Report: Beyond Rhetoric* in 1991.

.839 percent increase in birth probability. Translated into dollars and people, this figure suggested that a mere $30 increase in the value of the exemption would increase overall U.S. fertility by 8 percent, or 312,000 *additional* births in 1988! This study also showed that the value of the exemption positively influenced not only the timing of births but completed family size as well.[4] Another investigation found that this strong positive relationship between the value of the exemption and fertility held remarkably firm for the whole 1913–1984 period.[5]

In this chapter, I review the treatment accorded the family by U.S. federal tax policy since 1944 and its effects. In order to judge the latter, however, one need have an operational definition of "family." Mine, resting on historical, anthropological, and biological precepts, is: "A family is a man and a woman bonded in a socially approved covenant of marriage, to bear, raise, and protect children, to provide mutual protection and support, to create a small domestic economy, and to maintain continuity with the generations which came before and which shall come in the future."[6]

MEASURES OF FAMILY HEALTH

Although this definition allows for a number of possible measures of family health and decline (including abuse statistics and scales of intergenerational contact), I focus in particular on three:

1. *Encouragement to stable marriage.* At best, a tax system should deliver a positive economic incentive to marriage, as the foundation of social order, the first community. A good system would also embrace a direct or indirect financial penalty on divorce. At the very least, a tax code should never provide an individual with an incentive to avoid marriage, cohabit outside of wedlock, or seek a divorce.

2. *Encouragement to the birth of children.* In an era where *every* modern nation has either a zero-growth or (more commonly) a negative total fertility rate, the birth of additional children should be welcomed and encouraged by a tax system. Some would justify this instead as a logical extension of the "ability to pay" criteria for taxation. Others would view this as setting a minimum level of household existence, before taxation sets in. Family advocates of a more social democratic bent might argue for this as a means of redistributing income across one's lifespan: the "tax relief" granted when one raises children is compensated for by the payment of higher taxes both before and after the children are present.

I would emphasize two more justifications. First, tax preferences for dependent children—be they exemptions, deductions, or credits—are the least intrusive way to adjust income in compensation for the "market failure" regarding children. Competitive wage markets simply pay no attention to the number of dependents a worker might have. While many nations have adopted state child allowances as a response, these tend to draw governments into family life, welfare, and decision making. In contrast, *universal* tax exemptions, deductions, or credits require no investigations, means-testing, or payment schemes, beyond proof of a child's existence. In short, they have the same potential beneficial effects of child allowances, without the consequence of excessive state intrusion.

Second, families deserve targeted tax relief as partial compensation for the state's prior socialization of their children. This began in the nineteenth century with the imposition of mandatory school attendance laws, which took from parents control over their children's time and training and transferred it to the states. Early in this century, child labor laws, culminating in the Fair Labor Standards Act of 1938, placed a still larger block of children's time under social controls. In the same decade, the new Social Security Act began to socialize the insurance value of children. The full process took forty years. As late as 1957, 51 percent of persons over age sixty-five still reported receiving direct income support from their own children, compared to 42 percent who received some income from Social Security. However, by 1980, a mere 4 percent received help from their children, while over 90 percent drew on Social Security.[7]

In effect, the federal government and the states have already socialized the potential economic gains provided by children. Meanwhile, the direct costs of raising children are left with parents. One consequence is a sharply diminished birthrate. This "demographic contradiction" inherent to the welfare state has long been apparent to observers.[8] The proper compensation is massive tax relief targeted on families with dependent children, where *progressivity of taxation* is offset by the fact of marriage and the presence of children: indeed, where marriage and children serve as normal taxpayers' most prominent tax shelters. This would mean that single adults and childless married couples would bear a significantly higher share of the tax burden than their "child rich" neighbors. Yet since these categories of persons are, in effect, "free riders" in a pay-as-you-go Social Security system (where children, not money, are the real investment for the future), they *should* be paying a larger share of the income tax bill.

3. *Favored treatment of the home economy.* Each individual actually lives in two economies. The more visible of these is the market economy, characterized by the production and exchange of goods and services through cash, with a substantial proportion going to the state through taxes. The other economy is the home, or household economy, where goods and services are produced and

exchanged on a noncash, altruistic basis. It is through these latter acts and exchanges—ranging from child care and meal preparation, to home repair, carpentry, and gardening—that the institutional life of a family takes form. As the home economy *grows* relative to the market economy, the family's claims on the individual—relative to other institutions—grow as well. Moreover, because it operates outside the cash nexus, the household economy is difficult to count and tax, normally leaving all of its gains to the family.[9]

Even in the wake of industrialization, these actions and exchanges represent economic activity of considerable value. Working with U.S. data in the mid-1970s, Scott Burns calculated its overall worth to be at least 50 percent of the official Gross National Product.[10] Working with a more sophisticated model and Australian figures from 1992, economist Duncan Ironmonger calculated a "Gross Household Product" almost *equal* to what he calls the "Gross Market Product," roughly $350 billion each.[11]

Experience shows that taxation policy has a direct effect on the degree of household commitment to the two economies. Sociologists Janet and Larry Hunt have shown that the net effect of higher marginal tax rates is to encourage the substitution of home production for market production: with a one-point increase in marginal tax rates, the average woman will work thirty-nine fewer hours annually in the market economy and devote twenty-nine more hours to home production, as the family defends its living standard (and shelters income from taxation) by turning toward home.[12] On this same question, Harvey Rosen emphasized that "[m]arried women do in fact seem to react to tax rates in the 'rational' manner of standard economic theory."[13] Surprisingly, this turn to home production by "women in families with higher after-tax cash income contributes more to their families' economic well-being than that of women in lower after-tax income families."[14]

Accordingly, tax policies that encourage home production can be viewed as strengthening the institutional family. Those that discourage home production can be viewed as weakening the family. In a break with conventional wisdom, this measure suggests that a *favorable* nonrevenue effect of high marginal taxation is the encouragement it gives to family production and the home economy.[15]

THE HISTORICAL RECORD

Relative to these measures, how has the federal tax burden evolved over the past fifty years? In broad terms, by the end of the 1940s, the federal government had achieved a solidly promarriage, prochild, profamily income tax structure. However, the next forty-five years showed a steady dismantling of this structure, continuing to the present.

Each of the two major tax reforms of the 1940s introduced a new concept to the taxation of personal income.[16] While both of these had powerful pro-family effects, the primary motivation in each case actually had little to do with social issues.

The Reform Act of 1944 created the uniform per capita exemption. In prior decades, personal exemptions had varied widely, depending on one's status. In 1925, for example, a married couple received a $3,500 exemption, a single person $1,500, and each dependent $400. For reasons primarily of simplicity in administration, Congress adopted a uniform $500 per person exemption in 1944 for the wartime income surtax and extended it to normal taxation in 1946. A secondary purpose, though, appears to have been profamily in intent. As a Ways and Means Committee Report explained, the 1944 act was expected to impose a "lesser burden on the taxpayers with a large family and a greater burden on taxpayers with a smaller family."[17]

In 1948, a Republican Congress—over President Harry Truman's veto— forced through a new tax reform measure. With the Treasury running a surplus that year of $8.4 billion, the primary goal was to cut taxes, and Congress did so in a family-supportive way. Forty percent of the tax cut was achieved by raising the personal exemption by one-fifth, to $600 per person. Another 13 percent of the tax cut came through the introduction of an altogether new treatment for household taxation: income splitting.[18] This radical, yet strongly promarriage, measure came largely in response to state actions over the prior ten years. As federal taxation had begun to mount in the 1930s and 1940s, a number of states had switched their family legal codes toward the "community property" concept in marriage, a legacy of Spanish law. Under court rulings, this allowed the couple to use "income splitting" in filing federal taxes. Under its provisions, married couples would add up their total income, and then "split" that sum down the middle, with each person effectively being taxed on his or her half alone. Within progressive tax rates, this gave a strong bonus to marriage. Compared to single persons, effective tax brackets for married couples became twice as wide. Conversely, a divorce would eliminate this favored tax treatment and in most cases would raise net taxation of the broken home.

By 1948, a number of states were joining in this rush to help their citizens. To end the interstate competition, Congress voted to make "income splitting" the law of the land. In the context of 1948, where cutting taxes was the central goal, no one was worse off than before. Yet married couples—particularly at the middle-income levels—enjoyed a dramatic improvement in their status relative to singles.

The 1948 measure also expanded the generous treatment accorded owner-occupied housing: the "imputed rent" of the home was exempted from taxation;

the interest on mortgages was also exempted, as were the capital gains from the sale of a house if a new one was purchased within a given time. Veterans Administration (VA) and Federal Housing Administration (FHA) regulations, in conjunction with underwriters' guidelines, delivered most of these new, tax-favored mortgages to young married couples.[19] Econometric analysis showed that about 25 percent of the growth in homeownership in the 1945–75 period was a direct consequence of the tax system's favorable treatment of owner-occupied housing.[20]

Accordingly, by 1948, the United States could claim a powerfully profamily tax code:

1. The progressivity of tax tables was sharply reduced in a manner that favored marriage and children;
2. There was a strong financial incentive for adults to marry and a significant, indirect penalty for divorce;
3. The costs of child rearing were fairly recognized; indeed, the per capita exemption actually provided a kind of special bonus for truly large families;
4. As the tax code worked in conjunction with other government programs, family housing enjoyed a dramatic boom; and
5. The "household economy" was encouraged by high marginal tax rates in conjunction with income splitting.

Over the following fifteen years, the nation enjoyed both unprecedented economic expansion and remarkable social health. Marriages were more stable than in prior decades, and the proportion of adults who were married reached a historic high. Following a postwar "spike" in 1946, the divorce rate steadily declined. The "baby boom" also roared into high gear, with marital fertility nearly doubling between 1944 and 1957. Although other factors were surely in play, such as the return of men and women to "normal" lives after the disruptions of World War II, it also appeared that tax policy had been translated into family strength.

Almost from the beginning, though, critics began to assail the 1948 reforms. "Income splitting" drew the loudest complaints. A legitimate concern came from widows and other nonmarried persons with dependents. Congress responded wisely here and extended some of the benefits of "income splitting" to these categories of taxpayers in 1951, under the category "head of household."[21] But other complaints revealed a deep hostility to the very essence of the plan. One influential analyst claimed to see no virtue in a system that gave a benefit to a person just because he or she had acquired a spouse, rather than spending money in other ways.[22] Another argued that "[a]t the top of the income scale, the major rationale of income taxation is to cut down on the economic power of the family unit," a goal subverted by the 1948 reforms.[23] For a time, Congress turned a deaf ear to these arguments. The one troubling, although largely invisible, development in the 1950s was the slow erosion in the value of the personal exemption, both in terms of inflation and an offset against average per-capita income. According to Treasury analyst Eugene Steuerle, this change would become "[b]y almost any measure . . . the largest single change in the income tax in the postwar era."[24] Direct dismantling of the profamily tax code began in the 1960s. John F. Kennedy's 1963 tax cut, for example, did not raise the value of the personal exemption, as it should have done if the principles of 1948 had been followed. Rather, the measure implemented the new minimum standard deduction that paid no attention to the presence of children, focusing instead on relief for taxpayers with the smallest incomes.[25] This new "standard deduction" also introduced a modest "marriage penalty," since its value for married couples filing a joint return was less than twice that available to a single person.

Later in that decade, complaints that "singles" were treated unfairly under "income splitting" reached the ear of Wilbur Mills, chairman of the House Ways and Means Committee. In 1969, he expressed interest in extending tax relief to help "bachelors and spinsters as well as widows and widowers," while retaining the "marriage incentive" for those under age thirty-five. The House-approved bill carried this distinction. Yet the Nixon administration's tax reform proposal eliminated the age restriction altogether and limited the gains from income splitting to 20 percent of total tax. It was this universalized measure that won adoption in the Tax Reform Act of 1969. Not only did this abandonment of "income splitting" sharply reduce the "marriage incentive"; it also created a "marriage penalty," which affected some two-income couples with particular force. It created a situation where they would, in fact, be better off single, rather than married.

The 1970s were witness to a mounting critique of the favorable tax treatment accorded the "household economy." Some critics saw "income splitting" as giving too much benefit to families with a mother at home. As June O'Neill of the Urban Institute put it, "a system of joint filing is likely to discourage the market employment of married women."[26] Other critics said that it was unfair to leave "home production" untaxed, since this encouraged people to produce their own goods and services instead of buying them, which diminished the revenue base.[27] But since it was difficult to measure, and hence tax, home production, policy architects recommended instead that targeted tax cuts be given to households with working wives, which would have the same effect.

Accordingly, in 1972, Congress increased the value and availability of the tax deduction for child care. In 1976, it substituted the Dependent Care Tax Credit, which granted direct tax relief of up to $800 to working parents who put their children in institutional care. Similarly, Congress's attempt to reduce the "marriage penalty" in 1981 tax legislation (by permitting a partial deduction on the second income of a two-earner household) also enjoyed the same theoretical justification: this was an indirect way to tax the extra "implicit income" produced by the additional home labor within the "one-career" household.

At the same time, the housing provisions of the income tax code ceased to have a profamily effect. FHA and VA eligibility standards were loosened, with the effect being the funneling of substantially more loans to nonfamily households.[28] Indeed, by the early 1980s, some housing analysts suspected that a truly unusual, even perverse, process had emerged. As economists George Sternlieb and James Hughes explained: "The very decline in the size of household, with its nominal generation of increased demand for housing units, may in turn be a consequence of the availability and costs of housing units generally."[29] Put another way, the tax-favored housing system had now developed a vested interest in divorce and family disruption, where housing supply pushed artificial demand, and where federal housing subsidies—including tax benefits—now served as a substitute for the economic gains once provided by marriage.

Meanwhile, mounting inflation accelerated the erosion of the personal exemption. Even its increase from $600 to $1,000 in 1969 did little to help. Together with the changes cited previously, families with children became the big losers in the income tax sweepstakes. As Eugene Steuerle has shown, between 1948 and 1984, single persons and married couples without children showed no real increase in their average net federal tax rate. In contrast, married couples with two children saw their average income tax rate rise by 43 percent (from 6.9 to 9.9 percent), while a couple with four children faced a dramatic 223 percent increase (from 2.6 to 8.4 percent).[30]

On top of this, the pressure of the payroll tax was mounting rapidly. In 1947, the maximum payroll tax was only $30 annually, about 1 percent of mean household income. As late as 1965, the maximum annual tax was still a modest $174. But then came a steady expansion of coverage, benefits, and the mandatory FICA contributions to pay for them. By the early 1980s, this number had reached $2,400 (or $4,800, if one also included the employers' portion). As a regressive levy, the payroll tax fell most heavily on low- and middle-income workers, precisely the categories where potential new parents could be found.

One countervailing development was the creation of the Earned Income Tax Credit (EITC) in 1975, a modest income supplement made available to low-income working families with at least one dependent child at home. It is important to note that the EITC was conceived as a tax rebate to the working poor with children: its maximum benefit level was initially keyed to the combined total payroll tax rate (both employers' and employees' portions).

This measure aside, though, 1963 through 1985 were years of loss for the family, relative to federal taxation. Conscious policy changes, in league with inflation, had these consequences:

1. Families raising dependent children faced ever heavier federal taxes, both absolutely and in comparison to single persons and childless couples; and the larger the family, the greater the increased burden;
2. "Income splitting" disappeared as a guiding concept, reducing the incentive to marriage, creating a disincentive to marriage in its place, and largely eliminating the disincentive to divorce;
3. Indirect taxation of the "household economy" appeared for the first time, under the guise of the Dependent Care Tax Credit, followed by the 1981 "correction" to the "marriage penalty";
4. Tax incentives to owner-occupied housing ceased to have a profamily effect; indeed, there was mounting evidence that these incentives (in conjunction with other policy shifts) now damaged the interests of families and even encouraged family break-up; and
5. The mounting scope of Social Security and the financial pressures of the payroll tax eliminated remaining economic bonds between the aged and their grown children.

There can be little doubt that these shifts in the tax treatment of families had something to do with the negative turns in family life that began in the mid-1960s. The number of divorces climbed from 393,000 in 1960 to 1,213,000 in 1981, with the divorce rate rising 140 percent. The rate of first marriage fell 30 percent in the same period. Among women ages 20–24, the decline was 59 percent. The U.S. fertility rate tumbled from 118 (per 1,000 women ages 15–44) in 1960 to 65.6 in 1978. The number of legal abortions climbed from 745,000 in 1973 to 1,577,000 in 1981. The total fertility rate, which measures the ability of society to reproduce, slipped into the negative column for the first time in 1973.

Then came the Tax Reform Act of 1986. Partly as a response to its inability to balance the competing demands of married persons and singles, and of one-income and two-income families, Congress turned to a radically different approach. Its features included:

• The reduction of multiple tax brackets—ranging from 11 to 50 percent on regular income—to only two: 15 percent and 28 percent;

- An increase in the personal exemption to $2,000 by 1989, and its indexing thereafter to inflation; however, personal exemptions would also now be phased out for higher income households (above $71,900 for joint returns and $43,150 for singles), creating in effect a 33 percent tax bracket during this phaseout period;
- A repeal of the "marriage penalty" deduction;
- Modest expansion of the Dependent Care Tax Credit; and
- Retention of most of the tax preferences given to owner-occupied housing.

For the family, what were the effects? There were both gains and losses. On the positive side:

- The near-doubling of the personal exemption, from $1,080 to $2,000, was a significant gain, although the reduction in marginal tax rates (from 50 to 28 percent at the top level) blunted its effects at the middle- and upper-income levels. Nonetheless, the encouragement to child bearing was real. Whittington, Alm, and Peters predicted in 1987 that this change would result in a direct increase in the U.S. fertility rate of 7.53 births per 1,000 women, ages 15 to 44, by 1990.[31] The real increase turned out to be fairly close to this prediction: 5.5.
- Indexing the exemption to inflation was another major achievement, putting a halt to the continued erosion in its value.
- And elimination of the special deduction for two-income couples ended this indirect tax on imputed household income.

On the negative side, though:

- In the contest between participation in the "market economy" and the "home economy," the Tax Reform Act of 1986, by bringing tax rates down, generally shifted incentives toward the marketplace. One analysis predicted a direct 2.6 percent increase in the labor force participation of wives, due to the tax bill.[32]
- The tax benefit for out-of-home child care, and its indirect tax on the parent at home, grew in size and relative significance.
- The phasing out of the personal exemption abandoned the important principle adopted in 1944 of a uniform per-capita exemption. In practice, this phase-out also became a kind of indirect tax on the children of the relatively well-off.
- The significance and probable contemporary negative thrust of housing tax preferences remained unchanged.

- The so-called marriage penalty reappeared in a new form.
- And an increase in the relative value of the standard deduction for "heads of households" (normally, one-parent families) actually created a small incentive favoring divorce and an equal division of children.[33]

In all, for families, this act marked the continued erosion of support. While fertility was encouraged, marriage faced heightened disincentives, as did the operation of the home economy.

THE TAX AND FAMILY DEBATE IN RECENT YEARS

In 1991, the National Commission on Children, chaired by Senator Jay Rockefeller (D-WV), unanimously recommended "the creation of a $1,000 refundable child tax credit for all children through age 18."[34] Five years later, both the Republican and the Democratic platforms called for a $500 per child "family tax credit," with a phase-out at unspecified upper-income levels. In 1997, Congress passed and President Bill Clinton signed a measure creating this $500 credit for dependent children under age seventeen. Instead of making the credit refundable, Congress implemented a phase-out of the credit for household incomes of over $110,000 on joint returns. If Whittington's model is correct, the tax credit should have a modest positive impact on fertility.

The same measure also introduced two new tax benefits for families with dependent children attending colleges and universities. The Hope Tax Credit is worth up to $1,500 per dependent child for the first two years of post-secondary education. The Lifetime Learning Credit, more versatile in application, is worth up to $1,000 per dependent child. Both credits were phased out for "modified adjusted gross incomes" above $80,000. Since anticipated college costs appear to have a depressing effect on marital fertility, it is possible that these measures may have a small positive effect on the birthrate.

How would the tax plans of the major presidential rivals of 2000 affect the family? Looking back at the 2000 Republican platform, we found four measures that might significantly affect family well-being:

1. *"Replace the five current tax brackets with four lower ones, ensuring all taxpayers significant tax relief while targeting it especially toward low-income workers."* The primary result here would be a heightened incentive for men and women to engage in market labor, rather than home production. As in 1986, this could be expected to draw more secondary and tertiary workers out of the home and into the labor supply,

particularly married women with children. In consequence, the family as an institution would marginally weaken.

2. *"Help families by doubling the child tax credit to $1,000 [and] making it available to more families."* The consequence of this change would be positive toward the family, providing an increased incentive to child bearing and a slightly favorable rebalance of incentives in favor of home production.

3. *"Eliminat[e] the marriage penalty."* Results here would depend on the details. In 1999, the George W. Bush campaign proposed to reduce the marriage penalty by returning to the approach of 1981: permitting a partial deduction (10 percent up to $3,000) on the income of the second earner in the household. Meanwhile, the GOP congressional leadership in 2000 crafted a marriage penalty relief plan built on very different principles. The measure, finally passed by Congress (but vetoed by President Bill Clinton), took steps to restore "income splitting." The tax table for couples filing joint returns would have become double the single rate for the 15 percent tax bracket, and the standard deduction would also have been raised to a level double that of single taxpayers.

    The Bush plan would actually weaken the family by encouraging greater market activity among second earners and fewer children. In contrast, the congressional plan would strengthen the home economy and create a small disincentive to divorce. As a possible indication of a change of heart, as a candidate, Bush said that—given the opportunity—he would have *signed* the measure passed by Congress.

4. *"[W]e advocate choice in child care."* It is possible that this vague promise may include an extension of the Dependent Care Tax Credit to parents caring full time for their own children, an idea churning in some Republican circles. If so, it would reweigh tax incentives in favor of at-home care, thereby strengthening the home economy.

Democratic Party nominee Al Gore and the 2000 Democratic platform offered less specific promises:

1. *"Democrats want to give middle class families tax cuts they can use. . . . Democrats seek the right kind of tax relief. . . .These tax cuts would let families live their values by helping them . . . afford child care."* This implies an increase in the tax relief given to families that hire substitute, nonparental care, a measure that would diminish the home economy and weaken the family.

2. *"We should . . . fix 'the marriage penalty' so that parents can spend more time at home and less time trying to make ends meet."* As with the

Republicans, consequences would differ according to the details. Vice President Gore endorsed an increase of the Standard Deduction for married couples to twice that granted to singles. This would give a modest shift in favor of household labor and the home economy. At the same time, other Democrats have voiced support for a proposal similar to that of Bush, targeting the direct tax relief on two-earner couples. As with the Bush plan, this would encourage greater involvement by parents in the marketplace, fewer children, and a weaker home.

Taken at face value, the Republican platform of 2000 is more favorable toward family living than the Democratic alternative. While the GOP compression of tax brackets would work to the disadvantage of the home economy, the other proposed measures—a doubling of the Child Tax Credit, a solution to the marriage tax penalty similar to "income splitting," and the hint of favorable tax treatment for at-home child care—would more than compensate for this. Despite a rhetorical call for policies allowing parents to "spend more time at home," specific Democratic proposals would point to less functional, more market-oriented families.

If asked what would improve either document, I would advocate any or all of the following:

- A *tripling* (not just a doubling) of the existing child tax credit to $1,500 and its extension to all income levels;
- A larger, uniform, and universal personal exemption ($6,000 per person) in the context of enhanced progressivity of rates;
- Pure "income splitting" for married couples; and
- Fairness in child care, by turning the existing dependent care credit into a fixed credit ($2,500 per child under age five), and granted to *all* families with preschoolers.

The record strongly suggests that these measures would give an incentive to marriage, discourage divorce, favor the birth of children, and encourage a greater commitment to family autonomy and institutional strength, through home production.

NOTES

1. Gary S. Becker, "A Theory of the Allocation of Time," *Economic Journal* 75 (1965): 493–517.

2. See Robert T. Michael and Gary Becker, "On the New Theory of Consumer Behavior," *Swedish Journal of Economics* 75 (1973): 379–96; Michael C. Keeley, "The

Economics of Family Formation," *Economic Inquiry* 15 (April 1977): 247; Robert J. Willis, "A New Approach to the Economic Theory of Fertility Behavior," *Journal of Political Economy* 81 (March–April 1973): S14–S69; and Gary S. Becker, *A Treatise on the Family* (Cambridge, Mass.: Harvard University Press, 1981).

3. See James A. Mirrlees, "Population Policy and the Taxation of Family Size," *Journal of Public Economics* 1 (1972): 169–98; Marc Nerlove, Assaf Razin, and Efraim Sadka, "Income Distribution Policies with Endogenous Fertility," *Journal of Public Economics* 24 (1984): 221–30; and Alessandro Cigno, "Fertility and the Tax-Benefit System: A Reconsideration of the Theory of Family Taxation," *The Economic Journal* 96 (1986): 1035–51.

4. Leslie A. Whittington, "Taxes and the Family: The Impact of the Tax Exemption for Dependents on Marital Fertility," *Demography* 29 (May 1992): 215–26.

5. Leslie A. Whittington, James Alm, and H. Elizabeth Peters, "Fertility and the Personal Exemption: Implicit Pronatalist Policy in the United States," *American Economic Review* 80 (June 1990): 545–56.

6. A justification for this definition can be found in A. C. Carlson, *From Cottage to Work Station: The Family's Search for Social Harmony in the Industrial Age* (San Francisco: Ignatius, 1993), 4–6.

7. Steven Crystal, *America's Old Age Crisis* (New York: Basic Books, 1982): 16–18, 32, 57.

8. Gunnar Myrdal ably described the problem in *Population: A Problem for Democracy* (Cambridge, Mass.: Harvard University Press, 1940), 197–200; a more recent analysis of the antinatalist effects of state old-age pensions, on a global basis, is Charles F. Hohm et al., "A Reappraisal of the Social Security-Fertility Hypothesis: A Bi-Directional Approach," *The Social Science Journal* 23 (December 1986): 149–68.

9. A compelling case against efforts to measure "imputed" income from home production is found in Michael J. McIntyre and Oliver Oldman, "Treatment of the Family," in *Comprehensive Income Taxation,* ed. Joseph Pechman (Washington, D.C.: Brookings Institution, 1977), 205–39.

10. Scott Burns, *The Household Economy: Its Shape, Origins, & Future* (Boston: Beacon Press, 1977).

11. Duncan Ironmonger, "The Domestic Economy: $340 Billion of G.H.P.," in *The Family: There Is No Other Way,* ed. B. Muehlenberg (Melbourne: Australian Family Association, 1996), 132–46.

12. Janet G. Hunt and Larry Hunt, "The Dualities of Career and Families: New Integrations or New Polarizations?" *Social Problems* 29 (June 1982): 499–510. Also, Glen C. Cain, *Married Women in the Labor Force: An Economic Analysis* (Chicago: University of Chicago Press, 1966), 122.

13. Harvey Rosen, "Tax Illusion and the Labor Supply of Married Women," *Review of Economics and Statistics* 58 (1976): 170.

14. W. Keith Bryant and Cathleen Zick, "Household Production, Taxes, and Family Income Distribution," *Human Ecology Forum* 15 (1985): 12–14.

15. See C. Lowell Harriss, "Important Issues and Serious Problems in Flat-Rate Income Taxation," *American Journal of Economics and Sociology* 43 (April 1984): 159–62.

16. H. Seltzer, *The Personal Exemption in the Income Tax* (New York: National Bureau of Economic Research, 1968), 38–57.

17. *House Ways and Means Committee Report No. 1365,* 78th Congress, 2nd Session, 5; quoted in Seltzer, *The Personal Exemption in the Income Tax,* 42.

18. For a detailed treatment of this concept, see Harold M. Groves, *Federal Tax Treatment of the Family* (Washington, D.C.: Brookings Institution, 1963), 56–83.

19. See Gertrude Sipperly Fish, ed. *The Story of Housing* (New York: Macmillan, 1979), 472–75; and David Laidler, "Income Tax Incentives for Owner-Occupied Housing," in *The Taxation of Income from Capital*, ed. Arnold C. Harberger and Martin J. Bailey (Washington, D.C.: Brookings Institution, 1969), 50–64.

20. Harvey S. Rosen and Kenneth T. Rosen, "Federal Taxes and Home Ownership: Evidence from Time Series," *Journal of Political Economy* 88 (1980): 59–75.

21. Groves, *Federal Tax Treatment of the Family*, 68–69

22. Groves, *Federal Tax Treatment of the Family*, 59.

23. Joseph A. Pechman, *Federal Tax Policy* (Washington, D.C.: Brookings Institution, 1966), 83.

24. Eugene Steuerle, "The Tax Treatment of Households of Different Size," in Rudolph G. Penner, ed., *Taxing the Family* (Washington, D.C.: American Enterprise Institute, 1983), 74.

25. *Report of the Committee on Ways and Means to Accompany H.R. 8363* (Washington, D.C.: U.S. Government Printing Office, 1963), 24.

26. June O'Neill, "Family Issues in Taxation," in Penner, *Taxing the Family*, 13.

27. On this point, see Ake Blomquist and Michael McKee, "Eliminating the 'Marriage Exemption' in the Canadian Income Tax: The Erola Proposal," *Canadian Journal of Economics* 19 (May 1986): 309–317.

28. See Carlson, *From Cottage to Work Station*, 78–84.

29. George Sternlieb and James W. Hughes, *America's Housing: Prospects and Problems* (New Brunswick, N.J.: Center for Urban Policy Research, Rutgers University, 1980), 58–66.

30. Steuerle, "The Tax Treatment of Households of Different Size," 75.

31. Whittington, Alm, and Peters, "Fertility and the Personal Exemption," 553.

32. Jerry A. Hausman and James M. Poterba, "Household Behavior and the Tax Reform Act of 1986," *Economic Perspectives* 1 (Summer 1987): 108.

33. Noted in Thomas J. Espenshade and Joseph J. Minarik, "Demographic Implications of the 1986 U.S. Tax Reform," *Population and Development Review* 13 (March 1987): 119.

34. The National Commission on Children, *Beyond Rhetoric: A New American Agenda for Children and Families* (Washington, D.C.: U.S. Government Printing Office, 1991), 94–95.

9

Observations on Some Proposals to Help Parents: A Progressive Perspective

William A. Galston

The National Parenting Association has asked me to address taxes and housing—to spur discussion on proposals to assist parents. But before I reach policy specifics, let me offer some personal reflections that may provide a framework for deliberations across ideological as well as partisan lines. Although I spend a great deal of time in dialogue with conservatives of good will (and there are many), I address these remarks especially to potential members of what might become a new progressive coalition.

One of my early ventures in national politics was an extended stint (June 1982–November 1984) as issues director in Walter Mondale's presidential campaign. That was a formative and deeply sobering experience. By the end, it was clear to me that the Democratic party had—with the best of intentions—allowed itself to become a coalition of the top and the bottom (or as someone unkindly put it, "the overeducated and the undereducated"), with limited appeal to ordinary working families. I came to the conclusion that the party had lost touch with both the material interests and the moral sentiments of those families and that it would take a systematic, long-term effort to reforge the connection. My guiding thesis was simple: We could not hope to regain majority support for a progressive program unless our economic and social policies rested (and were seen to rest) on moral premises that average families could accept.

While it was misleading, I believed, to divide the public agenda into "moral" and "economic" issues (for the simple reason that many economic

---

William A. Galston is professor and director of the Institute of Philosophy and Public Policy at the School of Public Affairs, University of Maryland. He is the author of *Liberal Purposes: Goods, Virtues, and Diversity in the Liberal State*. During the first two years of President Clinton's administration, he was deputy assistant to the president for domestic policy.

questions have an overtly moral dimension), I argued that Democrats would have to restrain their tendency toward economic reductionism. That is, they would have to recognize that while some morally laden disputes involve economic issues, others of equal human importance and political salience do not. In that context, I came to advocate programs such as the Earned Income Tax Credit, which based income support on work. I also began speaking out on the importance of stable, intact families for children, neighborhoods, and our society and on the imperative for progressives to support programs to assist and strengthen such families.

At the beginning, my efforts were poorly received. I vividly remember a Democratic party conclave in the fall of 1986 when my profamily remarks created such a firestorm among feminists and welfare-rights advocates that the meeting's leaders, including the chair of the DNC, felt compelled to publicly distance themselves from me. But the center of gravity of the discussion gradually shifted, as more Democrats and progressives got comfortable with the idea that support for stable, intact families did not mean either restoring patriarchy or anathematizing single mothers. Bill Clinton's embrace of a public vocabulary rooted in the moral mainstream accelerated this convergence.

In a recent essay, Theda Skocpol writes:

> Some may feel that it is best to avoid talking about families, lest we exacerbate racially charged divisions between dual- and single-parent families. But I disagree. Family-friendly conditions are vital for both sets of families. And progressives need not adopt a morally relativist stance. We can champion moral understandings and practical measures that acknowledge the complexities that all Americans live with on a daily basis. Most people accept that two married parents are best for children, even though each of us is personally acquainted with mothers or fathers who have to soldier on outside this ideal situation. As policies are formulated, progressives can acknowledge the tension between ideals and second-best necessities.[1]

Speaking as a charter "New Democrat," I would not change a single word of this statement, offered by one of our country's most distinguished social democratic scholar-activists. I hope (and believe) that it can become a point of consensus within an emerging twenty-first-century progressive coalition.

A second framing observation: During the past generation, social policy discussion has been dominated (and distorted) by the corrosive debate over welfare, while fiscal policy has been driven by the budget deficit. Whatever one thinks of the 1996 welfare bill and the 1997 balanced budget agreement, their passage meant that this long unfortunate cycle, which placed progressives on the defensive, has come to an end. As President Clinton anticipated, the new welfare regime shifted the responsibility (and burden of proof) to those who have insisted that adequate numbers of entry-level jobs would be available and that states and localities would act effectively to link former welfare recipients to those jobs. Meanwhile, budget surpluses encouraged even congressional Republicans to offer expensive new proposals.

My conclusion is simple: Even with the new constraints imposed by the Bush tax cut, it is now possible to think less defensively and more expansively about the role of the public sector in helping hard-pressed parents and families. Although the people remain generally mistrustful of government (particularly the federal government), Democrats and progressives have perhaps their best opportunity in a generation to offer sensible proposals rooted in the moral sentiments of working-class and middle-class Americans and addressed to the concrete needs of America's families.

A final framing point: While progressives remain unswerving in pursuit of historic ends, we must become more open-minded and innovative regarding means. Just as the British Labour Party finally recognized that public ownership of the means of production is not the best way of realizing the dreams of workers and their families, so U.S. Democrats and progressives must acknowledge that direct public provision of basic goods and services is not necessarily the best way of discharging public responsibility for broad access to these basics. If we have decided that food stamps rather than government supermarkets and food banks are the right way to eliminate hunger among low-income Americans, why can't we consider a resource-based strategy for housing or even (dare I say it) education?

TAX REFORM TO STRENGTHEN MARRIAGE AND FAMILIES

The late 1940s witnessed the creation of a strongly profamily tax system. As a result, families at the median income with two children paid virtually no federal income taxes. While scholars disagree about the extent of the relation between economic incentives and family behavior, it is difficult to believe that the stability of marriage, explosion of child bearing, and decline of divorce during the postwar years were unrelated to these developments in the law.

Over the past three decades, however, some basic features of the tax code shifted against the interests of married couples, especially two-earner couples with children. The real value of the personal exemption has been allowed to erode by nearly 75 percent since the 1950s. The ability of married couples to combine and then "split" their incomes, with each person taxed on his or her half directly, was effectively eliminated in 1969. Special provisions to compensate couples for the "marriage penalty" were curtailed. The tax code shifted in favor of single individuals, and the tax burden on median income families with children increased nearly tenfold. Here again, it is difficult to believe that adverse family trends since the 1960s are entirely unrelated to these changing incentives.[2]

In 1975, lawmakers came together across party lines to create the Earned Income Tax Credit, principally designed to supplement the incomes of low-income working families with dependent children. (A five-year, $21 billion increase in the EITC was the single largest social policy success in Bill Clinton's first term.) While the 1986 tax reform act virtually doubled the personal exemption, it totally eliminated provisions to counter the marriage penalty. The Clinton administration's successful effort in 1993 to increase the progressivity of the tax code had the unintended effect of exacerbating this penalty.

Although the 1997 tax bill did create a $500 per child tax credit, it also included numerous provisions that further increase the code's tilt against married couples. For example:

- Under this law, interest on student loans is deductible during the first five years that payments are required. But the deduction phases out for single incomes between $40,000 and $55,000, and for married incomes between $60,000 and $75,000. So two single college graduates who start work at $39,000/year can each deduct $1,000, for a total of $2,000; if they get married and have a joint income of $78,000, they get no deduction.
- The Roth individual retirement account allows tax-free withdrawals in retirement and permits holders of current IRAs to convert them to Roth accounts if their adjusted gross income (AGI) is under $100,000. So two singles each making $51,000 could convert without penalty; if they were married, they couldn't.

  In addition, single workers cannot contribute to Roth IRAs if their income exceeds $110,000; the ceiling for couples is $160,000. So singles making $80,000–$110,000 each could contribute, but not if they get married.
- Similar limits apply to contributions to IRAs for education expenses, with similar antimarriage consequences.
- The $500/child tax credit is reduced by $50 for each $1,000 that income exceeds $110,000 (for married couples) and $75,000 (for single heads of households). So if two singles, each making $70,000 and with one child, were to marry, their child tax credit would disappear.
- The law creates a special low capital gains rate of 10 percent for married persons up to about $41,000 annual income and singles up to about

$25,000. So two singles with capital gains and incomes of $24,000 each would be taxed at 10 percent; if they married, their capital gains rate would double, to 20 percent.[3]

The prime source of the marriage penalty in the current tax code is the tension among three principles: progressivity; equal treatment of married couples with the same total earnings, regardless of the distribution of earnings between husband and wife; and marriage neutrality—the same tax treatment of individuals A and B, whether they are single or married.[4]

Box 9.1 A Marriage Penalty

A couple with $75,000 in total earnings, split evenly between the husband and the wife, would have incurred a marriage penalty of nearly $1,400 under 1996 tax law. The penalty results from two factors. First, the combined standard deduction for two individual tax filers would have been $8,000—$1,300 more than the standard deduction available on a joint return. At the couple's marginal tax rate of 28 percent, the lower deduction would have increased the couple's tax liability by $364 (28 percent of $1,300). Second, because tax brackets for joint returns were less than twice as wide as those for individual returns, $7,900 that is taxed at 15 percent on individual returns would have incurred a 28 percent rate on a joint return. That higher tax rate would have raised the couple's tax liability by an additional $1,027 (28 percent minus 15 percent equals 13 percent of $7,900). In combination, the two factors would have increased the couple's tax liability by 1.9 percent of their adjusted gross income.

	Husband	*Wife*	*Couple*
Adjusted Gross Income	$37,500	$37,500	$75,000
Less personal exemptions	2,550	2,550	5,100
Less standard deduction	4,000	4,000	6,700
Equals taxable income	30,950	30,950	63,200
Taxable at 15 percent	24,000	24,000	40,100
Taxable at 28 percent	6,950	6,950	23,100
Tax Liability	5,546	5,546	12,483
Marriage Penalty			$1,391
As a Percentage of Adjusted Gross Income			1.9

Source: Congressional Budget Office.

It turns out that there is no way of fulfilling these three principles simultaneously. For example, progressivity ensures that a couple in which each individual earns $37,500 will pay more total taxes if they marry than if they remain single.

Box 9.2   A Marriage Bonus

A couple with $75,000 in total earnings, all earned by the wife, would have received a marriage bonus of nearly $4,000 under 1996 tax law. The bonus results from three factors. First, filing jointly, the couple would have claimed $5,100 in personal exemptions, twice what they could have claimed on two single returns. At a 31 percent tax rate, the larger exemption would have reduced the couple's tax liability by $791 (31 percent of $2,550). Second, the standard deduction of $6,700 on a joint return would have been $2,700 more than the $4,000 standard deduction the wife could have claimed on an individual return. (The husband, filing individually with no income, could not take the deduction.) At the couple's marginal tax rate of 31 percent, the larger deduction would have reduced the couple's tax liability by $837 (31 percent of $2,700). Finally, because tax brackets for joint returns were wider than those for individual returns, $16,100 that is taxed at 28 percent on individual returns would have been taxed at only 15 percent on a joint return and $5,050 taxed at 31 percent rather than at 28 percent. Those lower tax rates would have reduced the couple's tax liability by an additional $2,245 (28 percent minus 15 percent equals 13 percent of $16,100 plus 31 percent minus 28 percent equals 3 percent of $5,050). In combination, the three factors would have lowered the couple's tax liability by 5.2 percent of their adjusted gross income.

	Husband	*Wife*	*Couple*
Adjusted Gross Income	$0	$75,000	$75,000
Less personal exemptions	2,550	2,550	5,100
Less standard deduction	4,000	4,000	6,700
Equals taxable income	0	68,450	63,200
Taxable at 15 percent	0	24,000	40,100
Taxable at 28 percent	0	34,150	23,100
Taxable at 31 percent	0	10,300	0
Tax Liability	0	16,355	12,483
Marriage Bonus			$3,872
As a Percentage of Adjusted Gross Income			5.2

Source: Congressional Budget Office.

Note that these same structural principles can lead to marriage *bonuses* in cases in which one spouse earns all or most of the married couple's total income.

So it is too simple to say that our current tax code is comprehensively biased against marriage. Rather, it tilts against certain kinds of marriages—namely, those in which husbands and wives are both in the paid workforce earning the same or similar salaries. This remains the case even after the modest reductions in the marriage penalty enacted as part of the 2001 tax bill.

There are two ways of looking at this balance: static and dynamic. Under one standard static analysis, 42 percent of all married filers in 1996 experienced penalties, while 51 percent received bonuses and 6 percent were essentially unaffected. The average penalty was $1,380; the average bonus was slightly less ($1,300); and the tax code awarded an overall marriage bonus of about $4 billion ($33 billion in bonuses minus $29 billion in penalties).

A dynamic analysis suggests a different picture. Between 1969 and 1995, the share of all married couples in which both spouses worked outside the home increased from 46 to 60 percent, while the proportion with just one worker fell from 46 to 25 percent. The increase for married couples with children was particularly sharp: from 54 to 74 percent for couples with one child, and from 33 to 67 percent for couples with two or more children. In 1969, only 17 percent of working-age married couples were characterized by rough equality of earnings between husband and wife (the technical definition: each spouse contributes at least one-third of the couple's total earnings). By 1995, that percentage had doubled, to about 34 percent. This statistic suggests that if all other variables had remained constant, the percentage of couples experiencing marriage penalties would have increased sharply between 1969 and 1995. To put it the other way around: If the demographic profile of married couples had not changed over the past quarter century, two-thirds of couples would get marriage bonuses (versus today's actual figure of about one-half) and fewer than one-third would pay penalties (versus today's actual figure of about two-fifths).

Based on this history, the case for tax reform to promote the interests of contemporary married couples appears strong. Let me suggest a few principles that might guide this effort.

1. The tax code should not create a substantial group of married taxpayers that is worse off than its members would be if they were unmarried.
2. There should be no bias in the tax code for or against work in the household economy. (In an earlier chapter, Allan Carlson has proposed a bias

in favor of the household economy. I disagree; I believe neutrality between the household and the paid economy is the correct standard.)

3. There should be no bias in the tax code against the decision to have children (as distinguished from the explicit pro-natalist policy Carlson suggests). As a related issue, the code should embody a social recognition of
the internalized family costs and external public benefits of child rearing.

4. There should be no substantial group of married taxpayers that would
be worse off under reform proposals than under the status quo.

Joint versus separate taxation. As we debate the reluctance or elimination of the marriage penalty, the American people and their representatives
should discuss these principles in some detail—especially the fourth, because
it screens out options that many might find appealing. For example, 19 out of
27 countries in the OECD impose income taxes separately on the earnings of
husbands and wives. (Only 3 other OECD nations have embraced the U.S.
strategy of joint taxation.) For all practical purposes, separate taxation eliminates the effect of marriage on a couple's taxes (fulfilling the criterion of marriage neutrality discussed previously), while violating the criterion of equal
tax treatment for couples with the same total incomes.

Prior to 1948, the United States employed separate taxation. The movement to joint taxation in that year was defended as promarriage. And in the
context of a social structure dominated by single-earner households, it was.
But today, joint taxation divides married couples into winners ("traditional"
households with a single dominant earner) and losers (modern two-earner
households with two significant contributors to total family incomes). Restoring and mandating individual filing would be roughly revenue-neutral (it
would increase federal revenues by a modest $4 billion annually) and would
eliminate the marriage penalty for the nearly 21 million couples now incur-
ring them. But it would also increase taxes by an average of $1,300 for the 25
million couples enjoying marriage bonuses under the current system.

By themselves, these raw numbers would constitute a formidable political
barrier to change. To complicate matters further, the tax increases would fall
disproportionately on couples where one spouse has made the decision to remain at home to care for young children, exacerbating the perception of an
economic and cultural bias against the home economy.

The alternative is to hold all married couples harmless by allowing them
to choose between filing jointly or separately. Assuming that each couple
made the economically rational choice, this approach would reduce annual
federal revenues by an estimated $29 billion—roughly the value of all mar-
riage penalties in the existing code. It is not unreasonable to wonder
whether the social benefits of this approach are commensurate with its hefty
price tag.

Reforming the Earned Income Tax Credit (EITC). The tension among the principles of progressivity, equal treatment of equal family incomes, and marriage neutrality operates with special intensity on the EITC. Consider the choice faced by two low-wage earners, each an EITC recipient with one child. With a family income of $22,000, the marriage penalty is $3,700, a staggering 17 percent of adjusted gross income.

Box 9.3   A Marriage Penalty for a Low-Income Couple with Children

A couple with two children and $22,000 in total earnings, split evenly between the husband and wife, would have incurred a marriage penalty of $3,701 under 1996 tax law. The penalty results from two factors. First, if they were not married, both the husband and the wife could file as heads of household, each claiming one child as a dependent. As heads of household, their combined standard deductions would have been $11,800, $5,100 more than the $6,700 standard deduction available on a joint return. At the couple's marginal tax rate of 15 percent, the lower deduction would have increased the couple's tax liability by $765 (15 percent of $5,100). Second, filing separate returns, the husband and wife each could have claimed the maximum earned income tax credit (EITC) for a filer with one child, $2,152. Filing jointly, the couple would have received only one, smaller EITC of $1,368. Thus, filing jointly the couple would have received a payment of $603, about $3,700 less than the $4,304 they would have gotten if they could have filed separately.

	Husband[a]	*Wife*[a]	*Couple*
Adjusted Gross Income	$11,000	$11,000	$22,000
Less personal exemptions	5,100	5,100 ·	10,200
Less standard deduction	5,900	5,900	6,700
Equals taxable income	0	0	5,100
Tax (at 15 percent)	0	0	765
Less earned income tax credit	2,152	2,152	1,368
Tax Liability	−2,152	−2,152	−603
		Marriage Penalty	$3,701
	As a Percentage of Adjusted Gross Income		16.8

Source: Congressional Budget Office.

[a] Baseline for calculating marriage penalty assumes that both husband and wife file as head of household with one child.

This may seem like a somewhat atypical case; after all, relatively few single men have sole responsibility for children. So let's vary it slightly: Assume that the man is a childless minimum wage worker, while the woman is a former AFDC recipient with two children (see table 9.1).

The EITC rewards work, fights poverty, and promotes tax fairness. But while it is one of the most morally admirable portions of our tax code, it is also the principal source of the marriage penalty for low-income couples. Removing this penalty is neither cheap nor straightforward, however, as a recent study by the Congressional Budget Office makes clear.

One option analyzed by the CBO would totally eliminate the penalty by allowing each parent to receive the EITC on the basis of his or her individual income. This approach would have a number of negative or counterintuitive consequences. For example, it would remove all limits on the total combined income of families receiving the credit, and it would expand the number of recipient families by more than 11 million—many at the upper end of the income spectrum. (A model case: the husband makes $60,000 and the wife, $10,000. Under existing family income limits, these taxpayers would not be eligible for the EITC; under the individual income option, the wife would receive payments.) In addition, the CBO estimates the overall annual cost (lost revenues plus increased outlays) of this approach at about $14 billion.

A second option, with an annual price tag of roughly $10 billion, would preserve the current family basis of the EITC while setting income eligibility limits for couples at twice the levels for individuals. (The current cutoff, which applies to both individuals and couples, is $28,495; the new cutoff for married couples would be almost $57,000.) Ninety percent of the benefits under this approach would go to couples making less than $50,000, and it would eliminate the marriage penalty for the family discussed earlier with two earners at the minimum wage. Still, it seems more than a bit odd to allow families with incomes almost 50 percent above the national median to qualify for a program intended to benefit the working poor.

Table 9.1. An Example of the EITC's Marriage Penalty

	Husband	Wife	Couple
Adjusted gross income	$11,000	$11,000	$22,000
Less personal exemptions	2,550	7,650	10,200
Less standard deduction	5,900	5,900	6,700
Taxable income	2,550	0	5,100
Tax (at 15 percent)	385	0	765
Less EITC	0	3,556	1,368
Tax liability	385	−3,556	−603
Marriage penalty			$2,568
As percent of AGI			11.7

A third option, which would make an additional 3.7 million couples eligible for the EITC and cost about $4 billion per year, requires spouses to pool and split their earnings and then allows them to qualify for the EITC as individuals. Like the second option, this approach would resolve the problems faced by the dual minimum-wage family. In contrast to the second option, it would mean lower payments for some couples—those in which one spouse earns substantially more than the other. Virtually all the benefits would go to families with incomes below $50,000 who are now experiencing marriage penalties.

Dependent exemptions and credits. During the 1950s, at the peak of the family-friendly tax code, married couples with two children at the median income paid federal income taxes at an effective rate of 5.6 percent, versus about 9 percent in the early 1990s. Similar families at half the median income (the working poor) paid no federal income taxes whatever, compared to an effective rate of about 5 percent by the early 1990s. The principal cause of these shifts is not higher marginal tax rates (which are in fact lower than they were forty years ago), but rather a decline in the value of the dependent exemption, in real inflation-adjusted terms and as a percentage of median income.

A rough calculation indicates that restoring the value of the dependent exemption to the level of the 1950s would require a dependent exemption of at least $8,000; the actual figure today is about $2,300. But this overstates the size of the problem. The $500 per child tax credit enacted in 1997 is the equivalent of an increase of $3,300 in the dependent exemption for working-class families in the 15 percent bracket and $1,800 for middle-class families in the 28 percent bracket. So working-class families now enjoy dependents' tax benefits totaling $5,600 (2,300 + 3,300) per dependent, while the total for middle-class families is $4,100 (2,300 + 1,800).

This simple calculation shows that an additional $500 credit per child (above and beyond what was done in 1997) would just about bring families with dependents back to where they were forty years ago. This strategy would be especially effective if the credit were targeted to lower- and middle-income families and made applicable to payroll as well as income taxes. For example, a low-income family with two children may not pay $1,000 in federal income taxes but would receive the full $1,000 credit, a portion of which would in effect reduce its payroll tax burden. The child credit provisions of the 2001 tax act move some distance in this direction.

Payroll taxes. For many families with dependent children, the increase in the federal income tax has been dwarfed by increases in the payroll tax. In the mid-1950s, working-class families paid payroll taxes at the rate of 4.0 percent, and middle-class families at 3.4 percent, versus 15.3 today. Even upper-middle-class families, much of whose income is excluded from the Social Security taxable base, have experienced major increases (table 9.2).

Given these trends, it is reasonable to look for ways of reducing the payroll tax burden for families with dependent children. The difficulty, of course, is that these efforts take place against the backdrop of projected long-term financing problems for the Social Security system and increasing political challenges to the program in its current form.

There are three basic strategies available for reducing families' payroll tax burdens: (1) increasing the payroll tax for other workers; (2) shifting some of the financing to general revenues; or (3) not compensating for revenue losses, further increasing the long-term financial pressures on the Social Security system. In my judgment, strategy 3 is substantively irresponsible and a political nonstarter. Strategy 2 is unwise to the extent that it weakens the moral basis of the system—namely, retirement benefits in return for (though not in proportion to) contributions during one's working life. By process of elimination, strategy 1 emerges as the most promising, though hardly free of difficulty.

What could be done? One possibility would be to reduce the employee portion of the payroll tax by (say) 1.5 percent per dependent child. A working-class family with two children at half the median income would see its payroll taxes cut by about $600 a year; families at the median income would see an annual cut of roughly $1,200. (This would roll back payroll taxes for these families to roughly the levels that prevailed in 1980.) Another possibility in the same vein would be to exempt from the Social Security tax base an amount equal to the value of the dependent deduction ($2,300) multiplied by the number of dependents. A very rough calculation suggests an annual revenue loss of roughly $25–30 billion; compensating for it would require a significant payroll tax increase for all workers without dependent children.

Table 9.2.   Federal Income and Payroll Taxes as a Share of Family Income, 1955–1991

	Half Median Income			Median Income			Twice Median Income		
Year	Federal Income Tax	Social Security Tax	Total	Federal Income Tax	Social Security Tax	Total	Federal Income Tax	Social Security Tax	Total
1955	0.0	4.0	4.0	5.6	3.4	9.1	10.8	1.7	12.5
1960	0.2	6.0	6.2	7.8	4.6	12.4	12.1	2.3	14.4
1965	2.2	7.3	9.4	7.1	4.5	11.6	11.1	2.2	13.4
1970	4.7	9.6	14.3	9.4	6.7	16.1	13.5	3.4	16.8
1975	4.2	11.7	15.9	9.6	10.4	20.0	14.9	5.2	20.1
1980	6.0	12.3	18.3	11.4	12.3	23.7	18.3	6.5	24.8
1985	6.6	14.1	20.7	10.3	14.1	24.4	16.8	8.5	25.3
1990	5.1	15.3	20.3	9.3	15.3	24.6	15.1	9.5	24.6
1991	4.8	15.3	20.1	9.2	15.3	24.5	15.0	10.6	25.6

Source: C. Eugene and Jon M. Bakija, *Retooling Social Security for the 21st Century: Right and Wrong Approaches to Reform* (Washington, D.C.: Urban Institute Press, 1994), 160.

A very different strategy would avoid the need to shift tax burdens among classes of workers, focusing instead on ways of allowing workers to shift burdens and benefits from one period of their lives to another. So, for example, workers who take advantage of the payroll tax reduction for minor children might be required to pay higher rates for the remainder of their working lives after their children are grown. Conversely, as is suggested in chapter 15 of this volume, it might be possible to allow young workers to draw from their Social Security accounts for some family-related purposes (e.g., financing an extended leave from the paid workforce after the birth of a child). This would require these workers to choose between higher tax rates later on and retirement benefits that are actuarially reduced by the value (principal plus interest over time) of the funds withdrawn.

A wild new idea. Consider a thought experiment comparing two stylized societies. In society A, virtually every couple is married, but no marriage lasts for more than a few years. (There is a very high rate of divorce and remarriage.) In society B, only half of the adults ever marry, but every marriage lasts until the death of a spouse. I don't know of many people who would consider society A to be a model for families and child rearing. Most people who care about these things probably want a society that combines the high marriage rate of A with the stability of B. But my guess is that if forced to choose, most of these people would opt for B. If this is right (every reader will have to run the thought experiment for him- or herself), it reveals a significant fact: Our interest in the stability of marital relations exceeds our concern for the statistical incidence of couples in the legal category of marriage.

Suppose we wanted to create a tax code that encouraged and rewarded marital stability rather than just status. What would we do? Here's a blue-sky proposal: After five years of marriage, begin reducing a couple's overall taxes by 1 percent a year for each subsequent year, up to a maximum of (say) thirty years. So, for example, a couple married for fifteen years would calculate its gross taxes for that year and then reduce that figure by 10 percent (fifteen years minus the base of five years multiplied by 1 percent/year). Couples married for thirty years or more would experience a tax reduction of 25 percent. My hunch is that these numbers are big enough to serve as a significant disincentive to divorce in a large number of cases.

HOUSING

The story of public housing assistance over the past three decades is not a happy one. The oldest and best known form of assistance is publicly owned and operated housing, initially authorized by the Housing Act of 1937. While quantitatively disappointing (only 1.2 million units have been produced during the past sixty years), this program still works reasonably well in some areas. In many central cities, however, the quality of this housing (typically, though not invariably, high-rise apartments) has declined dramatically, crime has surged in and around the buildings, and working-class married couples have been squeezed out in favor of the extreme poor—typically, single mothers with minor children. The physical deterioration was so severe that in 1996 the Department of Housing and Urban Development established a goal of demolishing 100,000 of the worst units by the year 2000. In several cities, including Washington, D.C., pervasive management failures prompted federal takeovers.

Still, there is a huge waiting list (estimated at 1 million families nationally), suggesting that for many poor people this housing represents the best available combination of quality and price. Recent efforts to improve public housing include enhanced security, expedited eviction procedures for drug dealers and other offenders, and the relaxation of strict income eligibility limits to increase the percentage of married and employed tenants.

Other housing programs—notably, subsidies to private developers to stimulate the creation of low-income housing, direct assistance to tenants, and efforts to promote the "deconcentration" of the poor—have been more successful. But many of these programs have proved vulnerable to political manipulation and scandal, and some of the most highly touted efforts (for example, the conversion of public housing to private ownership) have involved unsustainably high costs per beneficiary.

Most experts agree that the core housing problem for low-income people is not availability but rather affordability. This suggests that programs focused on the supply side needlessly divert resources from the intended beneficiaries to private developers and building managers. It is also widely agreed that the expansion of ownership (as opposed to renting) creates significant advantages for both individuals and communities.[5]

What would we do if we were able to mobilize the resources to realize the National Housing Goal, promulgated by Congress nearly fifty years ago, of a "decent [affordable] home and suitable living environment for every American family"? The following proposals are intentionally unconstrained by political and fiscal realities.

To begin, we would establish as an entitlement a housing voucher keyed to income and family size. The voucher's purpose would be to fill the gap between median housing costs (around $600 per month) and 30 percent of family cash income, defined as the sum of earned income and EITC payments. (Thirty percent of income is the affordability standard used by most existing

HUD programs.) So, for example, a family with two children and gross earned income of $11,000 now receives an annual EITC payment of $3,560, for a total cash income of $14,560. Thirty percent of that total is $4,368, or $364 per month. So the family would be eligible for a monthly voucher worth $236 ($600 minus $364)—an annual housing subsidy of $2,832. To avoid large transfers to nonworking families (and to increase work incentives for very low-income individuals), no family's housing voucher would be allowed to exceed its EITC payment. And because the lion's share of the EITC goes to families with children (the annual maximum for childless individuals is only $323 and payments phase out altogether when annual income reaches $9,500), the housing voucher would principally benefit parents and their dependents.

I don't have a very precise estimate of the cost of this proposal. But note that the housing voucher phases out entirely for families with incomes above $24,000, which is almost $4,500 less than the EITC cutoff. So because fewer families would be eligible for the voucher than for the EITC and each family's voucher would be capped at the EITC amount, the total cost of the program would be somewhat less than the EITC, which now has annual outlays of about $25 billion. (To provide some sense of relative size: annual federal support for low-income housing is less than $10 billion; the annual cost of the mortgage interest deduction is $66 billion.)

If home ownership is an important policy goal, there would be no reason to limit the use of the voucher to rental expenses. Recipients would be allowed to combine it with other income sources to qualify for home mortgages and meet monthly payments. The federal government could reinforce the push toward increased home ownership by transferring its inventory of single-family homes to local public housing authorities or community development corporations for quick resale and by supporting community-based groups such as the Industrial Areas Foundation that forge effective housing partnerships with the public, private, and voluntary sectors. And to help families that can afford monthly mortgage payments but cannot scrape together funds for down payments and closing costs, the government could create a fund for loans that would be secured by equity in homes and recovered with interest from proceeds at the time of resale.[6]

One possibility for financing these and related housing proposals would be to shift the structure of the mortgage interest deduction in a more progressive direction. At present, taxpayers are not allowed to deduct interest payments for the portion of their mortgage that exceeds $1 million. One straightforward proposal is to lower this cap to (say) $250,000. An alternative would be to directly limit the amount of interest deductible annually to (say) $20,000, an amount roughly equivalent to annual interest costs on a home mortgage of $250,000 at current interest rates. The latter proposal, unlike the former, would leave borrowers exposed to nondeductible interest costs when interest rates rise significantly.

SUMMARY: PUBLIC POLICY, FAMILY INCOME, AND WAGES

Enacting the principal proposals discussed thus far—reducing the marriage penalty, doubling the $500 per child tax credit while applying it to payroll as well as income taxes, lowering payroll taxes for workers with minor children, and instituting a housing credit keyed to family income and the EITC—would increase the disposable incomes of working-class and middle-class families with dependent children by thousands of dollars annually. But these public policy instruments do little to affect underlying patterns of income derived from work.

Over the past decade, median family income rose from $46,344 to $49,940. Married couples did better, increasing from $51,922 to $56,827. Female-headed families lagged far behind, with median incomes rising from $23,163 to $26,164.[7]

Despite the tight labor markets and across-the-board wage gains in recent years, the long-term trend remains one of wage stagnation in the middle, sharp drops at the bottom, and even sharper increases at the top. I subscribe to the conventional explanation that globalization has reduced the ability of key players—business, organized labor, and government—to maintain the terms of the social contract that characterized the quarter century after World War II. Still, there are some strategies that should be tried:

1. The ability of workers to organize should not be impeded by antiquated or unenforced labor laws.
2. Someone should announce a new moral norm of compensation: chief executive officers of firms shouldn't make more than (say) one hundred times the wages of their lowest-paid workers. The names of the firms and CEOs that violate this norm should be publicized regularly, and the offenders should be asked to justify their conduct. (Responses that simply invoke "the free market" would receive a grade of F.)
3. Another norm, which *might* be reinforced through the tax code (although I'm not sure just how): Compensation options available to top officials in a firm should be available to all employees as well. So if CEOs can receive stock options and profit-sharing plans, everyone should. In a period in which profits and stock prices are increasing faster than base wages, a strategy of "universal gain-sharing" offers the best hope for increasing the total compensation of average workers.

Having said this, I incline to the contrarian view that the role of government in leaning against rising market-induced inequality will increase rather than decrease over the next generation. But efforts to discharge this responsibility through measures that restrain market competition (e.g., restrictive international trade agreements, new regulations on domestic business activities) are not likely to succeed. Rather, government will have to act directly to reduce inequality and increase opportunity. I call this the "progressive market strategy." The EITC, child tax credit, and proposed housing credit are all examples of policies consistent with this strategy. In the next decade, we will have to work harder, intellectually and politically, to find ways in which government can act to compensate the sectors of society that are harmed by global competition and to make the sources of upward mobility in the new economy available to all.

In a spirit of speculative adventure, let me sketch two largish policy concepts under the "progressive market" rubric. (I'm not sure of the merits or practicalities of either one, but they strike me as being worthy of discussion.)

Wage insurance. When I was serving in the Clinton administration, I tried without much success to promote discussion of a plan for "wage insurance." The basic idea was straightforward: In the new economy, pressures from technology, trade, and other factors are producing downward pressures on wages. Many individuals who lose high-paying jobs discover that their next job will pay significantly less and that it will take several years (sometimes longer) to struggle back to prior levels of compensation. In the new economy, in short, wage loss is a problem independent of unemployment. The old model of cyclical unemployment, to which unemployment insurance was a reasonable policy response, must now be modified to include the risk of noncyclical wage loss, about which the current UI system does nothing.

That raises an obvious question: Would it be possible in principle to design a system of wage insurance that builds on the UI system? The answer, I believe, is yes. Imagine a contributory system into which all workers pay (say) one-half of 1 percent of their wage income, generating a trust fund of (depending on the details) $10–20 billion annually. Workers who experience involuntary wage losses would be eligible for insurance compensation of (say) half their losses for a period of three years or until they recover their previous wage levels (whichever comes first).[8]

Translating this concept into a workable program would not be easy. We would have to answer detailed questions about eligibility criteria, actuarial soundness, and administerability, among others. But the idea should be sustained by its underlying moral power: The distribution of benefits and burdens in the new economy is highly uneven, and many of us are exposed to risks that are hard to anticipate and mitigate under current circumstances.

Wage insurance represents meaningful recognition of the fact that we're all in it together and that those of us who are gaining from changes in technology and patterns of competition have a responsibility to share our gains with those who aren't.

Wage subsidies. Columbia University's Edmund Phelps has proposed a bold plan for increasing wages flowing to low-wage labor. Under his plan, firms would be subsidized for hiring low-wage workers on a sliding scale that would phase out at $12 per hour. Although some portion of this subsidy would go to the firm, much of it would help bid up the price of low-wage labor while dramatically reducing unemployment among lower-skilled workers.

The gross cost of this program would be enormous—on the order of $100 billion per year. Its net cost would be significantly lower, perhaps only half the gross: it would replace the EITC (currently $35 billion/year) and reduce costs for programs such as Medicaid, food stamps, and TANF (the successor to AFDC). But most important, it would improve the attractiveness to employers of potential workers now at the end of the labor market queue. And it could "make work pay" for young people now living in communities where alternatives to legal employment have proved so appealing. If Phelps is right, this will also increase incentives for these potential workers to obtain the education and job skills they need to succeed in the new economy, and it could also increase the propensity of employers to invest in these workers, who are now overlooked in most workplace-based training programs.[9]

NOTES

1. Theda Skocpol, "A Partnership with American Families," in *The New Majority: Toward a Popular Progressive Politics,* ed. Stanley B. Greenberg and Theda Skocpol (New Haven: Yale University Press, 1997), 123.

2. For more detail on this sad history, see Elaine Ciulla Kamarck and William A. Galston, "A Progressive Family Policy for the 1990s," in *Mandate for Change,* ed. Will Marshall and Martin Schram (New York: Berkley Books, 1993).

3. See Albert B. Crenshaw, "For Two-Income Couples, More Reasons Not to Get Tied," *Washington Post,* August 24 1997, H1.

4. See "For Better or for Worse: Marriage and the Federal Income Tax" (Congressional Budget Office, June 1997), 3. This careful study is the source for most of the statistics in this section of my chapter.

5. See Chester W. Hartman, "Memo to the Social Science Research Council Regarding U.S. Housing Policy," prepared for the SSRC's Committee for Research on the Urban Underclass, October 1993.

6. For a useful summary of federal home ownership strategies, see "Moving Up to the American Dream: From Public Housing to Private Homeownership" (U.S. Department of Housing and Urban Development, July 1996).

7. *Money Income in the United States, 1999* (U.S. Census Bureau P60–209, September 2000), x.

8. I note with interest that Robert Z. Lawrence and Robert E. Litan have suggested something along these lines in a Brookings "Policy Brief" (September 1997, no. 24).

9. Edmund Phelps, *Rewarding Work* (Cambridge: Harvard University Press, 1997). My comments are based on summaries by Alan Wolfe, "The Moral Meanings of Work," *The American Prospect* (September/October 1997): 87; and the staff of the *Economist* (September 20–26, 1997): 47.

10

Back to the Future: A GI Bill for the Twenty-First Century

Peter Winn

The postwar era that culminated in the 1950s is viewed by many as the golden age of the American family, an era in which stable two-parent families were the norm as well as the ideal, and middle-class family values shaped popular culture as well as personal lives. In the 1990s, an era in which the personal was political, the 1950s and its families became political banners, viewed nostalgically by conservatives as the last great age of the traditional American family, before the challenges of the 1960s and changes of the 1970s undermined its structure and ended the values consensus that had supported it. Much of the current political stress on "family values" looks back to the 1950s as an ideal to be recaptured and a model to be reconstructed.

LESSONS FROM THE 1950s

Revisionist historians have pointed out that what conservatives refer to as the "traditional" American family was really a creation of the 1950s. Not only did this era reverse earlier trends in marriage, fertility, and divorce, but it was the first era in this century in which most American families lived in a house of their own, as well as the first era in history of mass consumption centered around the family. It was also the first epoch in which the middle class became a majority in the United States and the first in which its image and values dominated. Moreover, it was the first era in which the family was viewed as the primary arena for achievement and fulfillment for both women *and*

Peter Winn is professor of history at Tufts University.

175

men, in which the goal of the family was happiness and children were its central focus. It was, concluded Elaine Tyler May, "the first wholehearted effort to create a home that would fulfill virtually all its members' personal needs through an energized and expressive personal life."[1]

The fact that the 1950s family was not "traditional" but a new phenomenon, the product of new postwar conditions, however, does not make it any less valid or valuable as a benchmark or a model. What it underscores is that our notions of the "traditional" and the "new" are not absolutes, but are revised and reimagined over time. In seeking to reconstruct or reimagine the family in the twenty-first century, we have several models and "traditions" that we can draw upon—and update. What makes the 1950s family so appealing today is that it was in many ways the opposite of the crisis-ridden family of the 1990s.

In many ways, the two decades seem similar. Like the 1990s, the 1950s were an era of conservative politics, economic growth, and "family values" in the United States. But one area where they differ is in the state of the nation's families. Today the American nuclear family is in crisis, and the call for a return to family values has an edge of desperation to it. During the 1950s, family values were consensus values, and Americans of all social strata, race, ethnicity, and religion embraced them in theory and generally lived them in practice. For proponents of family values in the 1990s, the 1950s seemed a success story, even a golden age.

Golden ages—by definition—are impossible to recapture, and, despite some surface similarities, there are many differences, in conditions, experiences, and problems between the 1950s and the 1990s, from labor union strength, women's work, and economic expectations to divorce law, tax structures, and popular culture. Yet much can be learned from exploring the 1950s family that can be useful to the families of today as well. In particular, much can be learned from examining the policies that supported and sustained the nuclear family in the 1950s—and from reflecting on how those policies might be reproduced in the very different world of today. For all of these reasons, an exploration of the American family and government policy in the 1950s may yield valuable lessons for the twenty-first century.

THE AMERICAN NUCLEAR FAMILY IN THE 1950s

The 1950s remain a controversial era in U.S. history. A self-defined success at the time, the decade, its families, and its values were rejected and ridiculed in the 1960s by its adolescent offspring. Later historians, many of them children of the 1950s, have continued this critical stance in their scholarship, adding feminist, African American, or postmodern critiques to the rebellions of their youth.[2]

The 1950s provide considerable grist for their mills. The decade was an age of conformity, when teenage rebellion was seen as "without a cause." It was a Cold War era of nuclear hysteria, when Joseph McCarthy attacked civil liberties in the name of anticommunism. It was an epoch of racial segregation in the South and racial violence throughout the country. It was a time when women were pressed back into traditional roles and their daughters taught that success in school meant getting their man with their degree.

Yet despite all the critiques by revisionist historians and social activists, the postwar period that culminated in the 1950s remains the golden age of the American nuclear family. It was a time when the boys came back from war glad to be home and ready to start the families they had feared they would never have. It was an epoch in which Rosie the Riveter returned home to marry her man and exchange her drill for a vacuum cleaner and the other new appliances that enticed women into being full-time homemakers.

These appliances—refrigerators, washing machines, dishwashers, televisions—were material symbols of the relative wealth of the postwar United States, which in 1950 was the sole global economic superpower, accounting for 80 percent of world trade. It was a wealth that was sufficiently diffused to lift many blue-collar workers into the "middle class" and to allow members of that middle class to acquire the American dream—a house of their own and a car to go with it. Was it any wonder that Americans in the 1950s were confident that their values and their way of life were models for the world?

Within this context, the U.S. nuclear family enjoyed its statistically finest hours. By 1950, both men and women were marrying earlier than at any time in this century. So desirable was wedded bliss that by 1957, "an incredible 97 percent of Americans of 'marriageable age' had taken the vows."[3] For another broad recent view of the 1950s, see James T. Patterson, *Grand Expectations: The United States, 1945–74* (New York: Oxford University Press, 1996). For a statistical analysis of marriage patterns, see Andrew Cherlin, *Marriage, Divorce, Remarriage* (Cambridge, Mass.: Harvard University Press, 1981). It was a phenomenon that cut across socioeconomic, racial, and cultural divides, with white middle-class values shaping those of other groups. Not only were Americans marrying more and sooner in the 1950s, they were also having more babies, often as soon as they married. And they were staying married, with divorce rates stable in the 1950s at around ten per thousand. An entire generation seemed to believe that marriage was "the natural state of adults" and "the Family the center of your living."[4] And the image of family was now a *nuclear* (not an extended) family, with the father at work, the mother at home, and the children in school or at play.

For most American families, the income of their male head of household was sufficient to provide, allowing their women to stay at home and their children to stay in school. In 1950, 65 percent of the workforce was composed of married men whose wives were home caring for children in a nuclear family. Still, during the 1950s, women entered the workforce at an accelerating rate, in part to pay for those appliances in an age of inflation, and by 1960, nearly 40 percent of women worked outside the home. Yet this women's work did not challenge the patriarchal norm of the era, nor did it often lead to marriage-ending tensions. Divorce, socially discouraged and legally difficult, affected only a small minority of families. Even among the poor, fathers were more likely to stay than leave and families were more likely to stay together than to split apart. Neighborhood fields sprouted Little Leagues and schools PTAs. That distinguishing American tendency to form civic groups that Alexis de Tocqueville had noted a century before seemed to reach new heights, with the nuclear family as its base and raison d'être.

It is true that this idyllic picture of the 1950s largely ignores minorities excluded from its benefits by racial discrimination and injured by racial violence.[5] It also underestimates the personal costs paid by women who surrendered their career possibilities for lives as homemakers. Moreover, we now know that off-camera Lucy and Desi had a far from ideal marriage and the family of Ozzie and Harriet was far less functional than it seemed on our television screens. Nor should we forget the pain of those who felt compelled to spend their lives in abusive or alienating marriages because of the pressures of conformity and the difficulties of divorce—or the traumas of homosexuals in a homophobic age.[6]

Yet despite these caveats, the product of hindsight, revisionist scholarship, and social activism, the 1950s remain the golden age of the American nuclear family. This seems particularly true by comparison to the family crisis of the present, when the American nuclear family seems an endangered species and the most functional family on television is the cartoon Simpsons, "a *nuclear* family." Fathers in the 1950s may have been more emotionally distant than today, but at least they "overwhelmingly stayed married and supported their families with their paychecks."[7] Moreover, today's images of paternal involvement, from Saturday Little League games to Sunday barbecues, all have roots in the 1950s.

Thus, it is not surprising that those who espouse "family values" and look back nostalgically to a less problematic nation, look to the 1950s as the last golden age. Conservatives, surveying this history and the rocky road that the American family has traveled since, tend to ascribe much of the hallowed past to family values and much of the current crisis to the Great Society programs of the 1960s and the intrusion of and dependence on government that they contend has sapped the individualism and self-reliance that made this country great.

This nostalgic view of the past is understandable, but it is profoundly ahistorical. What it ignores is the central role of government and its programs in helping the postwar generation to fulfill the American dream in the years before the 1960s. Some of these measures were targeted at helping middle-class families make it. Most of this help was an unintended consequence of policies created for other purposes. But, at bottom, the American dream family of the 1950s depended upon public subsidies and government programs to an extent that today's conservatives—who espouse family values, but attack government social spending—do not realize, yet need to accept if the American family is to transcend its current crisis and traverse the new century on solid ground.

THE GI BILL AND THE AMERICAN FAMILY

During the postwar period, federal tax policy directly encouraged family formation. It promoted marriage through income tax schedules that halved the married wage earner's tax liability and did not compute his wife's housework as income in kind. It offered an incentive to have children, in its sizable tax exemptions for each dependent. It helped make housing affordable through its home mortgage deduction.[8] In addition, a host of government policies, from highway and sewer construction to public education, provided indirect encouragement to form families and aid in sustaining them. But perhaps the most important government policy as far as family formation and maintenance were concerned was the GI Bill.

The "GI Bill of Rights"—as the Serviceman's Readjustment Act of 1944 was popularly known—was one of the most universally acclaimed government programs in U.S. history. It was promoted by both the American Legion and the American Federation of Labor and passed Congress with the unanimous support of both Republicans and Democrats, all of whom later claimed credit for its provisions. Its educational benefits helped 2.2 million World War II veterans attend college. It helped pay for the training of 450,000 engineers; 180,000 doctors, dentists, and nurses; 360,000 school teachers; 150,000 scientists; 243,000 accountants; 107,000 lawyers; and 36,000 clergy, raising "the levels of education and skills of the Nation."[9] Its housing benefits helped 12 million Americans buy a house, farm, or business. It offered disability pensions and mustering-out payments, retirement pensions and emergency relief, medical care, and unemployment insurance.[10] Moreover, it provided a model for how to treat veterans of later wars, such as the Korean War. More than any other government program, the GI Bill helped World War II and Korean War veterans secure their share of the American dream. Moreover, its considerable costs were more than repaid by the higher income taxes paid by veterans as a result of their increased education and training. All in all, the Veteran's Administration concluded, the GI Bill "was one of the most successful pieces of legislation ever enacted."[11]

But the GI Bill also had important unintended consequences. Through its promotion of housing construction, with its large multiplier effect, it accelerated economic growth and prosperity. Together, its programs added $14.5 billion to the economy, helping to avert a feared postwar recession, in effect a counter-cyclic policy.

Box 10.1   African American Experiences of the GI Bill

Although African American veterans did not take advantage of their GI Bill educational benefits to the same extent as white veterans, many of them did. They swelled the student body at the South's Negro colleges, whose enrollments nearly doubled between 1940 and 1950. There were so many black veterans applying to these colleges in 1946–47 that some 20,000 were turned away. Many of them joined the postwar migration of African Americans to the North, using their GI benefits to escape the segregated South and enroll in northern universities.*

African Americans also used their GI Bill educational benefits to get vocational training that opened the door to a good job. "One very important impact of the GI Bill on the African American community," recalled Edward Pitt, Director of the National Practitioners Network for Fathers and Families at the Families and Work Institute in New York, "was that many young men, many school dropouts who were marginal economically, were drafted into the army in large numbers, and they became economically viable on exiting from the military."

Many of these African Americans had families, and the GI Bill helped them sustain those families. "Tremendous numbers of people in my town [in North Carolina] were given the option of going to jail or going to the army. And once they were in the army, were given allotments and a matching of their income so that they could support a family. So you had a lot of early marriages," Pitt related. "I don't want to romanticize it. Many people had their rights violated. Many came back and weren't able to find jobs and just had their mustering-out pay that was supposed to tide them over.

"But the educational benefits steered them to colleges. I attended a school in Greensboro that had a big technical program and lots of African American veterans attended that—not the four-year liberal arts program but

(continued)

the technical school. Many of them then transferred into the regular school. But for many, the GI Bill and these technical schools were an access point that made it possible for young African Americans to literally construct careers without having what is now called the basic requirement, without even a high school education. They were brought in and they were pushed through," Pitt explained. "Now there were racist components, but certainly there was a benefit system that benefited young African American men who had what we would now consider very little prospects for positive outcomes and benefited their families with reinforcing family supports."

Black veterans had less access to the GI Bill's housing benefits, because of redlining and other discriminatory practices toward residents of the inner-city ghettos in which many lived. But for those who were able to use these benefits, they were often key to their own version of the American dream. They may not have made it to the suburbs, but access to the GI Bill's housing benefits transformed their social status and sense of self-worth, as well as that of their family.

"It was all relative," James Cox explained. "There certainly were more goodies available to blacks than ever before. We got to get the benefits, but it was proportionate, not equal."

Jim Cox's father was from South Carolina. But after serving in the army in both the European and Pacific theaters and earning his sergeant's stripes, he joined a growing number of African Americans who sought their postwar future in the industrial north. A job with General Electric in Schenectady, New York, led to a lifelong job on the assembly line of its Maytag subsidiary in Milwaukee. He arrived in Milwaukee with a young wife and little money, but was able to buy a house from a white family in an inner-city neighborhood that white ethnics would soon leave for the suburbs. For Cox and his family, this was a turning point.

"My family bought its first house with my father's GI Bill benefits," Jim Cox recalled, "and because he was a GI, every subsequent house they bought also benefited from the GI Bill. . . . My father didn't go to college, but just that economic boon of having the security of a house—and the psychological boon, because in this country we made home ownership so important to your own sense of self-worth—made a difference. So the fact that he owned his own home put him several steps up in the community. Even though the community was segregated, it was *his*.

"Even though they weren't Ozzie and Harriet, they had a house of their own. And even though my father wasn't going off to the office, he was going off to work at a regular job and bringing back wages," Cox stressed. "For us, as children growing up, that gave us some self-worth, because our parents owned a home."

(continued)

Today, Jim Cox is vice-president for urban services of the Boys and Girls Clubs of America, and a pillar of his community. Even though the GI Bill was not implemented in a color-blind way, it helped create the solid family and self-esteem that launched him on his own career, one in which family and the self-esteem of children remain central concerns.

*Keith W. Olson, *The G.I. Bill, the Veterans, and the Colleges* (Lexington: University of Kentucky Press, 1974), 74–75.

The GI Bill also had a major impact on higher education, which now had to deal with an enlarged and varied student body. As one-half of the GI Bill students were married, it legitimated the married student at institutions that had previously regarded marriage as grounds for expulsion. In addition, "by providing an excellent example to the contrary," concluded one scholar, the GI Bill "eased fears that massive federal aid to education invariably meant federal control," indirectly facilitating subsequent federal aid to education. Moreover, its success showed that "increased government support of education, especially for minority groups who required assistance, was an investment which paid rich dividends to society."[12] In view of its direct and indirect consequences, Texas Senator Ralph Yarborough called the GI Bill "one of the most beneficial, far-reaching programs ever instituted in American life"[13]—a conclusion shared by analysts and policymakers across the political spectrum.

Yet despite this bipartisan praise for the GI Bill as veterans' policy, as economic policy, and as educational policy, few noticed that the GI Bill was also a de facto *family* policy. In fact, it was one of the most effective profamily programs and a major factor in the 1950s golden age of the nuclear family.

The mustering-out pay financed more than one wedding and served many veterans as a down payment on married life that encouraged them to believe that they could afford a family. The educational provisions of the GI Bill persuaded many that there was no contradiction between pursuing their education and starting a family and enabled those who were already married to complete their education. Moreover, the degrees and training that they received made it possible for the GI Bill's beneficiaries to get better jobs and earn higher incomes, which both encouraged them to start families and enabled them to sustain those families. The GI Bill also made it possible for many who could not have afforded higher education to go to college. In the end, the subjective perception that the GI Bill would enable them to get the education, the jobs, and the incomes to support a family may have been as important in their decisions to form families as the financial aid they received. The GI Bill was a major source of optimism, and optimism about one's prospects is often a precondition for taking on the responsibility of starting a family.

Box 10.2   The GI Bill and the Family Economy of Student Veterans

The GI Bill paid for tuition, fees, and books. It also provided a maintenance allowance. Before April 1948, these monthly allowances were $65 for single veterans and $90 for married veterans, rising to $75 and $105 after that, with $120 paid to veterans with two or more children. These were substantial sums for the era, but not enough to meet veterans' expenses. Only 1 percent of veterans at the University of Iowa said they could subsist on their allowance. At the City College of New York (CCNY), the average single veteran in 1947 spent $85 a month and married veterans $182 to live "with a minimum of comfort," while at Stanford University they spent $120 and $180. These gaps between GI Bill benefits and expenses were echoed across the country.

How did the student veterans balance their budgets? By the same means as college students today: loans, savings, family gifts, and part-time work. As veterans were older than other college students—twenty-five years old on the average when they entered college—they were more accustomed to being financially independent and more likely to work. In Iowa City, 80 percent of the janitors were student veterans; at CCNY, 43 percent of the married vets worked, as did one third of the single vets. Half of the vets who benefited from the GI Bill were married and half of these had children. Still, many wives worked to balance the family budget. Almost half of married student veterans at Michigan State had working wives, and at Stanford the total approached two-thirds of married vets.

Student veterans also took advantage of subsidized housing provided by colleges or the government, often using war surplus facilities. Single vets paid $8.50 a month to sleep on bunk beds in a gymnasium at the University of Illinois, while Alabama Tech berthed vets in cabins on ninety-three tugboats given by the U.S. Maritime Commission and R.P.I. turned four surplus LSTs (Tank Landing Ships) into floating dormitories (with New York State subsidies). Married veterans sometimes lived at nearby military facilities, but most moved into Quonset huts or other temporary quarters near their college, "vetsvilles" that developed their own way of life. "Wives' organizations, nursery schools, baby-sitting exchanges, self-government units, and even food cooperatives" were created. "Similar ages, experiences, interests, housing and incomes generated a strong sense of community" (Olson 77). In the Hawkeye trailer camp at the University of Iowa, vet families paid about $25 a month for a furnished trailer, including electricity and the use of communal bathrooms. The cramped trailers lacked plumbing and were badly heated, but the mood was upbeat. When asked, "Do you think you did the right thing in going to college?" every one of the veterans of Iowa answered, "Yes" (*Life* 112).

(continued)

Close quarters and limited incomes also led fathers to share child-rearing chores, including baby-sitting, changing diapers, and doing the laundry (*Life* 109). Family and studies were interwoven. As a result, many would have agreed with the wife who affirmed that the time her husband spent as a college student constituted " 'three of the happiest years we had known' " (Olson 77).

Sources: "Veterans at College," *Life* (April 21, 1947), 105–13; Keith W. Olson, *The G.I. Bill, the Veterans, and the Colleges* (Lexington: University of Kentucky Press, 1974), 76–78.

Box 10.3   White Ethnic Experiences of the GI Bill

George K. was a young refugee from Nazism who enlisted in the army shortly after arriving in the United States. He served in the Pacific and in postwar Japan, where he met his wife, who was working with the Red Cross. Although George's father had been a wealthy doctor in Germany, his family had been forced to leave everything behind when they fled Berlin. He had begun his college education in England before coming to the United States, but when he left the army after World War II, he had no money of his own with which to complete his education.

That is where the GI Bill came in. With the help of the GI Bill he was able to go on to Harvard Business School and become a successful management consultant. The GI Bill also paid for the first house that he bought north of Boston. "Without the GI bill," his daughter concluded, "he couldn't have ever gone to school. He would have just been another immigrant without a college degree."

Joe D., on the other hand, had grown up in a working-class Boston Italian family in which no one had ever gone to college. He served in the army in Europe during World War II and married his childhood sweetheart when the war ended. The GI Bill enabled him to go to a local college, while starting a family. It also paid for his first house in the Boston suburbs. Without the GI Bill, he probably would never have made it to college—or into the middle class. Nor, in all likelihood, would he have had the resources to pay for his children's college education. For Joe and his family, the road to the American dream was paved by the GI Bill.

George and Joe were not alone. A poll at the University of Iowa revealed that nearly half of the student vets would not have gone to college without the GI Bill. And by April 1947, half of the country's college students were

(continued)

veterans.* They would use their degrees to get the jobs—and the GI Bill to buy the houses—that secured their rise into the middle class. The GI Bill underlay the newly middle-class families of the 1950s.

* "Veterans at College," *Life* (April 21, 1947), 105 and 112.

If the educational assistance of the GI Bill enabled veterans to get the education and training they needed to secure jobs that could support a family, its housing provisions made it possible for them to obtain a home of their own, one within which they could both found and sustain a nuclear family. During World War II, the marriage and birthrate had begun to rise, after a decade of decline during the Depression, spurred by the prospect of separation and government payments to the dependents of servicemen. They continued to climb during the postwar era, with housing the biggest bottleneck to family formation and expansion. By 1947, some 6 million families were living with relatives or friends, with another half million housed in temporary dwellings. In Omaha, a 7-by-17-foot ice box was advertised as a dwelling—hardly the kind of place to bring home your bride or raise a family![14] During the decade that followed, 12 million families became homeowners, with the U.S. government subsidizing the cost. Single-family housing starts rose from 114,000 in 1944 to a record 1,692,000 in 1950. Most of these units were in the suburbs and many were in low-cost subdivisions like Levittown, N.Y., where government subsidies built into mortgages and taxes brought a house within reach of blue-collar workers—many of them returning veterans—and made it cheaper to buy than to rent.

The boom in single-family housing was accompanied by a baby boom so pronounced that it gave birth to the term. This baby boom, which peaked in 1956, did not result so much from an increase in family *size*—although the wives of the 1950s did average three children—as from an increase in family *formation*. Everyone was getting married and everyone was having babies, often as soon as they got married, at younger ages than before.[15] The lure of a home of one's own, complete with appliances—Levittown houses came with a washing machine and a television—helped promote this family boom by assuring prospective partners and parents that they could obtain and afford an appropriate space in which to raise children. Even the architecture of Levittown houses—no stairs, kitchens near front entrances, living rooms with picture windows facing the backyard—facilitated child safety and supervision. It was little wonder that Levittown became known as "Fertility Valley." It was an ideal "starter house" for a young family. As one unsympathetic scholar concluded: "In effect, these federal programs provided subsidies and incentives for couples to marry and have several children."[16]

They also transformed the suburbs from exclusive communities for the wealthy into family communities for the new middle class of blue- and white-collar workers and professionals. It was here that skilled blue-collar workers found their piece of the American dream—a house and a car. It was a modest version of the dream, scaled down and mass-produced, but it was a home of their own and their passport to middle-class status (even while they remained manual workers, a status transformation that was key to the U.S. becoming a "middle-class" society during this era). Moreover, it was a *family* community, complete with backyard barbecues and Welcome Wagons, safe streets and schools, Little League teams and shopping centers.

The 1950s were the decisive decade in the suburbanization of America. Federal programs—from the GI Bill and the FHA loan to the Interstate Highway Act (1956) and the Income Tax Home Mortgage Deduction—played a decisive role in this process, along with local government investments in sewers, schools, and other aspects of suburban infrastructure.

Much can be—and has been—said against this suburbanization of American life. For the most part, African Americans and other poor minorities were excluded from it by redlining, zoning, and other practices in which government played a central role.[17] Although the single-family home suburbs promoted the *nuclear* family, they weakened the *extended* family, leaving grandparents a Sunday's drive away in the old urban neighborhood from which the young parents had moved. Moreover, the governmental subsidy to home owners penalized renters, while urban public housing never received its fair share of governmental support—or attention. One result was an accelerating process of white flight to the suburbs, as poor blacks (many of them recently arrived from the South) moved into the rental units vacated by upwardly mobile white ethnics. Another was urban decay, accentuated by the decline of public services in underfunded cities suffering from a shrinking tax base provoked by suburbanization. Moreover, although the 1950s saw a rededication of both men and women to family life and parenting, it was women who bore the biggest share of its burdens. The gendered costs of suburban married bliss were seen in sacrificed careers, alcoholism, and other manifestations of psychological problems.[18] Lastly, urbanists and architects have criticized the quality of life and aesthetics of the 1950s' suburbs, with their uniformity of architecture and lifestyle, their conformity of values, and their "caricature of the historic city."[19]

But as Kenneth Jackson, in a generally critical history of suburbanization, concluded: "The young families who joyously moved into the new homes of the suburbs were not terribly concerned about the problems of the inner-city housing market or the snobbish views of social critics. They were concerned about their hopes and their dreams. They were looking for good schools, private space and personal safety. . . . The single-family tract house—post–World War II style—whatever its aesthetic failings, offered growing families a private haven in a heartless world. If the dream did not include minorities or the elderly, if it was accompanied by the isolation of nuclear families, by the decline of public transportation, and by the deterioration of urban neighborhoods, the creation of good, inexpensive suburban housing on an unprecedented scale was a unique achievement in the world."[20] Government programs, from subsidies to sewers, played a central role in this achievement, with the GI Bill leading the way.

Moreover, for a generation born into the deprivations of the Depression and brought up amid the sacrifices of the world war, even this modest version of the American dream was good enough. It would be their children, raised in an age of affluence and opportunity, who would insist that they could (and should) have it all—often at the cost of the families they took for granted.

A GI BILL FOR THE TWENTY-FIRST CENTURY?

If the GI Bill played so central and positive a part in promoting and sustaining the nuclear family of the 1950s, could a similar program play a comparable role now? A comparison of the similarities and differences between the two eras suggests that it could.

Like the 1950s, the 1990s were a decade of economic growth and a concern with "family values." But there were also great differences between the two decades. Although both saw sizable job growth, in the 1990s the greatest job growth was in low-wage service jobs, not in the well-paid factory jobs that enabled workers with even limited education to buy houses and start families in the 1950s.[21] In the 1990s, unions were weaker and jobs less secure. Inequality increased, and the poverty rate among working families grew by half.[22] There was no war and few young veterans to reintegrate. There was no fear of a new depression or of a renewed fascism or expanding communism. Nor was there a consensus on values or culture. Most of these differences remain true today.

Yet despite these differences, there are striking parallels between the motivations for the original GI Bill and the reasons to establish a similar program today. The American Legion may have fought for the original GI Bill as an advocate of veteran interests, but it understood that the nation's gratitude to those who had risked their lives to defend it was insufficient to assure its passage. The Serviceman's Readjustment Act of 1944 was motivated by several mutually reinforcing *national* concerns, most of which have 1990s equivalents.

Economics was the most powerful motivation for many supporters of the GI Bill. Many policymakers, including important voices within the Roosevelt administration, feared that the end of wartime spending would mean a new depression or at least a return to the high unemployment and low wages of 1939. They saw the GI Bill as a way to avoid this danger, by the billions in government spending involved and by removing millions of veterans from those seeking work. "At its root," concluded one historian, "the Serviceman's Readjustment Act of 1944 was more an antidepression measure than an expression of gratitude to veterans."[23] Today we may not be afraid of a new depression, but we do fear that the United States may not be able to compete in the globalized economy because of an uncompetitive labor force. We also fear high unemployment and lower wages and salaries due to downsizing as part of the adjustment to that global economy.[24] We worry that the bursting of the "New Economy" bubble and high energy costs could lead to recession.

A further motivation behind the educational benefits of the GI Bill was "to do what is necessary to overcome the educational shortages created by the war."[25] Behind this concern was a fear that the United States would be unable to compete in the postwar era because of the educational deficits in its labor force. Today, the fear is similar, but the source of concern is different: the failures of the U.S. educational system, together with the soaring cost of higher education, in a postindustrial globalized economy where information is itself a leading economic sector and an educated labor force is a competitive necessity. A recent nonpartisan study concluded that a third of Massachusetts' workers "lack the basic technical skills required for the jobs in today's economy," underscoring that this was "a situation that threatens the state's economic growth," as well as the future prospects of these 1.2 million workers.[26] The nation's educational deficiencies were a recurring theme of the 2000 election campaign, and remedying them is a stated priority of President George W. Bush.

A fear of the social and political consequences of large numbers of unemployed youths is also common to both eras, even if the images of anxiety differ. In 1944, the American Legion evoked a national fear of 9 million unemployed veterans selling apples on a corner as a destabilizing, even a revolutionary force, like the Bonus Army of World War I veterans descending on Washington in 1932, only on a far larger scale.[27] Harry Truman himself underscored that the veterans could comprise the "most potent" voting bloc in the country.[28] In the 1990s, the fear was rather of crime on the streets and urban riots in the ghettos and of millions of unemployed—and unemployable—minority youths turning to crime or having babies without the means to support them. Moreover, minority youths—and their parents—could be a potent voting block, *if* they voted—as African Americans and Hispanic Americans did in unprecedented numbers in 2000.

The sustained economic expansion of the 1990s that reduced the previously high unemployment rate among minority youths and adults to near historic lows persuaded many that the problem of a future for minority and other disadvantaged youths had been solved. Nothing could be further from the truth.

As a recent study of New York City shows, the boom of the 1990s produced a sharply segmented labor market in which the number of low-wage jobs paying under $25,000 a year grew four times as fast as jobs paying $25,000–75,000 a year. Many of these jobs do not pay enough to support a family. "Despite the strong pace of private-sector job growth," the report concludes, "an alarming number of families in New York City are unable to earn enough to achieve an acceptable standard of living."[29] Throughout the country, charities reported serving a growing number of working families that could not make ends meet, despite a booming economy.[30] Part of the explanation is the lack of growth in manufacturing jobs, part is the privileging of computer skills and education in the New Economy.

What this means is that even in the best of times, the New Economy is adding a digital divide to the preexisting deepened inequality in the United States. Unless poor and minority youths get the educational opportunities to bridge that divide, they will be at a growing disadvantage in the New Economy of the twenty-first century. It will be a disaster for them and for the country.

Moreover, the boom of the 1990s—like all booms—did not last forever, and by 2001 had slowed so much that it had been replaced by fears of recession. The New Economy has not repealed the business cycle, and as the business cycle slows into recession, the number of jobs will fall and the last hired will be the first fired. The low minority and youth unemployment of the mid-1990s may become a nostalgic memory, and preparing our country's youths for the job markets and business cycles of the twenty-first century will once again become a theme of public policy and political debate.

One of the differences between the two eras, however, would seem to be prevailing attitudes toward government programs and dependence on government spending, but this is not the case. In fact, in the postwar era there was a great deal of suspicion of so large a government program affecting so many lives as the GI Bill, along with concerns over the large sums it would require and the dependency that it might create. These concerns help explain why the GI Bill did not fund housing directly, nor did it dictate to veterans what educational institution to attend, courses to study, or career to pursue, allowing the market and existing institutions to shape those choices. They also explain why the spending on loans and study programs was capped at a level below the actual cost of housing or maintenance, and why the government agencies involved stressed the ways in which the sums expended were repaid in later taxes and benefits to society. The two eras are more similar in these concerns than might initially appear. And common to both is the need for the argument for a GI Bill to be made in terms of *national* interests and not just the interest of the beneficiaries.

Also similar is the concern for "family values," although the consensus on family values in the 1950s was unusual and is difficult to reproduce today. On the other hand, even adolescents from broken homes or nontraditional families are reaching adulthood today with the same ideal and dream of marrying, living in a stable two-parent family, and raising children as their grandparents did in the 1950s. Moreover, like that 1950s generation, which grew up in years in which families were weakened by economic crisis and separated by war, and for that very reason prized a stable nuclear family, the generation coming to adulthood today has also experienced the pains and costs of dissolved or dysfunctional families. They, too, may value a successful family life all the more for their own negative experiences as children.

Still, despite these similarities, today would seem a more difficult *political* environment to enact and finance a GI Bill for nonveterans. Therefore, it is important to frame such a program so as to maximize its political support, to design it to minimize political opposition, and to finance it creatively.

A NATIONAL YOUTH SERVICE: TOWARD A POLICY PROPOSAL

Conservatives are right in arguing that government programs have not and cannot reverse the decline of the nuclear family in the United States. A change in values, a return to "family values," they contend, is needed for that to happen.[31] Here, too, they are correct, although some may disagree with their definition of "family values." The experience of the 1950s, the golden age of the nuclear family, points to the importance of values promoting family life as personal fulfillment and to the role of mass media and popular culture, as well as church and community, in creating that family values consensus.

Yet the experience of the 1950s also underscores the central role of government policies and programs—targeted and unintended—in creating the conditions within which strong and stable nuclear families can be formed and sustained. Governmental support at the federal, state, and local level in the areas of housing, education, and vocational training in particular was a crucial precondition for the millions of individual decisions to marry, have children, and sustain a nuclear family. Without this public support, it is unlikely that the 1950s would have been the golden age of the American family—or that millions of Americans would have made it into the middle class.

What was true for the 1950s is likely to be even more true of today, a time of job insecurity and culture wars, following decades of family decline, in which divorce, illegitimacy, teenage pregnancy, drugs, and disease have all taken their toll on the nuclear family, which no longer has the support of popular culture, a values consensus, or a strong local community. Today, the American family needs all the help it can get!

Despite the differences between the two eras, what *is* likely to be the same is the American nuclear family's need for supportive governmental policies, if it is not to face the new century from the endangered species list. Conservatives who want to see a resurgence of the nuclear family as the core of American society must accept that just as government programs alone can't solve the problem, neither can rhetoric about family values. The 1950s strongly suggest that what is needed is a *mutually reinforcing combination* of private values and public subsidies and incentives, as well as an economy that generates optimism for the future by creating jobs with prospects of security and increasing real wages.

Box 10.4   The 1950s: When Jobs Were Expanding and Unions Were Strong

Veterans in the 1950s benefited not only from the GI Bill, but from an expanding economy, with increasing numbers of both blue- and white-collar jobs. They also benefited from strong unions, which ensured that those jobs were secure, paid well, and came with medical, vacation, and retirement benefits.

The GI Bill may have enabled young Americans to get an education and technical training, but this vocational preparation would not have translated into higher living standards if these jobs had not been there. The 1950s were years of economic expansion so great that its most recent historian called it "the biggest boom yet."* During this decade, the U.S. economy grew by 37 percent, while real median family income rose 30 percent. Many factors combined to account for this prosperity. The United States still enjoyed an advantage over the war-damaged economies of Japan and Europe, which it increased through large investments in science and industrial research and development. It was also an era of inexpensive energy, with cheap oil fueling an industrial boom. U.S. defense spending remained high even in peacetime, sustaining a military industrial complex that the

(continued)

Cold War made permanent. The baby boom and housing boom also spurred economic growth, increasing consumer spending on everything from automobiles to toys. The U.S. population grew by nearly 29 million people, and the number of cars nearly doubled in a decade, from 39 million to 74 million automobiles. In part, this buying boom reflected the readiness of Americans, confident in their futures, to go into debt to enjoy the lifestyle they desired. The 1950s saw the debut of the credit card, a rise in private indebtedness from $105 billion to $263 billion, and the emergence of a society of mass consumption stimulated by an advertising industry that itself became one of the era's growth industries. Together, these factors were responsible for a 2 million increase in blue-collar jobs, to which were added record number of white-collar and service positions, with college graduates soon matching the incomes of their elders.

What made these jobs particularly good bases for stable families was that they were secure, with increasing real wages and good benefits. Although the labor needs of an expanding economy accounted for part of this optimistic picture, strong labor unions deserved a large share of the credit. Although women and minority workers were underrepresented among the unionized, in the mid-1950s the newly united AFL-CIO had almost 18 million members, nearly 35 percent of nonagricultural workers. Under conservative leadership, American unions concentrated on bread-and-butter issues, winning higher wages, more extensive benefits, shorter working hours, and improved working conditions. By 1960, half of the major unions had secured cost-of-living adjustments that protected wages against inflation. Seniority clauses in many of these contracts guaranteed job security in case of economic downturns, while the establishment of grievance procedures decreased the arbitrariness of management and on-the-job friction. Together, these advances by strong unions made the jobs of their members a solid base for forming and sustaining a family.

---

* James T. Patterson, *Grand Expectations: The United States, 1945–1974* (New York: Oxford University Press, 1996), chap. 11.

In constructing this mix of the public and the private, it is important not to ask government to do things that it is not good at or that are likely to be viewed as intrusive—such as trying to impose values, however laudable they may be in themselves. But it is equally important for those who want to reverse the decline of the American nuclear family to ask government to do what it can in this difficult and complex enterprise.[32]

The 1950s suggest that what government *can* do is to create the infrastructure and offer incentives and subsidies for people to help *better themselves* and pursue *their* dreams. Government has been less successful in transforming lives where it has just sought to create a social safety net for those who have not made it—and it is frustration with these programs and those failures at a time when the security of the middle class is itself in question that underlies the flight from government social programs among most of the U.S. electorate.[33]

A campaign for family values without these other supports will fail as surely as a reliance on government programs alone to do the trick. If anything, the far more difficult task of shoring up and reconstructing the weakened nuclear family of the 1990s will need even more help from government. In other words, Republicans and Democrats, conservatives and liberals will have to come together around their common concern for the family and set aside other ideological priorities to construct a vision that combines public policy, private initiative, and community support that can command broad public acceptance. Only so broad-based an approach and alliance can hope to reverse the decline of the American nuclear family in the 1990s and relaunch it in the new century with the "right stuff" to succeed.

Given the current political atmosphere in the United States, proponents of a family policy have to be as creative in their political strategies as in their policy proposals. Corporate downsizing, compounded by government budget cuts, created anxiety in the middle of macroeconomic prosperity, a job anxiety affecting large sectors of both the blue-collar and white-collar middle class, including professionals and managers who had thought themselves beyond such concerns—an anxiety that the end of the dot-com boom and the start of a recession exacerbated. Within this context of economic insecurity, a middle class that already sees itself as paying too much taxes and receiving too few benefits from government programs is going to be even more reluctant to accept more "handouts" to the poor.

Both of these sentiments will strengthen conservatives eager to reduce the *role* of government, as well as its spending. Moreover, given the composition of Congress and a Republican president, programs will need the support of Republicans if they are to be enacted—and implemented. All this points to the need to devise policy proposals that can have a broad political appeal. This argues for proposals that promise to address the needs of business and the anxieties of the middle class, as well as the plight of the poor, and to craft policies that prepare poor children for work, not welfare.

What lessons can be learned from the 1950s, an era without this employment anxiety, when jobs were not only expanding, but also propelling real wages and upward mobility, with strong unions consolidating these gains in contracts and protecting them on the factory floor? One lesson is that family formation takes optimism about being able to support that family in a reasonable style—an optimism that was abundant in the 1950s, but is rare today. We need to talk about the "sustainable family," as others have talked about "sustainable development" and "sustainable democracy." Governmental job promotion is beyond the scope of this chapter; tax policy is the subject of another chapter.[34] Both were important in shaping the 1950s as the golden age of the nuclear family.

But as this chapter has shown, two other large areas—housing and education—also played central roles in the 1950s, with the GI Bill the key program in both areas. The GI Bill won easy political acceptance, despite concerns about its cost, for several reasons. It was patriotic—the country owed something to those who had risked their lives to defend it. But even more important in its popularity were other concerns. It solved a social problem—how to reintegrate 13 million young men and women into civilian life. It averted a political crisis, which many feared would occur if millions of veterans ended up unemployed. It made economic sense: preventing a postwar slump with its spending and giving the workforce of the future the education and training it needed to sustain the United States' competitive position in the world. Its benefits were broadly distributed—it benefited people from different classes, races, and regions.

The 1990s, with a more austere fiscal climate than the 1950s, were not propitious for a new GI Bill, although they did witness the creation of Ameri-Corps, which could be viewed as a pilot for a larger National Youth Service. Today, although continued economic prosperity seems less certain, political debate centers around how to spend record national budget surpluses, with tax cuts and debt reduction the chief alternatives, all couched in terms of assuring the country's future. But what better way to assure the nation's future than to invest in its youths—who *are* the future.

Even so, it might not be possible to enact a full new GI Bill, particularly without the justification of wartime service. But it might be possible to pass a scaled-down version—a National Youth Service in exchange for educational benefits—that might accomplish some of the same goals, as well as others unique to this era.

A deep fear of today's middle class is the uncertain future of its children in this new downsizing global economy, along with the escalating costs of educating them to compete within it. Significantly, this is the first generation of Americans to expect that its children will do *worse* than it did. Moreover, as the experience of countries in East Asia and elsewhere has shown, education and training are keys to national as well as individual competitiveness in the postindustrial era. The Clinton proposals for special tax credits and deductions for postsecondary education pointed in this direction. But what was missing was the element of national service that might justify this government spending to the skeptical, the childless, and the elderly.

One solution might be a one- to two-year program of National Youth Service, military or civilian, depending on individual choice. In return, the young men and women would be entitled to an educational "GI Bill" that would help them pay for college, community college, or vocational training. Although one can imagine many different kinds of national service, a flexible program that would have maximum appeal to both participants and their parents would be best. It might well combine training and service, military and civilian options. Training components could include a common basic training (military or nonmilitary) to assure a minimum level of physical fitness and competence. It should also include remedial education, a second chance as young adults for those whose education as children was deficient. Business and labor, Republicans and Democrats, would all agree that it is imperative that all adults in this country should be functionally literate. But this training component could also include computer literacy and other vocationally useful skills, perhaps in combination with military or civilian public service work. It could include forestry, teaching, recreation, child care, construction, and public health work, depending on national and community needs. It is no secret that budget cuts have frayed or curtailed public services in many areas. A National Youth Service might well be the solution to some of the problems this has caused. At the same time, it might imbue America's youths with a sense of citizenship, purpose, and self-worth that comes from being part of something larger than yourself. This could translate into higher rates of voting and other forms of political participation from which many young Americans are shying away, a worrying development for our democracy.

In shaping a National Youth Service, we should draw on the experience of what worked best in such past and current programs as the Civilian Conservation Corps, Habitat, Vista, Teach for America, and AmeriCorps. The last, in particular, might be viewed as a pilot for a National Youth Service. Since its founding in 1993 as a "domestic Peace Corps," AmeriCorps has enrolled more than 150,000 young Americans (ages eighteen to twenty-four) in service that centers around the National Civilian Community Corps, where they work to improve the environment, enhance education, increase public safety, and address unmet human needs through community service. In return for 1,700 hours of community service over ten months, the members receive nearly $5,000 to help pay for college tuition or repay student loans. Youths can also do their service with Vista or with national charitable groups like the American Red Cross, Habitat for Humanity, the Boys and Girls Clubs, or with local community centers and places of worship. In effect, there are hundreds of ways that participants can serve. Some teach literacy; others build community centers or mentor poor children. Members have seven years to use their education awards and do not have to make student loan payments while they serve. The program has been so successful that it has expanded steadily, to enroll some 50,000 youths in 2000, with a proposal to expand to 100,000 by 2004.[35] A National Youth Service could be built on AmeriCorps.

AmeriCorps has also been a political and civil society success. It has enjoyed bipartisan support in Congress and cosponsorship from business. One example is Yahoo, which has pledged $1 million to promote a proposed "E-Corps" within AmeriCorps to help bridge the digital divide by teaching computer literacy to disadvantaged youths and teaching regular school teachers how to use computer technology in the classroom. AmeriCorps is also linked to the "PowerUp" initiative for bridging the digital divide, while building character and competence in youth through an online environment, an initiative supported by a dozen corporations, federal agencies, and nongovernmental organizations.[36] It was established as a commitment to America's Promise—The Alliance for Youth, until recently headed by Gen. Colin Powell, who celebrated National Youth Service Day 2000 with AmeriCorps members at one of their Washington projects.[37]

Although his appointment as secretary of state eliminates General Powell as the preferred choice to lead a National Youth Service, it should ensure support for such an initiative at the highest levels of the Bush administration. Moreover, in view of the bipartisan support for AmeriCorps in Congress, a National Youth Service could well serve as an issue around which President Bush could build the bipartisan cooperation that he has signaled is his preferred style and that the parity between the parties requires.

Their National Youth Service experience would also give its young participants a greater sense of direction when they came to use the program's educational benefits. These benefits ideally should be a full subsidy of tuition and maintenance costs that would vary with the beneficiary's needs. But even a limited sum available to all to help pay for either higher education or vocational training would be worthwhile. The fuller the subsidy, the greater the incentive to utilize it and the greater the freedom to pursue the education or training involved. But the original GI Bill demonstrated that something less than a full subsidy was sufficient to motivate millions to take advantage of the opportunity offered, with part-time earnings, savings, and loans making up the difference. There is every reason to believe that a National Youth Service/GI Bill would elicit a similarly positive response today.

Such a program should appeal to a beleaguered middle class that believes that education is the key to its children's future, but is worried about the high cost of higher education and fearful of indebting itself or its children in an era of job insecurity. It should also appeal to poor Americans who do not have the resources to pay for higher education and often do not have the credentials to gain admission to it—or to the good jobs that increasingly require higher education or special skills.

A National Youth Service could have other advantages as well. If it included a basic training component—perhaps in its first six months—it would serve a national strategic interest in creating a larger reserve of trained troops in case of war or some other emergency. For that reason it might appeal to patriotic conservatives and the military itself. Such a program could also help address the physical fitness problems of young Americans, which the health industry has warned will cost the nation dearly in future medical expenditures.

Between the postservice educational benefits and the remedial education and vocational training within the National Youth Service, this program could also have an important effect on the nation's economic preparedness, as well as on the job prospects of the young Americans who participated in the program. It would create the possibility of this country entering the new century with the educated and trained labor force it will need to compete globally. It would offer to the poor and ill-educated another chance to get the training they will need to get jobs that pay more than the minimum wage—a wage that can support a family.

In addition, if the selective service of the 1950s is any guide, a National Youth Service could play other positive roles for children in inner-city ghettos and elsewhere, who now see no future for themselves but what the streets have to offer. In the 1950s, for youths not headed for college, there was the army. It represented an end to childhood and a rite of passage into adulthood, a place of discipline and training, a place away from home and 'hood where horizons could broaden and friendships could be formed, where skills could be learned, responsibilities assumed, and leadership displayed. A National Youth Service might serve some of these same functions in the years ahead. It may be an exaggeration to claim that in the 1950s eighteen-year-olds entered the army as boys and came back as men, but transformations did take place. Similar changes could also help the youths of our times. They might even emerge from the program ready to raise a family—and with the education and training to get a job that could support one.

A National Youth Service could also address the problem of youth crime and delinquency, by taking young people off mean streets, placing them in a less corrosive context, and giving them the education and training to build a future—as the army and GI Bill did in an earlier era. At a minimum, a National Youth Service would remove an age cohort from the streets for one to two years of prime time for youth crime. Today nearly one out of three African American young men are in the criminal justice system—in prison or jail, probation or parole—and states like California are spending more money on prisons than on education, prisons that have all but given up on reforming their inmates. A program that would decrease this prison population

and reduce the crime rate could be both cost effective and politically popular—as well as less wasteful of human resources and more humane and eq-
uitable. It might even turn potential criminals into productive citizens, a savings both for them and for society.[38]

Moreover, such a hiatus between secondary school and college could serve
the interests of students of all classes and races, too many of whom arrive at
college with a lot of anxiety about the future but less sense of direction and
educational purpose. This immaturity is a major reason why most undergrad-
uates do not take full advantage of the opportunities college offers—and a
large percentage end up taking time off to try and figure out what college education they need or want. At $30,000 a year for private elite colleges, even
wealthy parents might welcome a chance for their children to acquire the ma-
turity and focus that would help them to get the most out of that costly higher
education. And given the growing stress on community service in college ad-
missions—and on "service learning" in college curricula—participation in a
National Youth Service could help young men or women get accepted by the
college of their choice and make the most of their experience. In other words,
a National Youth Service would also be a sound educational policy.

Last but not least, a National Youth Service could be a powerful instrument
of family policy. At first glance, it may seem strange to propose a program for
single young adults as a central part of a family policy. But this program is
projected to help children and their families in several crucial ways. For families with children approaching young adulthood, this program will offer a solution to financing higher education. This would allow families to spend
scarce resources on other things and not incur huge educational debts. It
would also permit parents *not* to take that extra job in order to pay for college,
enabling them to spend more time with their children instead. For their children, the advantages of the program will be higher education and vocational
training without indebtedness, and thus more resources (and optimism) as
young adults with which to form a family of their own.

For teenage children, particularly poor inner-city teenagers from minority
backgrounds, the creation of a horizon beyond the 'hood and a future beyond
the streets could be critical in helping them avoid the despair and tempta-
tions that have landed too many in prison and fed the rise in teenage pregnancies. It would also decrease the corrosive effect on families of having to
deal with troubled teenagers. It could help reverse the vicious circle of decline that has decimated the families and childhoods of generations of poor
Americans, many of them people of color facing racial prejudice as well,
leaving members of the current generation of young adults eager for a family but pessimistic about their own chances of success in creating and sustaining one.

In view of the broad range of *national* benefits that a National Youth Service could confer, it should be possible to assemble a political coalition broad enough to enact it. Liberals should be attracted by its educational and job training benefits, as well by its efforts to help the poor in a nonpunitive way, while also benefiting the middle class. Conservatives should find its basic training provisions appealing, along with its efforts to shore up the nuclear family, decrease teenage pregnancies, and put unemployable youths to work. It could even be sold as an anticrime program. After all, even mainstream Republicans agree that "in the long run, the best anticrime program is a renewal of family in America."[39] If a basic training component was included in the National Youth Service, this might garner the support of the military, in search of a new mission in the post–Cold War era and unhappy policing the world's most intractable conflicts. It could also win the program the support of the mostly rural areas with military bases that would benefit as sites of such basic training and of their mostly conservative congressional representatives. The increase in physical fitness as a result of such training could also gain the support of the health industry, worried about the costs of ill health in an obese, sedentary, unfit population.

The education and vocational training benefits, as well as the program's remedial education during the service period, should bring the support of business interests worried about the lack of preparedness of their workforce in a competitive global economy in the computer age, where an educated labor force is key to business success. These educational aspects of the program should also win the support of educators and administrators, including those in colleges worried about declines in enrollment.

Moreover, if the National Youth Service includes help in maintaining parks and forests that have suffered from budget cuts, as the Civilian Conservation Corps once did, it should enjoy support from conservationists. If it helps rebuild decaying communities and renew their schools and libraries, as Habitat, Vista, and Teach for America did on a smaller scale, it should receive the support of poor people and people of color. These provisions could also bring the support of state and local governments that are strapped for funds and trying to avoid cuts in services.

Lastly, as a program that will address the financial and educational worries of the middle class, it should appeal to and receive the support of that political majority of Americans—and the congressional representatives who need their votes to get reelected. Given the goals and character of a National Youth Service, it should be possible to get respected national figures, including Bush administration leaders such as General Colin Powell, to endorse it.

At the same time, a National Youth Service does not have the political liabilities of other kinds of government family programs. Because young people would participate as individuals, it doesn't raise the divisive question of *what* is a family. There is no need to argue the legitimacy of gay marriages, unwed mothers, or alternative lifestyles. Nor, given its broad spectrum of beneficiaries, does it call up the conflictual political question of *which*—that is, *whose*—families are being supported by this government program. It would benefit children from all family backgrounds. It cannot be attacked as a "handout" to welfare families or a poverty program. It also doesn't have to fight conservative criticisms that it is an effort to revive programs that have failed in the past—and therefore will fail in the future.[40]

On the contrary, promoting it as a "GI Bill" for the twenty-first century would underscore that this is a program that models itself on a program that everyone agrees was very successful in the past. It might even capture the support of the elderly, a constituency normally unsympathetic to programs for the young, because the GI Bill was part of *their* own life experience—as opposed to social programs that they can reject because they never needed them, so why should younger generations? Even conservative elders such as Bob Dole have affirmed that they could support a GI Bill for this era.

What remains to be confronted, however, is the likely objection of fiscal conservatives that a National Youth Service/GI Bill would be too costly. The anticipated record budget surpluses could have been one way to finance such a program in the short run. Moreover, the program would be self-financing in the long run, through the higher tax payments of beneficiaries as a result of their better education and training. Still, if this prospect does not convince fiscal conservatives that a National Youth Service is financially viable, an idea broached in Lyndon Johnson's administration might be revived. Beneficiaries could be required to pay a small percentile income tax surcharge, with those whose incomes rose most as a result of their subsidized education and training paying the most in return. Although in the short run government funding will be necessary, in the long run such additional tax payments should fund the program—making it the *reverse* of the Social Security program, where the young are asked to pay for the elderly.

Still, devising a way to finance the initial program through the public purse will require creativity as well as sobriety—and political skill. A costing out of the program that is beyond the scope of this chapter would be necessary. Parts of the program, however, might well be paid for out of the budgets of the Departments of Defense, Labor, Education, Interior, and Housing and Urban Development, with state and local governments also contributing, depending upon the nature of the training and services involved.

Politically, what must be kept in focus during both the legislative process and the administration of the program is that to succeed, a National Youth Service must enjoy broad popular support and avoid unnecessary conflicts.

That means designing and promoting it as a program that will benefit the middle class, while making sure that it also benefits those lower down in the social scale and that it is accessible to women and minorities who wish to take advantage of its benefits.* At the same time, for political reasons, it may be necessary to make the program a voluntary one, rather than an age group draft. This would avoid clashes over the issue of conscripting women and conflict with those opposed to any draft, as well as with those youths who don't need the financial benefits and don't want to serve.

Box 10.5   Women Veterans and the GI Bill

Far fewer women than men served in the U.S. armed forces during World War II. Still, several hundred thousand women veterans were mustered out at the war's end, almost all of whom were eligible for GI Bill benefits, even if these benefits were not always equal to those of male veterans, as was the case with married female vets, who did not receive an additional allowance if they had dependent husbands. Although the failure of the Veteran's Administration to keep statistics on women vets makes it impossible to calculate with any precision, there is general agreement that women veterans made proportionately less use of the GI Bill than male vets. In part, this was because of ignorance. Many women vets recall that, unlike the male vets, they received little counseling about benefits when they left military service. Some, like Audrey, a WAAC captain, mistakenly believed that they were not entitled to the housing benefit.[†]

But for the most part, women veterans did not take advantage of their GI Bill benefits for cultural reasons. The same values that led 1 million women to leave their wartime jobs and return to their homes after the war also

(continued)

---

* In devising a GI Bill for the twenty-first century, therefore, it will be important to keep in mind the criticisms that have been leveled at the original GI Bill, that women and minorities did not have equal access to its benefits. In part, this was because of the ways in which these programs were promoted; in part, it was a result of values that led many female veterans to choose to become housewives after the war rather than go on to college. But it also reflected the stress on higher education over vocational training and the redlining policies inherited from the Federal Housing Authority that made home loans difficult for veterans of color. Yet the fact that those women who did take advantage of their GI Bill educational benefits did so as fully as male veterans and even more at a college level suggests that the inequities were not so much inherent in the program as in the way it was administered. The same conclusion is suggested by the numbers of black veterans who swelled the Negro colleges of the postwar era and escaped the segregated South to enroll in northern colleges. Still, what these critiques of the original GI Bill underscore is that any program for the twenty-first century should be color-blind and gender neutral and accessible to the poor and less-educated.

affected women veterans. Both popular culture and public policy promoted the priority of a gendered nuclear family in which the husband was the breadwinner and the wife the homemaker. Many women vets embraced this role, along with the boys they had left behind or met in the service. Jean C., a Midwestern WAVE, decided not to go to college when the navy pilot she married decided to go home to the family farm instead of becoming an airlines pilot. Others sacrificed their college education and professional careers to support those of their husbands. In these personal choices, women veterans were no different than other U.S. women of their generation. Moreover, because the education benefits expired before their children had grown, women veterans who wanted to go to college at that later stage in their lives found that the GI Bill was no help.

Yet equally striking is the fact that those women veterans who did use their GI Bill benefits utilized them as fully as male vets and more fully where college education was concerned. Nancy, a WAVE from Brooklyn, used her education benefits to get a B.A. at Brooklyn College and an M.A. in education from Teacher's College at Columbia University. "Looking back, she wonder[ed] whether she would have gone to school at all if it hadn't been for the service. Before she went into the service, she didn't have any particular aspiration."[†] She went on to have a lifelong career in teaching. Others used their educational benefits to get Ph.D.s or to become doctors or lawyers. Still others used their housing benefits, which did not expire, to purchase homes or businesses, with or without spouses. They blazed the trail that later generations of women veterans could follow more freely to subsidized education, careers, homes, and businesses.

[†]June A. Willenz, *Women Veterans: America's Forgotten Heroines* (New York: Continuum International, 1983), 58 and 78.

Clearly, a policy proposal this bold and broad will require fine tuning and political compromise. But for this program to succeed, it must be as bold and broad as the dimensions of the problem. Moreover, the consequences of inaction are clear: a continuation of the same downward spiral that has weakened the U.S. nuclear family and condemned millions of Americans to stunted childhoods and wasted lives. A National Youth Service/GI Bill will not by itself reverse that trend and save those families, but it is a good place to begin that task. Together with other measures and the growing concern about the fate of the family across the political spectrum, it can play a vital part in a revival of the American family in our time that historians of the future may yet compare to the golden age of the 1950s.

NOTES

I would like to thank James D. Cox, Jean Carden, Julia Kristeller, and Edward Pitt for sharing their family histories for this chapter.

1. Elaine Tyler May, *Homeward Bound: American Families in the Cold War Era* (New York: Basic Books, 1988), 11.

2. In addition to May, *Homeward Bound*, see, for example, Wini Breines, *Young, White and Miserable: Growing Up Female in the Fifties* (Boston: Beacon Press, 1993); Arlene Skolnick, *Embattled Paradise: The American Family in an Age of Uncertainty* (New York: Basic Books, 1993); Stephen Whitfield, *The Culture of the Cold War* (Baltimore: Johns Hopkins University Press, 1996); John Gaddis, *Strategies of Containment: A Critical Appraisal of Postwar American National Security Policy* (New York: Oxford University Press, 1982); Peter Biskind, *Seeing Is Believing: How Hollywood Taught Us to Stop Worrying and Love the Fifties* (New York: Owl Books, 2000); Manning Marable, *Race, Reform and Rebellion: The Second Reconstruction in Black America* (Jackson: University Press of Mississippi, 1991); Nicholas Lemann, *The Promised Land: The Great Black Migration and How It Changed America* (New York: Vintage Books, 1992); Marty Jezer, *The Dark Ages: Life in the United States, 1945–1960* (Boston: South End Press, 1981).

3. John Diggins, *The Proud Decades: America in War and Peace, 1941–1960* (New York, W. W. Norton, 1988), 213.

4. Paul Landis, Family Counselor; *The Woman's Guide to Better Living,* quoted in Diggins, *Proud Decades,* 212.

5. At the same time, recalling his own childhood, Cornel West reminds us that those segregated black communities were often more solidary and supportive of children than today's drug-ridden ghettos and that they had many more intact families, with fathers who built Little League fields and served as positive role models. For a fuller discussion, see Sylvia Hewlett, *Seedbeds of Violence* (New York: National Parenting Association, 1995), 15–16.

6. See, for example, Betty Freidan, *The Feminine Mystique* (New York: Dell, 1963); May, *Homeward Bound,* chaps. 8 and 9; John D'Emilio, *Sexual Politics, Sexual Communities: The Making of a Homosexual Minority in the United States, 1940–70* (Chicago: University of Chicago Press, 1983), chaps. 2–4.

7. *Newsweek* (June 17, 1996): 60. This part of the article draws on David Blankenhorn and his book *Fatherless America* (New York: HarperCollins, 1996).

8. See chap. 8 in this volume, Allan Carlson, "Taxes and the Family: A Conservative Perspective."

9. U.S. House of Representatives, Committee on Veteran's Affairs, *Hearings on Legislation to Provide G.I. Bill Benefits for Post-Korean Veterans*, 89th Congress, 1st sess., 1965, 3091.

10. *Going Back to Civilian Life: Official Information about the Privileges, Opportunities, and Rights of Returning Soldiers,* ed. M. B. Schnapper (Washington, D.C., 1944).

11. Cyril F. Brickfield, Deputy Administrator of Veteran's Affairs, Veteran's Administration, "The G.I. Bill Paid Off," *Employment Service Review* (June–July 1965); quoted in Keith W. Olson, *The G.I. Bill, the Veterans, and the Colleges* (Lexington: University of Kentucky Press, 1974), 108.

12. Olson, *The G.I. Bill,* 110.

13. Quoted in Olson, *The G.I. Bill,* 107.

14. Kenneth Jackson, *Crabgrass Frontier: The Suburbanization of the United States* (New York: Oxford University Press, 1985), 232.

15. See, for example, Cherlin, *Marriage, Divorce, Remarriage,* 19–21; May, *Homeward Bound,* chap. 6; and Ira Steinberg, *The New Lost Generation: The Population Boom and Public Policy* (New York: St. Martin's Press, 1982), 3–4. See also the classic sociological study of Levittown by Herbert Gans, *The Levittowners: Ways of Life and Politics in a New Suburban Community* (New York: Columbia University Press, 1967).

16. May, *Homeward Bound,* 171.

17. William Levitt himself argued: "We can solve a housing problem, or we can try to solve a racial problem. But we cannot combine the two" (quoted in Jackson, *Crabgrass Frontier,* 241). In 1960, there were no blacks among the 82,000 residents of Levittown, Long Island. The red-lining of nonwhite and ethnically mixed neighborhoods was a legacy of the Home Owners Loan Corporation (HOLC) and the Federal Housing Administration (FHA), created during the Depression to oversee federally guaranteed housing loans, the model for the GI Bill housing program. The HOLC mapped every city in the United States and divided them up by risk categories that the private banks then followed, a practice continued by the FHA and then, with the GI Bill, by the Veterans Administration (VA) (Jackson, 197–214). For a revealing case study, see Arnold Hirsch, *Making the Second Ghetto: Race and Housing in Chicago, 1940–1960* (New York: Cambridge University Press, 1990).

18. It was this empty side of *The Feminine Mystique* that Betty Friedan raised the curtain on in 1963, and a generation of feminist scholars—many of them children of those suburban marriages—have criticized it since. Significantly, many of the children of the 1950s would rebel against this suburban family ideal during the 1960s and 1970s.

19. They were attacked as a cultural and emotional wasteland, what Lewis Mumford criticized as "a low-grade uniform environment from which escape is impossible" (Lewis Mumford, *The City in History* [New York, 1961], 486).

20. Jackson, *Crabgrass Frontier,* 244–45.

21. Steven Greenhouse, "Low Wage Jobs Leading Gains in Employment," *New York Times,* October 1, 2000.

22. Anne Adams Lang, "Behind the Prosperity, Working People in Trouble," *New York Times,* November 20, 2000.

23. Olson, *The G.I. Bill,* 24.

24. For a critical analysis of these economic processes and U.S. responses to them, see David Gordon, *Fat and Mean: The Corporate Squeeze of Working Americans and the Myth of Managerial "Downsizing"* (New York: Free Press, 1996). For the relative decline in the incomes of families, see chap. 4 of this volume, Edward Wolff, "The Economic Status of Parents in Postwar America."

25. Report of the Armed Forces Committee on Post-War Educational Opportunities for Service Personnel (Osborn Committee), July 1943, quoted in Olson, *G.I. Bill,* 12. Formed by Pres. Franklin Roosevelt in late 1942 to study postwar educational needs, the Osborn Committee report was one of several studies upon which the GI Bill of 1944 was based.

26. Anand Vaishnav and Scott Greenberger, "Workers in State Lack New Job Skills," *Boston Globe,* January 7, 2001.

27. For American Legion lobbying and discourse in 1944, see Olson, *G.I. Bill,* 17–20. For the Bonus Army march on Washington, see Franklin Folsom, *Impatient Armies of the Poor: The Story of Collective Action of the Unemployed, 1808–1942* (Niwot: University Press of Colorado, 1991), 310–322.

28. Quoted in Olson, *The G.I. Bill,* 20.

29. Quoted in *New York Times,* October 1, 2000.

30. *New York Times,* November 20, 2000.

31. The most influential—and controversial—of these conservative critiques has been Charles Murray, *Losing Ground: American Social Policy, 1950–1980* (New York: Basic Books, 1984).

32. For a thoughtful reflection on this question by analysts with extensive governmental experience, see Henry J. Aaron and Charles L. Schultze, *Setting Domestic Priorities: What Can Government Do?* (Washington, D.C.: Brookings Institution, 1992), chap. 1.

33. For analyses of these failures and frustrations by liberal supporters of such programs for the family, see Gilbert Steiner, *The Futility of Family Policy* (Washington, D.C.: Brookings Institution, 1981), and D. Patrick Moynihan, *Family and Nation* (San Diego: Harcourt Brace Jovanovich, 1986).

34. See chap. 8, Allan Carlson, "Taxes and the Family: A Conservative Perspective."

35. AmeriCorps, "The Basics," http://www.cns.gov/americorps/joining/basics.html; "The Benefits," http://www.cns.gov/americorps/joining/benefits.html; "Money for College," http://www.cns.gov/americorps/joining/moneyforcollege.html; "Member Stories," http://www.cns.gov/americorps/joining/memberstories/member7.html; "Press Releases," http://www.americorps.org/news/media.html. (Site last accessed: January 2001.)

36. PowerUp, "Program Information," http://www.powerup.org/proginfo.html; "About the Digital Divide," http://www.powerup.org/digitaldivide.html; "PowerUpPartners," http://www.powerup.org/partners.html; "The Five Cyber Promises," http://www.powerup.org.html; "Major Digital Divide Initiative Launch," November 8, 1999, http://www.powerup.org/init.html. (Site last accessed: January 2001.)

37. "Powell and Hundreds of Volunteers Serve at the Kennedy Institute," AmeriCorps, *Service News,* April 6, 2000; http://www.americorps.org/news/40600.html. (Site last accessed: January 2001.)

38. Equally disturbing is the fact that African American women experienced a 78 percent increase in involvement with the criminal justice system during 1989–94, the largest of any demographic group in the country. (See Marc Mauer and Tracy Huling, *Young Black Americans and the Criminal Justice System: Five Years Later* [The Sentencing Project: Washington, D.C., October 1995]).

39. Senator Robert Dole, quoted in *New York Times,* July 17, 1996.

40. See, for example, Murray, *Losing Ground.*

PART FOUR

BUILDING PUBLIC WILL AND POLITICAL
POWER TO HELP PARENTS

11

The Paths from Here

Raymond Seidelman

The political portrait of American parents traced by Ruy Teixeira in chapter 7 seems to me to point to the obstacles, choices, and opportunities facing any future parents' movement. In this commentary, I want to avoid extended discussion of the methods and many of the specific data contained in his chapter.

Instead, I want to take Teixeira's findings at face value and focus on their various and complex political implications. Given what we know from his chapter, and the NPA's 1996 and 2000 surveys, could a stronger national parents' movement (or movements) be built? If so, what are the central strategic choices to be made, and where might each choice lead politically? Are there historical or contemporary examples that are relevant for a potential parents' movement, built around the "practical" concerns and policy suggestions unearthed by the National Parenting Association survey and other research?

My aim in this short commentary is to be provocative and even somewhat simplistic, if only to ground the discussion between two (possibly artificial) polarities. In the broadest terms, I see two very different paths that any parents' movement could follow, given Teixeira's analysis and the surveys. The first path is rooted in a "pessimistic," or some might say "realistic," reading of the Teixeira data. It leads to a political strategy that accepts, however regrettably, the basic patterns of parental political behavior pretty much as they are, but then attempts to move a parents' agenda forward. The second path is a longer and more adventurous one and presents bigger risks. It is rooted in

Raymond Seidelman, professor of political science at Sarah Lawrence College, Bronxville, N.Y., is author of *Disenchanted Realists: Political Science and the American Crisis* and co-author of *The Democratic Debate: An Introduction to American Politics*.

the idea that a parents' movement must be based on changing the huge participation and class gap unearthed by Teixeira.

A PARENTS' MOVEMENT? DREAM ON

The elements of "pessimistic realism" in the reported data are not hard to identify, for there are some discomfiting facts at work among parents and in U.S. society as a whole. Since the 1970s, the proportion of parents in the U.S. population has been declining. While American society as a whole is divided by income and wealth inequality, parents are if anything even more divided by class (broadly conceived) than are nonparents in the population. In American society, class is, of course, interlaced with the racial divide as well. A growing and disproportionate number of parents (and their children), and especially African American and Latino parents, live in poverty or near poverty, while others have ascended to relative affluence.

Perhaps even more ominous is the logical political result of these findings. Class divisions within the parent population have produced profound disparities in levels of voting participation. Participatory inequality, already great in U.S. society as a whole, is even more pronounced among parents. When most parents go to the polls (or don't), their political decisions are not based primarily on their identities as parents. [Ed. note: See chapter 14, table 14.8, which presents some evidence to the contrary.] In real life, parents are fragmented by radically different social and economic circumstances. Consequently, they lack both a political identity and political voice qua parents. Indeed, many parents seem to lack a political voice at all.

Moreover, class divisions are reflected in the difficulty of forming political bridges among parents across the divides of race and class. Just as in the rest of U.S. society, the corrosive effects of growing economic inequality provide few reasons to believe that the "disconnect" between most people and political power can be redressed. In theory, a common agenda and similar life circumstances in some respects may "unite" parents in a Las Vegas gated community with parents in the South Bronx. While our own NPA survey found such "unity" around certain issues, it cannot be forgotten that a consensus in a survey is far different than consensus built through the concrete actions and participation of parents in politics. If some of Teixeira's findings are right, being a parent is not now much of a political identity—it is submerged under other political identities, distorted by clichés about family values, or generally absent from the political debate entirely.

The difficulty of forging concrete political bonds based on parenthood also meets two other uncomfortable facts, well noted by Teixeira. The first fact is that political and personal efficacy is quite low among most ordinary citizens and is even lower among parents than among nonparents. To an even greater degree than nonparents, parents are skeptical about government and about their own ability to have an impact on it. The second fact derives from a general political climate of shrinking governmental spending and commitments, crystallized in the present balanced budget agreement, lower capital gains taxes, and the rightward march of both parties. Both facts seem to provide few reasons for confidence about the mobilization of a parents' movement or the capacity to expand governmental roles. Because parents lack a distinctive and self-confident political voice, their interests are left to be defined, articulated (or distorted) in politics by others. In 1996, "soccer moms" could be created as statistical artifacts and then could be appealed to on the basis of "small bore" initiatives like school uniforms, free beepers for neighborhood crime patrols, or experiments in private school vouchers. In present politics, a vicious circle of declining faith in government and the possibilities of democratic citizenship feed on each other.

A REALISTIC STRATEGY FOR PESSIMISTIC TIMES

Accepting these demographic and political realities as they are may preclude a broad-based parents' movement. Building a broad-based political movement would require a high level of mobilization and a degree of repoliticization of presently inactive parent-citizens. Yet that is simply unlikely in the present political context, and even more unlikely given the divides between parents. It would have to involve a reversal of long-term trends that depress political participation among median- and low-income citizens. It would involve the emergence of an organization or a set of organizations with an enormous amount of resources. However much this may be wished for, "realism" dictates that it cannot be achieved in the near future.

There are some obvious implications if this "realistic" reading is accepted. It does not mean giving up altogether, but working through a "politics of small steps" among *some* parents to make *some* issues more visible. This would mean concentrating *less* on changing long-term trends through attempts at voter and grassroots mobilization and more on building a parent-based *interest group*. Like every other interest group today, it would have to focus on the parents who already *do* participate in politics. Interest groups specialize in the intense mobilization of active citizens around specific and usually narrow demands. An interest group based on parents would set goals that are achievable in the present political context. In doing so, it would take the class and race gap, as well as the declining proportion of parents, for granted and would go on from there.

In today's politics, this top-down, interest-group approach to the organization of parents would seem to have a number of real advantages. First, it is based less on mobilizing large numbers of people for some action than it is rooted in targeting a select and already active few for intensive mobilization and selected appeals. As numerous studies have shown, interest groups of this kind can be effective by harnessing the financial support of the "fortunate fifth"—people of high affluence and formal education inclined to participate in politics as it is. Second, there are existing and successful models of the interest-group approach that present potential and immediate advantages, Trial lawyers, investment bankers, soybean farmers, doctors, broadcasters, beer brewers, and even gun owners have been generally effective these days by harnessing the money, media visibility, lobbying power, and expertise that are necessary to achieve access and respectability in today's Washington.

For top-down interest groups, money is the chief resource because it helps to build the think-tanks, PACs, experts, and lobbyists necessary to achieve immediate and concrete results. Grassroots participation isn't required, except for an annual donation or an occasional e-mail to a member of Congress when a crucial piece of legislation is being debated. Even the mighty AARP, in many ways a model of a successful, mass-based interest group, emerges as a spokesperson for America's seniors not because it encourages grassroots participation among its members, but because of its institutional visibility and professionalism in Washington. Its agenda and impact are thoroughly in the hands of its hired professionals. Its "mass" membership matters, but only insofar as those $5 and $10 annual fees can really add up.

All this tends to show that an interest-group approach for parents could be very effective and persuasive within the present political context of shrinking government and class- and race-based participation trends. Like other such interests, those that involve parents would almost by definition draw the financial support of the more affluent parents. The interest group model suggests that proparent measures of low cost to taxpayers and no threat to entrenched institutions could become more visible, as well as the type of small-bore initiatives undertaken by Clinton and proposed by Gore in 2000. Among such issues identified by the NPA/Penn + Schoen poll might be increased gun control, unpaid release time to care for child emergencies, compensatory time, extension of voluntary leaves, and increased tax breaks for parents with children.

There is a large flip-side to pursuing the path of interest-group conformism, however. An AARP-style interest group for parents would only spin the wheels of declining democratic understandings and decreasing inclusiveness that split parents. An interest group for parents would inevitably organize, and then represent, the affluent fifth. Frankly redistributive policies would as a result fall by the wayside, labeled as impractical in a generally conservative political era and undoable, given the low levels of political participation (and active support) one can expect from working-class and poor parents. Measures like comprehensive health-care coverage for all children, extension of the earned income credit, targeted tax cuts for median- and low-income parents, "living wage" initiatives, or much increased aid to education would find scanter support and would seem like "pie in the sky." So, too, would rollbacks of the so-called welfare reform bill—to me, the single most harmful strike at the economic basis of parenting. In short, the interest-group strategy is "realistic" at the very high cost of a stunted proparent agenda deprived of democratic breadth and inclusiveness.

BUILDING A PARENTS' MOVEMENT

The other reading of Teixeira's data leads to very different conclusions. It would be based on the idea that a parents' agenda could only succeed by means of closing in some measure the participation and class gap rather than working within its confines. Instead of an interest group based on financial contributions by the affluent and the expertise and access it buys, the chief potential resource of parents is "power in numbers and power in movement." Parents may be declining as a proportion of both the population and of the voting electorate, but their chief resource remains the fact that there are still 63 million of them. Saul Alinsky has called American politics a continuous struggle between "organized money and organized people," with the former currently in ascendancy. Surely, a parents' movement would have to rely on the latter to achieve its agenda.

The opportunity, from this perspective, is to build a parents' movement by taking advantage of numbers and mass participation as a vast and unique democratic resource. Seizing this opportunity would mean to begin to close the large class and racial gaps that fragment parents. In turn, as the concerns of parents achieve new visibility in politics, the participation and efficacy gaps would be thereby lessened.

There are some tentative reasons for optimism on this score, contained in both Teixeira's study and surveys conducted by NPA/Penn + Schoen and the Lake Research Group. For example, much could be made of the growing "conservative" orientation of parents. But this means little, or even nothing, when more depth is sought. Parents are "operational liberals" in practice. By broad margins and across many divides, parents support measures—even redistributive ones—that ease the economic burdens of child rearing, extend medical care to the poor and working poor, provide greater flexibility and security in the workplace, and promote greater federal spending on education (NPA poll, Lake Research survey). Perhaps even more telling throughout the research is what might be called the unmet *political needs* or unarticulated political interests of most parents. No matter which survey is read, the results confirm the sense that most parents are struggling economically and juggling increasingly incompatible roles as workers, spouses, parents, and citizens.

Objectively, the conditions for a cross-class, interracial, proparents' movement most definitely exist. Even a careful reading of parental political attitudes can reveal much common ground. Yet if parents are to arrive as a political force, surveys cannot be the chief instrument, for they must give way to the conversations and actions of real people who associate together, who build communities and ideas, and who make broader claims for justice in the name of the entire society. Instead of an interest group and its narrow claims, parents could become a social movement with its broadly democratic, moral, and civic claims.

A PARENTS' POLITICAL MOVEMENT: FIRST AND SECOND STEPS

Assuming that the interest group path is problematic on a host of grounds, the question becomes: How could parents, divided and inactive in so many ways, come together politically? Much has been made in intellectual circles about the "decline of civil society." Frequently and mistakenly, some "civil decline" theorists have associated the decline of civil society with the rise of "big government." At the risk of overgeneralization, it must be said that if there is a decline in civil society, it has much more to do with elite secession and insulation from society and the attendant professionalization of politics as a sport for the expert and the affluent than it has to do with government. Historically, participation and "volunteerism" are linked to democratization and are enabled and encouraged by democratic government, not separated out as two distinct fields of human action.

More practically, parents might be "participating" in lots of things, both on an informal and formal basis. The point of democratic politics is to maximize the opportunities for participation. But present-day politics, and most especially professionalized, money-driven electoral politics, is like a third rail for ordinary citizens. It seems like a distant battle involving monied politicians and interests, incomprehensible experts, and meaningless personal scandals and revelations. In 2000, present-day politics even meant that a popular electoral majority was thwarted. Why join that exclusive club of political participants?

Here, any future parents' movement might take lessons from two strange bedfellows—the Christian Coalition and the new labor movement. From the CC comes an organizational, not an ideological, lesson. The CC started from a network of extant religious organizations—Baptist, Pentecostal, and other congregations. Building from the ground up, it began to coordinate a national agenda from the top down. The organizers of the CC did not stand around lamenting apathy at the grass roots. Any organization or movement able to deliver 25 million voter guides through volunteers, as the CC has, employs techniques well worth emulating in a very different parents' movement.

Any parents' movement should seek similar places where parents congregate—churches, ballfields, schools, day-care centers, malls, and, most of all, workplaces. In this regard, the NPA's poll demonstrates something important about a grassroots strategy around a proparent agenda. Use the associations parents are presently in to network and to develop and propagate a proparent agenda. The numbers in traditional organizations like the PTA may be declining, but there is robust involvement across class and race lines in informal organizations linked to day care, school, sports, and other activities. Bemoaning the fate of civil society among parents is unduly pessimistic. Working to politicize the scattered and informal ways in which parents presently associate together is quite realistic.

The lesson from the AFL-CIO and its present attempts at revival are more directly to the point. The juggernaut of the global market economy is creating new inequalities, insecurities, and anxieties, and the genuine angst can be used to turn workers against workers, race against race, and "native-born Americans" against immigrants. Yet these poisonous juices need not freely flow. By concentrating on the centrality of the workplace and the conditions of work to democratic public life, the contemporary AFL-CIO has begun to fight back politically. In 1996, 1998, and 2000, the votes of union members enabled Democrats to advance in both the House and the Senate and provided a popular majority for Al Gore.

A future parents' movement would do well to recognize the workplace, and the global economic forces that shape it, as a site for democratic coalition building and the politicization of a parent/wage-earner agenda that cuts across class and race. One reason is quite obvious: in an era of shrinking governmental expenditures and responsibilities, government and politics nonetheless still possess the sovereign power to set conditions under which parents and workers live. At little or no expense to taxpayers or to the precious federal budget, government can still set the terms and conditions of family leave, the minimum wage, overtime, and the ability of workers to organize themselves. Second, the AFL-CIO and its natural concentration on the workplace and workers speak directly to the skepticism about big government programs, so tellingly revealed in Teixeira's chapter. "America needs a raise" could be broadened to include the idea that "America needs a raise because it needs strong families." Connecting to the labor movement, and helping to broaden its claims to include parents and their unmet needs, seems like an obvious and democratic strategy for a parents' movement.

Expanding union efforts to include a proparent agenda has advantages for a newly aggressive labor movement as well. For unions, the political potential is to move beyond the perception that they are a special interest group in the backchannels and at the margins of political change. For any set of parent organizations, unions provide a way of presenting a whole range of workplace and political issues, from the "time crunch" to economic insecurity through public education and the right to health care. It makes sense not to hark back to the welfare state but to attempt to change corporations and their policies through low-cost, nonbureaucratic reforms that promote economic democracy, personal security, and enhanced citizenship.

A TENTATIVE STRATEGY

In the immediate term, what could a parents' movement do to begin to form a distinctive identity and its own political voice? Why would politicians listen to parents in either 2002 or 2004?

- One first step would be the formation of a short parents' political agenda on matters ranging from flextime and the minimum wage through increased support for public education. This agenda could include a selected number of policy positions drawn from existing legislative proposals. But more important, the goal would be to refine further a parents' agenda that might begin to bridge the class/racial/participation gap by reaching out to the concerns of the broadest number of parents and especially to the kinds of parents presently inactive in politics. The general guidelines for a proparent national agenda are already contained in surveys taken by NPA, the Children's Partnership/Lake Research Poll, and other sources. Especially important here would be to coordinate formation of the parents' agenda with labor unions, community organizations, and workplace issues.
- The formation of this agenda could easily lead to a rating system for electoral candidates, most particularly for members of Congress but also, in some states, for state legislators. The rating system could judge key legislative votes of incumbents on parent-friendly legislation, as well as their support for proparent proposals currently absent from the Washing-

ton legislative agenda. It would help to identify proparent challengers to incumbents and become a way that a parents' agenda could achieve new visibility for voters (and nonvoters). It would promote increased media visibility for the issues most central to a parents' movement.

- The rating systems could be used to produce voter guides for the next elections. In the short term, parents' groups could work with labor and the many other groups involved in voter registration and mobilization among people of color (Southwest Voter Registration Project, NAACP, COPE, and other such efforts.) The idea would be to target a number of congressional districts where parent organizations, in combination with labor and other groups, could work together in common electoral efforts and around proparent candidates that stand a chance of victory. The voter guides could be distributed to extant parent, labor, civil rights, and other advocacy organizations, where they could be customized and extended for use in local races.

- Obvious "test cases" for the implementation of this initial strategy would be places where there is fertile ground for budding efforts to take root. Prime candidates are places where union and church groups are already engaged in voter registration efforts, where there are a number of in-cumbent officeholders who are likely to be friendly to a proparent agenda, and where there is the possibility of achieving electoral success through mobilization around the agenda.

These are very tentative suggestions. What does seem clear is that such efforts, minimal as they are, need to start at the *national* level. If a parents' agenda is to emerge, the worthy though scattered efforts of many groups need to be concentrated, if only through a limited amount of research and visibility, for a proparent agenda that can stimulate grassroots activity and a new national and local debate.

12

What It Will Take to Build a Family-Friendly America

Theda Skocpol

America today is badly in need of family-friendly politics, including new and renewed social supports for child-rearing families. All kinds of families at various stages of life must be supported, but working parents should be moved to the center of today's movements for family support.

The need for such a focus is very great. Since the 1970s most working families have become increasingly hard-pressed in an unforgiving economy (Boushey et al. 2001; Danziger and Gottschalk 1995). Except for elites, regular wage increases are few and far between; and ordinary employees cannot be certain of health coverage and other employer-provided benefits vital for themselves and their families. Yet the problems today's families face are more than economic. Working parents, in particular, face a double bind—not only a squeeze of economic resources, but also constraints on the time and energy people need to raise children and engage in activities in churches, schools, neighborhoods, and civic life.

With both men and women juggling jobs and family duties at the same time—in a market-oriented culture that proclaims individual satisfactions as the only meaningful goal in life—stable marriages are often difficult to form or sustain. Home and community life may suffer. Even if families hold together, at the very time that most working people are grappling with unnerving changes in the economy, domestic demands are greater and certainly more pressing. Grandparents live longer and, while they often help to succor their

Theda Skocpol is Victor S. Thomas Professor of Government and Sociology at Harvard University and director of the Center for American Political Studies. Among her books are *Protecting Soldiers and Mothers: The Political Origins of Social Policy in the United States* and *The Missing Middle: Working Families and the Future of American Social Policy.*

children and grandchildren, the elders themselves need caring attention from their adult children. At the same time, children require plentiful reserves of parental guidance—and a very long-term commitment of family resources— if they are to flourish and prepare to succeed in tomorrow's demanding world. Working fathers—and working mothers even more—find themselves under extraordinary pressures today.

The National Parenting Association (NPA) already knows these things, of course. Yet the NPA faces fundamental questions about how best to move forward. In my view, the association should ponder not only the details of specific proposals about tax cuts and regulatory adjustments and media campaigns. People should think more boldly and self-consciously about long-term developments in American democracy and public policymaking. Only by taking a longer view, longer into the past and into the future, can the NPA expect to arrive at a wise understanding of strategic opportunities and choices in the present. This contribution is meant to spur such broader reflection.

America in the late twentieth century has veered rather far away from earlier, deep-rooted traditions of popular politics and broad (though never fully inclusive) social policymaking. Today, the United States is in a period of socioeconomic polarization, with the top fourth of families pulling away from those in the middle, as well as from the least privileged people at the bottom (Danziger and Gottschalk 1995; Reich 1991; Wolff 1995).

Americans have become increasingly distrustful of government—and are being very much urged on in this distrust by privileged elites who stand to benefit from lower taxes and unfettered, winner-take-all markets (Frank and Cook 1995). Meanwhile, our national civic life is more and more dominated by superficial media campaigns, by consultants who measure aggregate opinions in narrow snapshots, but never encourage two-way dialogues about national issues, and by foundations and advocacy groups that seek to devise and apply expert solutions from the top down (Ganz 1994; Judis 1992; Tierney 1992). Money and expertise now count for more than participation in American politics and civil life (Skocpol 1999; Verba, Schlozman, and Brady 1995, 1997).

Without intending it, the National Parenting Association could end up simply "going with the flow" of these worrisome trends in American society and democracy. The easiest route forward is to commission and lobby for expert policy proposals, emphasizing only those apparently "realistic" notions that accept dwindling tax revenues and widening socioeconomic disparities as givens, while the NPA joins with other advocacy groups seeking to manipulate government regulations and advance media campaigns around the edges of the apparently inevitable. Family rhetoric could easily mask support for (more) tax cuts and "restructurings" of Social Security and Medicare that, in the name of helping the young instead of the old, would actually leave most ordinary working mothers and fathers worse off.

Another path forward involves searching for ways to reinvigorate and extend broad public supports for ordinary American families, while looking for ways to strengthen profamily forces and popular participation at local and state, as well as national, levels. As we are about to see, this would be a strategy in line with the best traditions of U.S. democracy and public policymaking. But it would not be an easy course to follow, given contemporary trends.

SUCCESSFUL SOCIAL SUPPORTS IN AMERICAN DEMOCRACY

Americans today who champion family supports do not need to imitate any foreign models or take any unprecedented leaps into an unhinged future. They do not even have to cling to the New Deal as their sole precedent. They can discover fresh ways to renew and extend long-standing traditions of U.S. social provision. Again and again—and starting long before Franklin Roosevelt's New Deal—successful social policies have furthered economic security and opportunity for many American families, while simultaneously expressing and reinforcing mainstream moral values about family integrity, individual responsibility, and the mutual obligations of individuals and the national community. A look at the past can provide a new perspective on what is missing today and what might be possible for the future.

While some might quibble here or there, most would agree that America's finest social policy achievements have included the following milestones. Whether a single program or a set of related measures, each milestone has offered security and opportunity to millions of individuals, families, and communities, inspiring broad and enduring political support in the process. The milestones of U.S. social provision span most of the nation's history:

- *Public schools:* The United States was the world's leader in the spread of widely accessible public education (Heidenheimer 1981). During the nineteenth century, primary schools, followed by secondary schools, spread throughout most localities and states.
- *Civil War benefits* were disability and old-age pensions, job opportunities, and social services for millions of Union veterans and survivors. By 1910, more than a quarter of all American elderly men, and more than a third of men over sixty-two in the North, were receiving regular payments from the federal government on terms that were extraordinarily generous by the international standards of that era. Many family members and survivors were generously aided as well (Skocpol 1992, 129–35).

- *Programs to help mothers and children* proliferated during the 1910s and early 1920s. Forty-four states passed laws to protect women workers and also "mothers' pensions" to enable poor widows to care for their children at home (Leff 1973). Congress established the Children's Bureau in 1912 and in 1921 passed the Sheppard-Towner Act to fund health-education programs open to all American mothers and babies (Ladd-Taylor 1986).
- *The Social Security Act* was passed in 1935, including unemployment insurance and public assistance to the poor, along with Old Age Insurance (OAI), which subsequently became its most popular part. OAI eventually took the name "Social Security" and expanded to cover virtually all retired employees, while providing survivors' and disability protections as well (Derthick 1979). Most employees and their dependents were included in Social Security by the 1960s. Modeled in part on retirement insurance, *Medicare* was added to the system in 1965 (Marmor 1973).
- *The GI Bill of 1944* offered a comprehensive set of disability services, employment benefits, educational loans, family allowances, and subsidized loans for homes, businesses, and farms to 16 million veterans returning from World War II (Mosch 1975; Olson 1974).

Although these giant systems of social support developed in different periods of American history and varied in many ways, they have important features in common, three of which we can consider here:

(1) *American social policy milestones and the movements supporting them have aimed to give social benefits to large categories of citizens in return for service to the community or else as a way to help people prepare to serve the community.*

The most enduring and popularly accepted social benefits in the United States have never been understood either as poor relief or as mere "individual entitlements." From public schools through Social Security, they have been morally justified as recognition of—or prospective supports for—individual service to the community. The rationale of social support in return for service has been a characteristic way for Americans to combine deep respect for individual freedom and initiative with support for families and due regard for the obligations that all members of the national community owe to one another.

A clear-cut rationale of return for service was invoked to justify the veterans' benefits expanded in the wake of the Civil War and World War II (Skocpol 1992, 148–51; Ross 1969). Less well understood, though, is the use of civic arguments by the educational reformers and local community activists who originally established America's public schools. They argued for common schools not primarily as means to further economic efficiency or individual mobility, but as ways to prepare all children for democratic citizenship (Emirbayer 1992; Tyack and Hansot 1982, part 1). Similarly, early 1900s programs for mothers were justified as supports for the services of women who risked their lives to bear children and devoted themselves to raising good citizens for the future (Skocpol 1992, part 3).

Today's Social Security and Medicare systems likewise have a profound moral underpinning in the eyes of most Americans (Kingson, Hirshorn, and Cornman 1986; Greenberg 1996). Retirees and people anticipating retirement believe they have "earned" benefits by virtue of having made a lifetime of payroll contributions. But contrary to what pundits and economists often assert, the exchange is not understood as narrowly instrumental or individualistic. Most Americans see Social Security and Medicare as a social contract enforced by, and for, contributors to the national community. The benefits are experienced as just rewards for lifetimes of work—on the job and at home—not simply as returns-with-interest on personal savings accounts.

(2) *Successful U.S. social policies have built bridges between more and less privileged Americans, bringing people together—as worthy beneficiaries and as contributing citizens—across lines of class, race, and region.*

Even if policy milestones started out small compared to what they eventually became, the key fact has been the structure of contributions and benefits. Successful social policies have built bridges, linking more and less privileged Americans. They have therefore not been considered or labeled "welfare" programs.

Public schools, for example, were founded for most children, not just for the offspring of privileged families, as was originally the case with schools in other nations (Katznelson and Weir 1985, chap. 2). Civil War benefits and the GI Bill were available to all eligible veterans and survivors of each war. Although mothers' pensions eventually deteriorated into "welfare," they were not originally so stigmatized (Skocpol 1992, chap. 8). During the early 1900s, a great many American mothers who lost a breadwinner-husband could suddenly find themselves in dire economic need. What is more, early federal programs for mothers and children were universal. The Children's Bureau was explicitly charged with serving all American children (Skocpol 1992, chap. 9), and its first chief, Julia Lathrop, reasoned that if "the services of the [Sheppard-Towner] bill were not open to all, the services would degenerate into poor relief" (from a letter quoted in Covotsos 1976, 123).

Social Security and Medicare are today's best examples of inclusive social programs with huge cross-class constituencies. Although Social Security is the most effective antipoverty undertaking ever run through government in the United States, its saving grace over the past several decades—during an era of tight federal budgets and fierce political attacks on social provision—

has been its broad constituency of present and future beneficiaries, none of whom understand it as "welfare" (Heclo 1986). Were Social Security and Medicare to be divided into residual social safety nets versus individualistic private market accounts, they would soon be on the road to moral, political, and fiscal demise. America would not just be making a technical or budgetary adjustment. Especially in the case of Social Security, even partial privatization would undercut a successful solidary program that, with minimal "bureaucratic" hassle, enhances dignified security for millions of working families.

(3) *Broad U.S. social policies have been nurtured by partnerships of government and popularly rooted voluntary associations. There has been no zero-sum relationship between state and society, no trade-off between government and individuals, and no simple opposition between national and community efforts.*

The policy milestones I have identified were developed (if not always originated) through cooperation between government agencies and elected politicians, on the one hand, and voluntary associations, on the other hand. I am not referring merely to nonprofit, professionally run social service agencies. I mean voluntary citizens' groups. The associations that have nurtured major U.S. social programs have usually linked national and state offices with participatory groups in local communities.

Public schools were founded and sustained by traveling reformers, often members of regional or national associations, who linked up with leading local citizens, churches, and voluntary groups (Tyack and Hansot 1982, part 1). The movers and shakers behind early 1900s state and national legislation for mothers and children were the Women's Christian Temperance Union, the General Federation of Women's Clubs, and the National Congress of Mothers (which eventually turned into the PTA) (Skocpol 1992, part 3). Civil War benefits ended up both reinforcing and being nurtured by the Grand Army of the Republic (GAR) (Skocpol 1992, chap. 2). Open to veterans of all economic, ethnic, and racial backgrounds, the GAR was a classic three-tiered voluntary civic association, with tens of thousands of local "posts," whose members met regularly, plus state and national affiliates that held big annual conventions (McConnell 1992).

Social Security has had a complex relationship to voluntary associations. Back during the Great Depression, a militant social movement and voluntary federation of older Americans, the Townsend Movement, pressed Congress to enact universal benefits for elders (Holtzman 1963). But Social Security definitely did not embody specific Townsend preferences, and the movement itself withered away during the 1940s (Amenta, Carruthers, and Zylan 1992). Today over 35 million Americans fifty and over are enrolled in the American

Association of Retired Persons (AARP), whose newsletters and magazines alert older voters to maneuvers in Washington, D.C., that affect Social Security and Medicare (Morris 1996). The AARP does not have very many local membership clubs (though it is currently working to establish more of them). Still, many elderly Americans participate in locally rooted seniors' groups, including the union-related National Council of Senior Citizens, which has played a key role in advocating for Medicare. Moreover, along with unions and religious congregations, federal, state, and local governments have done a lot over the past thirty years to create services and community centers for elderly citizens. An important side effect has been to foster considerable social communication, civic volunteerism, and political engagement among older Americans.

The final example of government-association partnership in the expansion of inclusive U.S. social provision is perhaps the most telling. A nationwide veterans' federation, the American Legion, was crucial in the enactment of the inclusive and generous GI Bill of 1944 (Ross 1969; Skocpol 1997). New Democrats today often praise the GI Bill for giving benefits in return for service, in ways that maximized the choices of individual veterans to enroll in any training program or college or university. All very true, and worthy of emulation (Skocpol 1996b). But what new Democrats need to notice is that the GI Bill took this shape only because the American Legion pressured conservatives in Congress as well as on the somewhat elitist "planners" of the wartime Roosevelt administration (Skocpol 1997). The Legion was a locally rooted, cross-class, and nationwide voluntary association that developed in close symbiosis with two very strong "federal bureaucracies"—the U.S. military and the Veterans Administration (Pencak 1989). In this story, there are no oppositions of state versus civil society—or of government versus individual autonomy and community engagement. The post–World War II American Legion—along with half of the nation's young workers and families— was enormously helped by an active federal government and by very generous public spending.

TODAY'S MISSING MIDDLE

During the Depression and World War II, many Western nations launched comprehensive systems to guarantee citizens full employment and social security. In the United States, too, New Deal reformers battled for broad protections for all citizens or wage-earners. But by the 1950s the United States was left with only one relatively universal permanent program—Social Security's contributory disability and retirement insurance. Other attempts to institutionalize broad social programs were defeated, and America was set on the road to a "missing middle" in social provision—the relative absence of protections for working-aged adults and their children that pertains today.

True, gaps in social protection were temporarily filled for many younger American families by the GI Bill of 1944 and subsequent veterans' legislation. Generous social investments in many young men and their families, along with hearty postwar economic expansion, ensured opportunity and security for millions of child-rearing families. Especially well served were those working-class and middle-class whites who entered the labor force, married, and raised children from the late 1940s into the 1960s. But after that, the impact of the GI Bill faded, just as the American economy was about to take a turn for the worse for young workers and families (Danziger and Gottschalk 1995).

Taken together, the War on Poverty, the Great Society, and many of the social policy initiatives sponsored by moderate Republican President Richard M. Nixon aimed to help poor children and working-aged adults, especially African Americans who had not been fully incorporated into the economic growth or social insurance protections of the postwar era. But when the dust settled, the broadest and costliest achievements focused on the elderly. The most important federal innovations were Medicare, enacted in 1965, and the indexing of Social Security pensions to inflation, which occurred in 1972. During the "Reagan era" of the 1980s, moreover, cutbacks occurred primarily in welfare programs for the poor and not in the popular social insurance programs, which covered the middle-class elderly, along with working and poor retirees.

At the dawn of the twenty-first century, American social provision is very generationally skewed, and grand schemes for reconstructing social policies are fought out in generational terms. The Concord Coalition asserts that government budget cuts are essential because too much is being done for the elderly (Peterson 1993), while the Children's Defense Fund (1994) wants government to do more to uplift poor children. Alas, this polarized debate overlooks millions of mid-life adults and their children, often in working families of modest means. Most working-aged parents, especially wives and mothers, are close to elderly parents and correctly feel a strong stake in Social Security and Medicare (Kingson, Hirshorn, and Cornman 1986; Lawton, Silverstein, and Bengston 1994). But young men, in particular, may see themselves primarily as taxpayers within late-twentieth-century America's uneven system of social provision. Many working parents see themselves as struggling in an unforgiving economy, trying to care for their families with stagnant wages and shrinking employer-provided benefits. "Why should I pay taxes to fund health care and child care for others," a working parent may think, "when I cannot afford those for my own family?"

People who want better family supports in America need to change the terms of the policy debate and inspire a new sense of democratic possibilities for the medium-run future. Rather than accepting the notion of zero-sum generational conflicts, advocates of family support can advance options that unite rather than divide generational and class groups. We must, moreover, advocate social support for all working families, not just a few who happen to qualify for one or another narrowly targeted program.

A more seamless and complete system of social insurance and family supports was, of course, the dream of many Progressives and New Dealers and the goal of farsighted black and white leaders during the 1960s. But regional and racial divides dashed hopes for completing a comprehensive American welfare state at the end of World War II. And since the 1960s, possibilities to achieve more complete social supports for all American families have been undercut, again and again, by bitterly racialized disputes over "welfare" (Edsall and Edsall 1991; Weir 1992). Whatever one may think of the "welfare reform" legislation that President Clinton signed in the summer of 1996, it creates the possibility of refocusing national debates on what it takes for all families, poor and middle-class alike, to work and raise children. Discussions about family supports in America can finally move beyond fruitless debates about programs or regulations focused on some of the very poor alone.

MOVING FORWARD FROM HERE

Stronger, more coherent support for America's families is not just a matter of giving benefits to—or adjusting taxes on—individuals. Equally at stake are social honor and our sense of mutual obligation between the community and citizens who serve it—just as such matters have always been at stake in each era of American social policymaking. Americans have always favored social benefits for those who contribute vitally to the national community. Nowadays, working parents can become the focus of such a moral argument. The future of the nation as a whole depends vitally on the work that families do— and especially on the efforts of parents during the years when they are both wage-earners and care-givers. The future growth of the economy, the vibrancy of our civic life and culture, and the well-being of the retirees of tomorrow all depend on how well families can manage to do both economically and culturally, as they raise the children who will become the citizens and workers of tomorrow (Adams and Dominick 1995; Leone 1997).

Of course, child-rearing families have *always* been important, so in a sense the current situation is nothing new. But in other ways, the challenges families must meet are greater than ever. In a high-tech, fast-changing economy,

the rearing of children and young people into productive workers and participating community members demands much greater reserves of parental and
institutional support than ever before. Marriages are fragile, however, and
men and women alike face intense demands on the job. So many parents may
actually find it harder to supervise and stimulate children, at the very time that
more, not less, is required for young people to flourish (Garbarino 1995;
Hewlett 1991).

The problems are not just at the level of individual behavior. National culture and public priorities are implicated, too. Right now, America is treating
parental work as a kind of private luxury. Higher incomes and glamorous
freedoms go to individuals who take off on their own or shirk their responsibilities. Workplaces and the economic rules of the game make life hard for
family men and women. Parents thus end up making disproportionate sacrifices—to do the very work of raising children on which we all depend.

In short, if ever there was an era when American working families need
strong social support, this is it. And the people who most require—and deserve—extra support are working parents. They are the ones at the vortex of
today's economic and family transformations. Working parents deserve honor
and support from the nation as a whole, because, under increasingly difficult
conditions, they are doing vital service on which all of us depend, today and
tomorrow.

If a family-oriented politics focusing especially on working parents is the
right strategy, then specific and bold measures would need to be simultaneously advanced in several areas at once. Many of these measures will require
bolder government regulation and the mobilization of greater public resources—there is no getting around that. Adequate family supports must include measures focused on work, family ties, and communities alike. Here are
the goals we must seek to achieve:

- *Make the economy family-friendly:* Parents will make their way for
  themselves and their children through work, so adults must be able to
  find jobs and take advantage of opportunities for education or training.
  All jobs (including part-time positions) must have decent wages and (full
  or partial) health and pension benefits, designed to make family life viable (Sweeney 1996). There must be rights to family leave on terms that
  make it truly available to all employees. And because parents need time
  as well as money, we as a nation should work toward the norm of a
  thirty-five-hour work week (with pay remaining at least at the level it
  was before the reduction in hours).
- *Ensure that every child has sustained contributions from both parents:*
  Taxes, benefits, and marriage rules should encourage married parent-

hood. At the same time, we should recognize that there are many divorced and single parents doing the best they can. If marriages fail, rules about child support should help children and the parent who takes responsibility for them. This means working toward an automatic, nationally coordinated system of minimum-benefit child support that allows a custodial parent to work less than full time and still provide for children. (Such a system, in my view, would also discourage divorce and unmarried parenthood from happening in the first place.)

- *Make communities and institutions safe and supportive for families with children:* Profamily advocates naturally want tough anticrime measures and active steps to make neighborhoods and schools and community facilities safe, clean, and orderly. We want schools that are held to high standards and are able to afford small classes, with administrators and teachers free to innovate. Governments at all levels must have the wherewithal and inspiration to encourage private-sector and voluntary activities to nurture and supervise children—and to honor and support mothers and fathers.

HOW TO DO IT?

I could say more about policy specifics in each of the previous areas. But let me defer for want of space and also because I want to make a point about the democratic political process. Experts can sit in universities or think tanks and outline detailed policy plans. But the results will not be what they intend if there is no popular power to prod Congress to enact measures that will truly make a difference for ordinary families (for a case study of such a failure, see Skocpol 1996a).

A parent-oriented movement today needs to be built up through organization and dialogues across many localities, states, and institutions, before it turns to outlining specific proposals about taxes or regulations or benefits. Successful movements for social support in America's past have always involved broad social movements and voluntary associations (or coordinated networks of associations). The National Parenting Association might ask itself what it could do to create, or take part in the creation, of such a widespread civic effort—an effort directly grounded in actual groups of parents and including local, state, and national meetings where, over time, popularly rooted groups could work out the details of a policy agenda for which real support could be galvanized.

Absent such a widespread, popularly rooted movement, the U.S. political system as it is will simply take specific ideas—such as Bill Galston's tax proposals (see chapter 9)—and twist them into an occasion for yet another set of massive giveaways of potential tax revenues to the very rich. We know perfectly well that this is what happens when Congress "reforms taxes." Another likely result of moving forward without popular involvement would be the evisceration of such shared social supports as the United States already has. "Social Security reforms" might be undertaken in the name of relieving the "payroll tax burden" on working families, only to create massive subsidies for Wall Street brokers and complicated individual market accounts that would, in the end, leave many more working-strata retirees in dire straits—burdening their children and grandchildren in the process. These kinds of twists on well-intentioned profamily proposals have happened again and again, under Republican and Democratic presidents alike. In a polity dominated by elite interest groups and narrow, professionally led advocacy groups, no other result can really be expected. Media campaigns might try to disguise the truth. But on the ground, more tax cuts and further assaults on shared governmental programs like Social Security would make life harder for most parents and children and encourage more broken families in the process.

In short, while I have the greatest respect for the intentions behind the specific policy proposals that Bill Galston outlines, I do not believe he is thinking boldly enough about either the policies or the politics we need to make twenty-first-century America truly family-friendly. If U.S. politics continues down the path of shrinking government and unleashing market forces in the name of "individual choice," the results may be just fine for those of us at the top: we won't have to contribute much to the commonweal through taxes or shared participation, and we will be able to buy the supports and enjoyments we want on private markets. But life will become steadily nastier, more brutish, and less rewarding for everyone else. And American democracy—the possibility of a shared civic community and national governance that buffers market forces and opens doors for the majority—will become but a nice memory from an ever-more-distant past.

There is, in short, no way to revive American democracy now, and no way to move toward adequate and inclusive social supports for parents and children, except by proceeding democratically. Another top-down advocacy campaign for adjustments within a diminishing public sector cannot help to turn the tide.

REFERENCES

Adams, Paul, and Gary L. Dominick (1995). "The Old, the Young, and the Welfare State." *Generations* 19 (3) (Fall): 38–42.

Aldrich, John H. (1995). *Why Parties? The Origin and Transformation of Party Politics in America.* Chicago: University of Chicago Press.

Amenta, Edwin, Bruce G. Carruthers, and Yvonne Zylan (1992). "A Hero for the Aged? The Townsend Movement, the Political Mediation Model, and U.S. Old-Age Policy, 1934–1950," *American Journal of Sociology* 98 (2) (September): 308–39.

Boushey, Heather, et al. (2001). *Hardships in America: The Real Story of Working Families.* Washington, D.C.: Economic Policy Institute.

Bronfenbrenner, Urie, Peter McClelland, Elaine Wethington, Phyllis Moen, and Stephen J. Ceci (1996). *The State of Americans: This Generation and the Next.* New York: Free Press.

Children's Defense Fund (1994). *Wasting America's Future: The Children's Defense Fund Report on the Costs of Child Poverty.* Boston: Beacon Press, 1994.

Covotsos, Louis J. (1976). "Child Welfare and Social Progress: A History of the United States Children's Bureau, 1912–1935." Unpublished Ph.D. dissertation, University of Chicago.

Danziger, Sheldon, and Peter Gottschalk (1995). *America Unequal.* Cambridge, Mass.: Harvard University Press; and New York: Russell Sage Foundation.

Derthick, Martha (1979). *Policymaking for Social Security.* Washington, D.C.: Brookings Institution.

Edsall, Thomas Byrne, and Mary D. Edsall (1991). *Chain Reaction: The Impact of Race, Rights, and Taxes on American Politics.* New York: W. W. Norton.

Emirbayer, Mustafa (1992). "The Shaping of a Virtuous Citizenry: Educational Reform in Massachusetts, 1830–1860." *Studies in American Political Development* 6 (Fall 1992): 391–419.

Frank, Robert H., and Philip J. Cook (1995). *The Winner-Take-All Society.* New York: Free Press.

Ganz, Marshall (1994). "Voters in the Cross-Hairs: How Technology and the Market Are Destroying Politics." *The American Prospect* 5 (December).

Garbarino, James (1995). *Raising Children in a Socially Toxic Environment.* San Francisco, Calif.: Jossey-Bass.

Greenberg, Stanley B. (1996). "The Economy Project." Washington, D.C.: Greenberg Research, January 16.

Heclo, Hugh (1986). "The Political Foundations of Antipoverty Policy." In *Fighting Poverty: What Works and What Doesn't,* ed. Sheldon H. Danziger and Daniel H. Weinberg. Cambridge, Mass.: Harvard University Press, 312–40.

Heidenheimer, Arnold J. (1981). "Education and Social Security Entitlements in Europe and America." In *The Development of Welfare States in Europe and America,* ed. Peter Flora and Arnold J. Heidenheimer. New Brunswick, N.J.: Transaction Books, 269–304.

Hewlett, Sylvia Ann (1991). *When the Bough Breaks: The Cost of Neglecting Our Children.* New York: Harper Collins.

Holtzman, Abraham (1963). *The Townsend Movement: A Political Study.* New York: Bookman.

Judis, John B. (1992). "The Pressure Elite: Inside the Narrow World of Advocacy Group Politics." *The American Prospect* 9 (Spring): 15–29.

Katznelson, Ira, and Margaret Weir (1985). *Schooling for All: Class, Race, and the Decline of the Democratic Ideal.* New York: Basic Books.

Kingson, Eric R., Barbara A. Hirshorn, and John M. Cornman (1986). *Ties That Bind: The Interdependence of Generations.* Washington, D.C.: Seven Locks Press.

Ladd-Taylor, Molly (1986). *Raising a Baby the Government Way: Mothers' Letters to the Children's Bureau, 1915–1932.* New Brunswick, N.J.: Rutgers University Press.

Lawton, Leora, Merrill Silverstein, and Vern L. Bengston (1994). "Solidarity between Generations in Families." In *Intergenerational Linkages,* ed. Vern L. Bengston and Robert A. Harootyan. New York: Springer.

Leff, Mark (1973). "Consensus for Reform: The Mothers' Pension Movement in the Progressive Era." *Social Service Review* 47 (3) (September).

Leone, Richard C. (1997). "Why Boomers Don't Spell Bust." *The American Prospect* 30 (January–February): 68–71.

Marmor, Theodore R. (1973). *The Politics of Medicare.* Chicago, Ill.: Aldine.

McConnell, Stuart Charles (1992). *Glorious Contentment: The Grand Army of the Republic, 1865–1900.* Baltimore, Md.: Johns Hopkins University Press.

McLanahan, Sara, and Gary Sandefur (1994). *Growing Up with a Single Parent: What Hurts, What Helps.* Cambridge, Mass.: Harvard University Press.

Morris, Charles R. (1996). *The AARP.* New York: Times Books.

Mosch, Theodore R. (1975). *The G.I. Bill: A Breakthrough in Educational and Social Policy in the United States.* Hicksville, N.Y.: Exposition Press.

Olson, Keith W. (1974). *The G.I. Bill, the Veterans, and the Colleges.* Lexington, Ky.: University of Kentucky Press.

Paget, Karen M. (1990). "Citizen Organizing: Many Movements, No Majority." *The American Prospect* 2 (Summer): 115–128.

Patterson, James T. (1981). *America's Struggle Against Poverty, 1900–1980.* Cambridge, Mass.: Harvard University Press.

Pencak, William (1989). *For God and Country: The American Legion, 1919–1941.* Boston: Northeastern University Press.

Peterson, Peter G. (1993). *Facing Up: How to Rescue the Economy from Crushing Debt and Restore the American Dream.* New York: Simon and Schuster.

Reich, Robert B. (1991). *The Work of Nations.* New York: Alfred A. Knopf.

—— (1997). "Rebuilding America's Broken Social Compact." *Boston Globe,* January 19, 1997, E7.

Rosenstone, Steven J., Warren E. Miller, Donald R. Kinder, and the National Election Studies (1995). *American National Election Study, 1994: Post-Election Survey.* Ann Arbor, Mich.: Center for Political Studies.

Ross, Davis R. B. (1969). *Preparing for Ulysses: Politics and Veterans During World War II.* New York: Columbia University Press.

Skocpol, Theda (1992). *Protecting Soldiers and Mothers: The Political Origins of Social Policy in the United States.* Cambridge, Mass.: Belknap Press of Harvard University Press.

—— (1996a). *Boomerang: Clinton's Health Security Effort and the Turn Against Government in U.S. Politics.* New York: W. W. Norton.

—— (1996b). "Delivering for Young Families: The Resonance of the G.I. Bill." *The American Prospect* 28 (September–October): 66–72.

—— (1997). "The GI Bill and U.S. Social Policy, Past and Future." *Social Philosophy & Policy* (Summer).

—— (1999). "Advocates without Members: The Recent Transformation of American Civic Life." In *Civic Engagement in American Democracy,* ed. Theda Skocpol and Morris P. Fiorina. Washington, D.C.: Russell Sage Foundation.

Sweeney, John J. (1996). *America Needs a Raise: Fighting for Economic Security and Social Justice.* Boston: Houghton Mifflin.

Tierney, John T. (1992). "Organized Interests and the Nation's Capitol." In *The Politics of Interests: Interest Groups Transformed.* Boulder, Colo.: Westview.

Tyack, David, and Elisabeth Hansot (1982). *Managers of Virtue: Public School Leadership in America, 1820–1980.* New York: Basic Books.

Verba, Sidney, Kay Lehman Schlozman, and Henry E. Brady (1995). *Voice and Equality: Civic Voluntarism in American Politics.* Cambridge: Harvard University Press.

—— (1997). "The Big Tilt: Participatory Inequality in America." *The American Prospect* 12 (May–June): 74–81.

Walker, Jack, Jr. (1991). *Mobilizing Interest Groups in America: Patrons, Professions, and Social Movements.* Ann Arbor: University of Michigan Press.

Weir, Margaret (1992). *Politics and Jobs: The Boundaries of Employment Policy in the United States.* Princeton, N.J.: Princeton University Press.

Wolff, Edward N. (1995). *Top Heavy: A Study of the Increasing Inequality of Wealth in America.* New York: Twentieth Century Fund.

13

The Emerging Fatherhood Movement: Making Room for Daddy

Wade F. Horn

The single biggest social problem in our society may be the growing absence of fathers from their children's homes because it contributes to so many other social problems.

—Bill Clinton, president of the United States, 1995

We have arrived at a consensus that fathers have been lost and must be found.

—Ellen Goodman, syndicated columnist, 1996

Dan Quayle was right.

—Barbara Dafoe Whitehead, *Atlantic Monthly,* 1993

Fatherlessness in America today is an unprecedented reality, with profound consequences for children and civil society. In 1960, the total number of children in the United States living in father-absent families was less than 10 million. Today, that number stands at *24 million.*[1] Nearly one out of three children in America do not live in the same home as their father. By some estimates, this figure is likely to rise to 60 percent of children born in the 1990s.[2] For the first time in our history, the average expectable experience of childhood now includes a significant amount of time living absent one's own father.

Wade F. Horn is assistant secretary for the Administration for Children and Families (ACF) in the U.S. Department of Health and Human Services (HHS). He is the former president of the National Fatherhood Initiative and former commissioner for Children, Youth and Families in HHS. An earlier version of this chapter originally appeared as "Did You Say 'Movement'?" in *The Fatherhood Movement: A Call to Action,* ed. Wade F. Horn, Mitchell Pearlstein, and David Blankenhorn (Lanham, Md.: Lexington, 1999). The views expressed in this chapter do not necessarily represent views of ACF, HHS, or the U.S. government.

For one million children each year, the pathway to a fatherless family is divorce.[3] The divorce rate nearly tripled from 1960 to 1980, before leveling off and declining slightly in the 1980s.[4] Today, 40 out of every 100 first marriages end in divorce, compared to 16 out of every 100 first marriages in 1960. No other industrialized nation has a higher divorce rate.[5]

The second pathway to a fatherless home is out-of-wedlock fathering. In 1960, about 5 percent of all births were out-of-wedlock. That number increased to 10.7 percent in 1970, 18.4 percent in 1980, 28 percent in 1990, and nearly 33 percent today.[6] In the United States, the number of children fathered out-of-wedlock each year (approximately 1.3 million annually) now surpasses the number of children whose parents divorce (approximately 1 million annually).

No region of the country has been immune to the growing problem of fatherlessness. Between 1980 and 1990, nonmarital birth rates increased in every state of the Union.[7] During this time period, ten states saw the rate of nonmarital births increase by over 60 percent. Furthermore, births to unmarried teenagers increased by 44 percent between 1985 and 1992.[8] In fact, 76 percent of all births to teenagers nationwide are now out-of-wedlock. In fifteen of our nation's largest cities, the teenage out-of-wedlock birth rate exceeds 90 percent. Overall, the percentage of families with children headed by a single parent currently stands at 29 percent, the vast majority of which are father-absent households.[9]

African Americans are disproportionately affected by the problem of father absence. Sixty-three percent of African American children live in father-absent homes. But fatherlessness is by no means a problem affecting minorities only. The absolute number of father-absent families is larger—and the rate of father absence is growing the fastest—in the white community. Currently, nearly 13 million white children reside in father-absent homes, compared to 6.5 million African American children.[10]

Research consistently documents that unmarried fathers, whether through divorce or out-of-wedlock fathering, tend over time to become disconnected, both financially and psychologically, from their children. Forty percent of children in father-absent homes have not seen their father in at least a year. Of the remaining 60 percent, only one in five sleeps even one night per month in the father's home. Overall, only one in six sees his or her father an average of once or more per week.[11] More than half of all children who don't live with their fathers have never even been in their father's home.[12]

Unwed fathers are particularly unlikely to stay connected to their children over time. Whereas 57 percent of unwed fathers visit their child at least once per week during the first two years of their child's life, by the time their child reaches seven and one-half years of age, that percentage drops to less than 25 percent.[13] Indeed, approximately 75 percent of men who are not living with their children at the time of their birth never subsequently live with them.[14]

Even when unwed fathers are cohabiting with the mother at the time of their child's birth, they are very unlikely to stay involved in their children's lives over the long term. Although a quarter of nonmarital births occur to cohabiting couples, only four out of ten cohabiting, unwed fathers ever go on to marry the mother of their children, and those who do are more likely to eventually divorce than are men who father children within marriage.[15] Remarriage, or, in cases of an unwed father, marriage to someone other than the child's mother, makes it especially unlikely that a noncustodial father will remain in contact with his children.[16]

The absence of fathers in the home has profound consequences for children. Almost 75 percent of American children living in single-parent families will experience poverty before they turn eleven years old, compared to only 20 percent of children in two-parent families.[17] Children who grow up absent their fathers are also more likely to fail at school or to drop out,[18] experience behavioral or emotional problems requiring psychiatric treatment,[19] engage in early sexual activity,[20] and develop drug and alcohol problems.[21]

Children growing up with absent fathers are especially likely to experience violence. Violent criminals are overwhelmingly males who grew up without fathers, including up to 60 percent of rapists,[22] 72 percent of adolescents charged with murder,[23] and 70 percent of juveniles in state reform institutions.[24] Children who grow up without fathers are also three times more likely to commit suicide as adolescents[25] and to be victims of child abuse or neglect.[26]

In light of these data, Urie Bronfenbrenner, noted developmental psychologist, has concluded:

> Controlling for factors such as low income, children growing up in [father-absent] households are at a greater risk for experiencing a variety of behavioral and educational problems, including extremes of hyperactivity and withdrawal; lack of attentiveness in the classroom; difficulty in deferring gratification; impaired academic achievement; school misbehavior; absenteeism; dropping out; involvement in socially alienated peer groups, and the so-called "teenage syndrome" of behaviors that tend to hang together—smoking, drinking, early and frequent sexual experience, and in the more extreme cases, drugs, suicide, vandalism, violence, and criminal acts.[27]

If ever there was a problem in need of a broad-based social movement, it is this one, for the evidence suggests that we can expect little improvement in the well-being of either our children or our communities without a restoration of responsible and committed fatherhood as a valued, respected, and widely practiced institution. In short, if a fatherhood movement does not yet exist, someone better start one.

CHARACTERISTICS OF A SOCIAL MOVEMENT

A social movement has been defined by sociologist John Wilson as a "conscious, collective, organized attempt to bring about or resist large-scale change in the social order by noninstitutionalized means."[28] Social movements are important because they frequently are the means through which new ideas and practices enter the social fabric. Indeed, the very appearance of a social movement is a sign that the old social order is being challenged.

Social movements typically view existing institutional structures as part of the problem and hence unlikely avenues for achieving social change. Social movements have broad goals and incorporate diverse groups of people as they seek to affect not just their own constituency, but society as a whole.

Social movements do not emerge or succeed by accident. Although they may capitalize on fortuitous events to further their goals, their founding is purposive and their activities transcend the vagaries of day-to-day events. In this way, they are different from temporary coalitions or mere aggregate action.

Successful social movements frequently go through a three-stage developmental process. The first stage is the setting of an agenda, during which the problem is defined and given urgency. Sometimes, this occurs through the appearance of an influential book. The modern environmental movement was, for example, largely triggered by the publication in 1962 of Rachel Carson's book *Silent Spring*. Alternatively, a social movement may have its agenda set by a major speech, a focusing conference, or even a television program. Some, for example, credit the airing of a 1990 Bill Moyers television special "A Gathering of Men" for kick-starting a modern men's movement.

This does not mean, of course, that there were no organizations or individuals working on behalf of the issue prior to the birth of a social movement. All social movements have roots that predate themselves. For example, as pointed out by noted columnist William Raspberry,

> Every single element of what was to become the Civil Rights Movement was already being carried out by someone, somewhere. Before there was a movement there were voter registration drives, demonstrations against segregated parks and swimming pools, attempts to desegregate residential areas, restaurants and other places of public accommodation.[29]

What defines the birth of a social movement, therefore, is that the disparate activities of various organizations and individuals are, for the first time, brought together under one overarching philosophical or organizational umbrella. In doing so, the movement is able to heighten the public's awareness of the issue in ways that no single group or individual would have been able to achieve, while at the same time giving new significance and power to the various organizations and individuals comprising the movement. In other words, with the birth of a movement, the total becomes greater than sum of the parts.

The second stage is recruitment of members from outside the initial group of originators. These members are recruited by various groups, whether formally or informally. Most successful movements do not draw their members using one charismatic leader, for when membership recruitment is too reliant on the activities of an individual, gathering converts is likely to be slow or highly episodic. Instead, the most successful social movements are those that develop more generalized strategies for membership recruitment, thereby enhancing their reach. The nineteenth-century temperance movement, for example, developed the strategy of convening revival-style gatherings to encourage individuals to take a pledge of abstinence as a signal of their allegiance to the temperance movement. In fact, over-identification of a single leader with a cause can be one distinguishing feature between a social movement and a cult or fad.

The third stage is the development of organizational structures capable of sustaining the movement. In some cases, one preeminent organization emerges, serving as the main vehicle for coordinating the movement and communicating its message. In other cases, several relatively autonomous organizations emerge, but with each dedicated to an overarching goal. As the movement progresses, the development of local chapters helps sustain it and nurture new leaders.

Given this understanding of social movements, is there a fatherhood movement?

THE BIRTH OF A MOVEMENT

If there is a fatherhood movement, one of its early stirrings revolves around thirty-nine words delivered by a public figure widely perceived at the time as an intellectual lightweight—Vice President Dan Quayle. While campaigning for reelection, Dan Quayle made a speech on May 19, 1992, at the Commonwealth Club of California in San Francisco, during which he asserted: "It doesn't help matters, when prime time TV has Murphy Brown—a character who supposedly epitomizes today's intelligent, highly paid, professional woman—mocking the importance of fathers, by bearing a child alone, and calling it just another 'lifestyle choice.'"

The importance of this event was not that Dan Quayle himself went on to lead, or even propose the formation of, a fatherhood movement. In fact, prior to Quayle's speech, several national commissions, including the National

Commission on Children and the National Commission on Urban Families, had already concluded that father absence was one of the most significant problems facing America. Rather, the importance of the Quayle speech was that it galvanized others to come to the defense, if not of him, at least of the larger point he was trying to make—that fathers matter to the well-being of children and that society experiments with father absence at its peril. His speech was not the creative moment but rather the defining moment.

One of the first spirited defenses of Quayle's point was the appearance in the _Atlantic Monthly_ magazine of an influential article by Barbara Dafoe Whitehead entitled "Dan Quayle Was Right." In this article, Whitehead laments that "every time the issue of family structure has been raised, the response has been first controversy, then retreat, and finally silence." Undaunted, she continues:

> The debate . . . is not simply about the social-scientific evidence, although that is surely an important part of the discussion. It is also a debate over deeply held and often conflicting values. How do we begin to reconcile our long-standing belief in equality and diversity with an impressive body of evidence that suggests that not all family structures produce equal outcomes for children? . . . How do we uphold the freedom of adults to pursue individual happiness in their private relationships and at the same time respond to the needs of children for stability, security, and permanence in their family lives?[30]

The themes laid out in Whitehead's article were further refined and expanded in a series of compelling articles and books, including _Life without Father_ (1996) by David Popenoe; _New Expectations: Community Strategies for Responsible Fatherhood_ (1995) by James Levine and Edward Pitt; _FatherLove_ (1993) by Richard Louv; "Marriage in America: A Report to the Nation" (1996) by the Council on Families; and, most especially, _Fatherless America: Confronting Our Most Urgent Social Problem_ (1995) by David Blankenhorn. These writings, in turn, spawned a renewed interest in programmatic activity on the fatherhood issue, including skill-building programs, outreach programs for unwed fathers, the development of public service announcements, and legislative advocacy. In fact, the most compelling evidence for an emerging fatherhood movement is the dramatic increase in the number of books and programs, both secular and sectarian, addressing fatherhood that have appeared over the past several years. In just a few short years, fatherhood has grown from a topic worthy of derision to an important and legitimate subject for serious journalists, social commentators, philanthropists, and social programmers.

But to be considered a social movement, the fatherhood issue must be more than a collection of disparate activities—more than a search for new knowledge about the institution of fatherhood, seminars to increase the skills of fathers, or the pursuit of legislative victories for divorced and unwed fathers. To be considered a social movement, there must, at a minimum, be evidence of a purposive, collective effort to organize under a single theme, and, in doing so, to seek broad social change.

On this score, there is evidence that we are witnessing, if not the actual birth, then at least the labor pains, of a fatherhood movement. Increasingly, fatherhood advocates, researchers, analysts, and programmers are coming together to seek common cause. Although these leaders and organizations certainly maintain a primary interest in their own activities and agenda, increasingly there is a sense that each is a part of a larger whole—that the work of each is contributing to a greater social good. Despite widely divergent perspectives on the causes of and strategies for overcoming fatherlessness, leaders in the fatherhood arena are demonstrating an increasing willingness to put aside their differences in the pursuit of a common goal—ensuring that an increasing proportion of children grows up with an involved, committed, and responsible father.

Probably the earliest manifestation of this desire to seek common cause under the fatherhood banner was the convening of the first-ever National Summit on Fatherhood in Dallas, Texas, in October 1994.[31] Hosted by the newly formed National Fatherhood Initiative, an organization for which I was the former president, this gathering attracted over two hundred fatherhood advocates, researchers, and public policy analysts, along with fathers' rights advocates, fathering-education and skill-building experts, advocates for low-income fathers, and religious leaders involved in fatherhood promotion. Other gatherings followed, including the formation by the philanthropic community in 1995 of the Funders Collaborative on Fathers and Families; a 1995 Father's Day gathering in the District of Columbia of major fatherhood activists; an Interfaith Summit on Fatherhood in June 1996; statewide, governor-sponsored fatherhood conferences in California (1995), Massachusetts (1996), Indiana (1996 and 1997), and South Carolina (1997); and a conference on the fatherhood movement in 1996 in Minneapolis, Minnesota, that resulted in a book, *The Fatherhood Movement: A Call to Action.*

THE ELEMENTS NEEDED

A bona fide movement requires more than simply a series of meetings and conferences. It also requires sufficient ideas, numbers, distinctiveness, and organization. The answer to the question of whether or not the fatherhood movement has these qualities is, at best, maybe.

The fatherhood movement certainly has no paucity of ideas. Everyone involved in the fatherhood issue believes passionately in his or her own perspective and idiosyncratic agenda. Religiously oriented advocates believe that fatherhood is part of God's plan, without recognition of which the institution of fatherhood will not be recovered. Fathers' rights advocates consider the current focus on deadbeat dads inaccurate and counterproductive and lobby for divorce and child custody reforms. Advocates for low-income men believe that poor economic circumstances are a primary cause of fatherlessness and see the solution in job training and education programs for disadvantaged and minority men. Culturalists believe that fatherlessness is a failure of our culture to reinforce a compelling fatherhood script and seek the definition of one. Marriage advocates believe that only a restoration of the institution of marriage will lead to a renewal of fatherhood. The list of ideas concerning the nature of fatherhood and the cure for father absence goes on and on.

Is There a Core Idea?

But for a social movement to survive, it must eventually coalesce around a single, core idea, while at the same time respecting diversity of opinion. This is, perhaps, the most immediate challenge facing the nascent fatherhood movement. It will require achieving a delicate balance between having a set of firmly held beliefs and accommodating a diversity of viewpoints. If, on the one hand, the movement is too rigid and uncompromising, it will have difficulty attracting followers and building momentum. If, on the other, the movement is overly accommodating to differing opinions, it will have difficulty sustaining an energized, passionate, and committed leadership and communicating a clear and unambiguous message to the public at large.

So, if there is a fatherhood movement, what is its core idea around which its member organizations can coalesce? Although there is certainly room for legitimate debate on what the core idea ought to be, here is my candidate: Every child deserves the love, support, and nurturance of a legally and morally responsible father. This core idea is based on three assumptions: (1) responsible and committed fatherhood ought to be a norm of masculinity; (2) fathers are different from mothers in important ways; and (3) the father–child bond is important to the healthy development of children.

But social movements are not just about establishing a core idea or mere consciousness raising. They are about changing behavior. Abolitionists in the nineteenth century were not content with having the public agree with them that slavery was wrong; they wanted it abolished. The temperance movement was not content with the public agreeing that alcoholic beverages, and especially "hard" liquor, were bad for one's moral and physical health; it wanted alcohol consumption dramatically reduced, if not stopped. So, too, the fatherhood movement cannot be about getting the public to agree that fathers are "good"; it must be about changing the behavior of men and women to ensure that a greater proportion of children grow up with involved fathers. This goal requires that the movement settle on at least the broad outlines of an agenda for social change.

But if achieving agreement on a core message is difficult, attaining consensus on an overarching agenda for achieving broad social change will be even more difficult. Will, for example, the divorced men's groups be able to reconcile their agenda to improve access of divorced and noncustodial fathers to their children with the agenda of those who seek greater accountability from noncustodial fathers through stronger child support enforcement? Will organizations dedicated to advancing the interests of noncustodial, unwed fathers be able to coalesce with a movement that also includes advocates for stronger statutory rape laws? And will those organizations that advocate marriage as the institution most likely to deliver fathers to children be able to coalesce with those that seek greater involvement of noncustodial fathers in the lives of children?

The answers to these questions are by no means clear. But social movements succeed only when its member groups, while still pursuing their own individual agenda, see themselves within a larger context. The alternative is a return to focusing on the parts, at the expense of the whole. If this happens, the nascent movement will surely be stillborn.

Is There Broad Appeal?

There do seem to be signs of a developing grassroots dimension to the fatherhood issue. For a time in the mid- to late 1990s, Promise Keepers, an evangelical Christian enterprise seeking, in part, to inspire men to be better husbands and fathers, routinely drew tens of thousands of devotees to football stadiums across the nation. Similarly, the Million Man March in the summer of 1995 drew over a half million African American men and their sons to the nation's capital. The message from these gatherings that fathers matter certainly does seem to have some resonance with the general public. What is still needed is a means for converting grassroots participation in these special events into mass identification with the core message and agenda of a fatherhood movement.

Thus far, this goal is unmet, primarily because the sponsoring organizations of these special events emphasize other issues in addition to fatherhood. Promise Keepers encourages not only responsible fatherhood, but also, and more centrally, reconciliation with God and the acceptance of Jesus Christ as one's personal savior. Speakers at the Million Man March organized by Louis Farrakhan preached not only the importance of responsible fatherhood, but also the need to organize politically to thwart the plans of a Republican-led Congress to downsize the federal government. Certainly, it is legitimate for these organizations to have a broader agenda than fatherhood. But doing so dilutes the fatherhood message at these gatherings and makes it harder to develop grassroots support specific to and identified with a fatherhood movement.

In addition to developing a strategy for greater identification of the grass roots with a common core message and agenda, the emerging fatherhood movement must also find ways to broaden its appeal beyond its natural constituency of men. Historically, many successful social movements found creative ways of forging coalitions with other organizations and constituencies. The abolition movement was able to forge an alliance with pro-union sentiments in its battle against slavery. Similarly, the women's movement creatively found connections with fathers of daughters in its pursuit of equal rights for women. So, too, the fatherhood movement will need to garner the active support of women and women's organizations if it is to be successful.

Is It Distinctive?

While the fatherhood movement has a number of historical roots, including the men's, fathers' rights, civil rights, and mythopoetic movements, it is distinct from these movements in a number of critical ways. First, the men's, fathers' rights, and mythopoetic movements tend to be inner-directed (toward the feelings, needs, and well-being of men and fathers), whereas the fatherhood movement is largely other-directed (toward the feelings, needs, and well-being of children). These former movements also tend to be focused on the "rights" of men and fathers, whereas the fatherhood movement is largely focused on the "responsibilities" of fathers. Thus, the fatherhood movement does not appear to be merely a branch of some other men's movement.[32]

A more crucial issue is whether or not the fatherhood movement is distinct from a marriage movement. Many people argue that fatherhood and marriage go hand in hand. One can not have the former, they argue, without first having the latter. Indeed, some even argue that, ultimately, the fatherhood movement's importance lies in its being a "stalking horse" for a marriage movement. If these critics are correct, there is no fatherhood movement; only the stirrings of a marriage movement. If so, some groups and leaders currently seeking to help establish a fatherhood movement will surely splinter away. In fact, we are already seeing the marriage issue develop into a dividing line within the fatherhood movement. Resolution of this issue is, therefore, one of the most critical challenges facing the fatherhood movement.

Is There Organizational Structure?

The establishment of a number of national fatherhood groups over the past several years, including the National Fatherhood Initiative, the National Center for Fathers and Families, the National Institute for Responsible Fatherhood and Family Revitalization, and the National Center for Fathering, suggests that the rough outlines of a movement "infrastructure" are starting to emerge. Although there is an attempt by a group of private philanthropic foundations to nurture and organize the fatherhood "field," thus far the chief organizational features of the emerging fatherhood movement are decentralization and specialization, not centralization and hierarchical command-and-control. Some fatherhood groups specialize in increasing public awareness, others in teaching fathering skills, others in stimulating research, and still others in public advocacy. No one national fatherhood group commands the allegiance or deference of any other.

Given this penchant toward specialized and decentralized organizational structures, it seems unlikely that the fatherhood movement will galvanize around a single organization, akin to the way the women's movement coalesced around the National Organization for Women. Instead, it appears likely that the fatherhood movement will function through a broad array of like-minded, and often specialized, organizations, similar to what has developed within the environmental movement.

The lack of a centralized organizational structure creates certain advantages for movement making, including a more flexible, diverse, and pluralistic movement; less reliance on any one leader or small group of leaders; and the ability to try different approaches and solutions. But a decentralized organizational structure also creates certain disadvantages. First, it makes the clarification of a core message all the more crucial, without which the movement may simply become an ever shifting series of temporary alliances among the various member organizations. Second, it makes it harder for member organizations to move beyond their idiosyncratic agendas and embrace a common overarching agenda for achieving social change. Third, it makes it more difficult for the grass roots to identify primarily with the broader fatherhood movement, as opposed to the parochial interests of a single organization. Still, as evidenced by the success of the environmental movement, it is an organizational structure that can work. But it does make movement building more difficult.

THE MEASUREMENT FOR SUCCESS

One key issue for all social movements is how to measure success. One possible measure is the degree to which the movement is able to increase public awareness of the importance of fathers to the well-being of children. Progress toward this goal could easily be measured through public opinion surveys. There are, in fact, indications that an increasing majority of Americans view father absence as the most significant social problem of our time. But while attitudinal change is helpful, it is not sufficient. Enhancing public awareness of the fatherhood problem does not guarantee that an increasing proportion of children will grow up with an involved, committed, and responsible father. In fact, numerous psychological and sociological studies indicate that while attitudinal change is frequently a precursor of behavior change, it is neither necessary nor sufficient.

Another possible measure is whether or not the number of children living with their biological fathers has increased. On the surface, this goal seems self-evident. If the problem is father absence, the solution must be father presence. As such, one could assess the success of the fatherhood movement by declining divorce and out-of-wedlock birth rates. But while reversing the historically high divorce and out-of-wedlock birth rates would logically reduce fatherlessness, father presence alone is not sufficient as the goal of the fatherhood movement. For a father to have a positive impact on the development of his children, he must not only be present, he must be involved. It is only when fathers are engaged in the lives of their children, not just as co-residents, but as nurturers, disciplinarians, teachers, coaches, and moral instructors, that their children evidence greater self-esteem, higher educational achievement, a more secure gender identity, and greater success in life. If the present father is, in actuality, psychologically and morally absent, or worse still, abusive, his presence may well make things worse, not better, for children.

Ultimately, though, I believe the most important outcome measure for a fatherhood movement is improvement in the well-being of children. As such, increasing father presence is really an intervening or process variable, one that may or may not improve the true outcome measure of interest: the well-being of children. Focusing on improving the status of children as the goal for the fatherhood movement holds the best promise for achieving a broad-based coalition of both men and women dedicated to revitalizing responsible and committed fatherhood as a respected and valued social institution.

Promoting fatherhood, then, is really a strategy for improving the well-being of children, just as promoting abstinence from alcohol was really a strategy for promoting civic virtue through moderation. In fact, an interest in improving the well-being of children is the entire rationale for the fatherhood movement, for if father absence did not increase the risk of poor outcomes for children, there would be no need for a fatherhood movement. If, in the end, increasing the proportion of children growing up with fathers does not enhance child well-being, the fatherhood movement ought to be judged a failure, and we all ought to move on to something else.

A MOVEMENT ENEMY

A final issue is whether or not the fatherhood movement needs an enemy — an opposition against which the troops can be energized. Abolitionists railed against the evils of slavery; the temperance movement against demon alcohol. What should fatherhood advocates rail against?

Some are tempted to designate absent fathers as the "enemy." Certainly, there are too many men who desert and abandon their families, and such men ought to be ostracized. But designating absent fathers as the bogeyman will undoubtedly alienate one potentially important constituency of the fatherhood movement: divorced fathers. Indeed, with a good measure of truth, divorced fathers frequently contend that they very much want to remain actively involved in the lives of their children but are prevented from doing so by a court system that treats them like "cash machines" and ex-wives who deny them access to their children. Unless the fatherhood movement is ready to write off this constituency—and some appear willing to do so—it designates absent fathers as the "enemy" at its peril.

Others assert that the enemy is feminism. But a fatherhood movement that seeks simply to turn back the hands of time to an earlier period when men were patriarchs and feminists were rare will surely fail. It is only by forging a movement that seeks a revitalization of fatherhood within a modern understanding of the enhanced choices, rights, and prerogatives of women that the fatherhood movement has a chance to succeed.

If an enemy there need be, here is my candidate: family relativism—the notion that all family structures are morally and socially equivalent, all equally deserving of support, and all equally good for children. Elevating family relativism to "bogeyman" status does not mean that one has to demean other family structures. One can assert that children do best when they are reared with the love and commitment of a mother and a father, bound in marriage and dedicated to each other, and still demonstrate compassion for the fatherless and provide support for widowed and abandoned mothers. But the argument must be made—frequently and with great passion—that society needs a critical mass of married two-parent families, both to raise their own children well and to serve as models for children growing up in alternative family structures.

Tragically, we are in great danger today of losing that critical mass; in some communities it has already been lost. Whatever else it does, the fatherhood movement must be, in large measure, about reclaiming that critical mass.

A WORK IN PROGRESS

For those who seek a fatherhood movement, there is evidence of one in the making. Delicate, certainly. Ill-formed, of course. In need of definition, yes. But a movement nonetheless. Its leadership is clearly committed to effecting broad-based social change, and it does seem to have sufficient ideas and a growing grassroots presence. Furthermore, the rough outlines of an organizational structure are appearing—although no one organization appears likely to emerge to lead it.

But pivotal issues remain. Can the movement achieve consensus on a common core message and, even more important, on a core agenda for achieving social change, without undue fragmentation and splintering of its member organizations? Can effective grassroots supporters be cultivated who will identify with the core message and agenda of the movement? Will the highly decentralized organizational structure that seems to be emerging serve the fatherhood movement well, or will it increase the pressure toward fragmentation? Is the fatherhood movement really only a stalking horse for a marriage movement?

Given the uncertain resolution of these questions, perhaps it is best to consider the fatherhood movement a work in progress. But important work it surely is. Let us get on with that work.

NOTES

1. Wade F. Horn, *Father Facts,* 3rd ed. (Gaithersburg, Md.: National Fatherhood Initiative, 1998).

2. Frank F. Furstenberg, Jr., and Andrew J. Cherlin, *Divided Families: What Happens to Children When Parents Part* (Cambridge, Mass.: Harvard University Press, 1991).

3. U.S. Bureau of the Census, *Statistical Abstracts of the United States 1997* (Washington, D.C.: U.S. Government Printing Office, 1997).

4. U.S. Department of Commerce, Bureau of the Census, *Statistical Abstract of the United States, 1993* (Washington, D.C.: Government Printing Office, 1993).

5. National Commission on Children, "Just the Facts: A Summary of Recent Information on America's Children and Their Families" (Washington, D.C.: U.S. Government Printing Office, 1993).

6. Harry M. Rosenberg, Stephanie J. Ventura, Jeffrey D. Maurer, Robert L. Heuser, and Mary Freedman, *Births and Deaths in the United States, 1995,* Monthly Vital Statistics Report 45 (1996).

7. Stephanie J. Ventura et al., "The Demography of Out-of-Wedlock Childbearing," in U.S. Department of Health and Human Services, National Center for Health Statistics, "Report to Congress on Out-of-Wedlock Childbearing," DHHS Pub. no. (PHS) 95-1257 (Washington, D.C.: U.S. Government Printing Office, 1995), 105.

8. *Kids Count Data Book: State Profiles of Child Well-Being* (Baltimore, Md.: Annie E. Casey Foundation, 1995), 125.

9. *Kids Count Data Book,* 125.

10. U.S. House of Representatives, Committee on Ways and Means, "1993 Green Book" (Washington, D.C.: U.S. Government Printing Office, 1993); Arlene Saluter, U.S. Department of Commerce, Bureau of the Census, "Marital Status and Living Arrangements: March 1993," Current Population Reports: Population Characteristics P20-478 (Washington, D.C.: U.S. Government Printing Office, 1994); Stacy Furudawa, U.S. Department of Commerce, Bureau of the Census, "Diverse Living Arrangements of Children: Summer 1991," Current Population Reports: Household Economic Studies (Washington, D.C.: U.S. Government Printing Office, 1994).

11. Frank F. Furstenberg, Jr., and Christine Winquist Nord, "Parenting Apart: Patterns of Child Rearing after Marital Disruption," *Journal of Marriage and the Family* (November 1985): 896.

12. Furstenberg and Cherlin, *Divided Families: What Happens to Children When Parents Part.*

13. Robert Lerman and Theodora Ooms, *Young Unwed Fathers: Changing Roles and Emerging Policies* (Philadelphia, Pa.: Temple University Press, 1993), 45.

14. Lerman and Ooms, *Young Unwed Fathers,* 45.

15. Kristin A. Moore, "Nonmarital Childbearing in the United States," in U.S. Department of Health and Human Services, "Report to Congress on Out-of-Wedlock Childbearing," DHHS Pub. no. (PHS) 95-1257 (Washington, D.C.: U.S. Government Printing Office, 1995), vii.

16. Linda S. Stephens, "Will Johnny See Daddy This Week?" *Journal of Family Issues* 17 (1996): 466–94.

17. National Commission on Children, "Just the Facts: A Summary of Recent Information on America's Children and Their Families" (Washington, D.C.: U.S. Government Printing Office, 1993).

18. Debra Dawson, "Family Structure and Children's Well-Being: Data from the 1988 National Health Survey," *Journal of Marriage and Family* 53 (1991); U.S. Department of Health and Human Services, National Center for Health Statistics, "Survey of Child Health," (Washington, D.C.: U.S. Government Printing Office, 1993).

19. U.S. Department of Health and Human Services, National Center for Health Statistics, "National Health Interview Survey" (Hyattsville, Md.: U.S. Government Printing Office, 1988).

20. Irwin Garfinkel and Sara McLanahan, *Single Mothers and Their Children* (Washington, D.C.: Urban Institute Press, 1986); Susan Newcomer and J. Richard Udry, "Parental Marital Status Effects on Adolescent Sexual Behavior," *Journal of Marriage and the Family* (May 1987): 235–40.

21. U.S. Department of Health and Human Services, National Center for Health Statistics, "Survey on Child Health" (Washington, D.C.: U.S. Government Printing Office, 1993).

22. Nicholas Davidson, "Life without Father," *Policy Review* (1990).

23. Dewey Cornell et al., "Characteristics of Adolescents Charged with Homicide," *Behavioral Sciences and the Law* 5 (1987): 11–23.

24. M. Eileen Matlock et al., "Family Correlates of Social Skills Deficits in Incarcerated and Nonincarcerated Adolescents," *Adolescence* 29 (1994): 119–30.

25. Patricia L. McCall and Kenneth C. Land, "Trends in White Male Adolescent, Young-Adults and Elderly Suicide: Are There Common Underlying Structural Factors?" *Social Science Research* 23 (1994): 57–81; U.S. Department of Health and Human Services, National Center for Health Statistics, "Survey on Child Health" (Washington, D.C.: U.S. Government Printing Office, 1993).

26. Catherine M. Malkin and Michael E. Lamb, "Child Maltreatment: A Test of Sociobiological Theory," *Journal of Comparative Family Studies* 25 (1994): 121–30.

27. Urie Bronfenbrenner, "What Do Families Do?" *Family Affairs* (Winter/Spring 1991): 1–6.

28. John Wilson, *Introduction to Social Movements* (New York: Basic Books, 1973).

29. William Raspberry, "Start with the Boys," *Washington Post,* April 19, 1996.

30. Barbara Dafoe Whitehead, "Dan Quayle Was Right," *Atlantic Monthly* (April 1993): 47–48.

31. One might argue that Vice President Al Gore's meeting in Nashville, Tennessee, in July 1994 was the first fatherhood gathering. Initially, that conference was to focus on fatherhood. As planning progressed, however, the focus changed from "fatherhood" to "male involvement," reflecting just how politically sensitive the topic of fatherhood was at the time. But encouraging *male* involvement in the lives of children is quite different from encouraging *father* involvement. Hence, Vice President Al Gore's meeting may have been an important precursor to the fatherhood movement, but its broader focus argues against portraying it as the initiating event of a fatherhood movement.

32. In its emphasis on responsibilities over rights, the fatherhood movement appears to be distinct not only from the men's and fathers' rights movements, but from many modern social movements as well. In fact, most large-scale social movements in the twentieth century have mostly to do with expanding the rights of a designated group, whether that group be minorities, women, or homosexuals. It remains to be seen whether or not the fatherhood movement's emphasis on personal responsibility and obligation to others will resonate with a culture more accustomed to calls for expanded rights.

14

The Parent Vote

Nancy Rankin

When the curtains close on the voting booths in coming elections, the deciding ballots could be in the hands of the nation's 63 million parents. Parents—including both mothers and fathers—have not been seen as a voting bloc by pollsters, press, and politicians. In an era of niche market politics, the American public is sliced and diced into slivers that candidates court with narrow appeals. We hear about suburban soccer moms and Joe six-pack, stay-at-home mothers and the Christian right, African American men and working women. Few have thought to look at whether there are issues that could unite a broad swath of the population because of their fundamental common interests *as parents*. Are moms and dads simply too divided by gender, race, income, and where they live to agree on problems, much less solutions? Or, like seniors, a similarly diverse group, could parents become a powerful voice that politicians heed?

The National Parenting Association has investigated the potential for parents to emerge as a voting bloc through a series of national surveys and focus groups. We thought it was important to understand what's on the minds of our nation's parents these days. What are their daily struggles? Are parents pretty much agreed or hopelessly fragmented on proposals to tackle major issues that concern them and their children? What do parents say should be the president's top priority? Do they think the politicians are paying attention to them? And when they decide among the candidates, how

Nancy Rankin is past executive director of the National Parenting Association and prior to that, director of research and programs. This chapter is based on survey research she directed with Ruth Wooden and Peggy Shiller of the NPA and conducted by Craig Charney of Charney Research. The September 2000 focus groups on voter identity were facilitated for the NPA by Margaret Mark.

does parenthood figure in among their other voter group identities, like race, gender, or income level?

To learn the answers, the National Parenting Association commissioned Charney Research to update our landmark 1996 research *What Will Parents Vote For?* with two national polls. Telephone interviews were conducted with 650 parents in late January and early February 2000 and with another sample of 550 parents and a comparison group of 200 nonparents in mid-September 2000.[1]

What we found in our January poll was that despite an unprecedented span of prosperity and dramatic drops in crime, parents are more worried now than four years ago about threats of violence and drugs, educating their kids, instilling values, and managing the time demands of both family and work. We also found lots of agreement among parents, with strong across-the-board support for a host of practical measures to keep guns away from kids, improve public schools, relieve the time crunch, and ease the economic burdens on young, low-income parents that make work-family stresses even tougher for them. Seven out of ten parents, regardless of gender, race, income, and, to a great extent, party, favor proposals that could emerge as a cross-cutting parents' agenda (see table 14.1).

Not only do mothers and fathers express substantial agreement, but they also differ in their political priorities from nonparents. In our September 2000 poll, we compared parents to a random sample of Americans without dependent children. Parents are much more likely to say "improving public schools" should be the president's top priority (28 percent) than tax cuts (19 percent), whereas nonparents rank tax cuts over education by 31 percent to 19 percent—almost exactly the reverse.

While it is hardly surprising that parents put education at the top of their political agenda, it is striking that they also agree on what they want the federal government to do to about it. Parents clearly see more and better teachers linked to accountability for higher standards as the key to improving public schools (see table 14.7).

On education as well as other issues, parents think that government *could* address their concerns—four out of five say that government can do a great deal or at least something—but less than half (46 percent) say that government is responding, a six point decline since this same question was asked in 1996. And nearly two-thirds (64 percent) of parents now believe that public officials "do not care much about what parents like me think"—up seven points from our earlier survey. It's not that parents think government cannot offer solutions, it's that they think no one is listening. In fact, this is one area where parents and nonparents agree. Despite all the political rhetoric devoted to "family values" by the Republicans and to "working families" by the Democrats in the 2000 elections, few thought that either party listened more to parents compared to the voices of campaign contributors, business, and union members.

WHAT DO PARENTS WANT?

Relief from the Time Crunch. The good news from our research is that employers—particularly in today's tight labor market—have begun to respond to the realities of contemporary family life. The majority of working parents now report that they have some flexibility on the job:

- Sixty-nine percent of working parents say they can work fewer hours regularly if family needs require it.
- Sixty-seven percent say they can work flexible hours—for example, starting earlier or later than normal working hours—and nearly half of working parents are currently doing so.

Most parents say it would not hurt their careers if they told their boss they need more time for their children, by a margin of 65 percent to 27 percent—a finding that is both surprising and heartening. After years of advocacy on the need for family-friendly work practices, attitudes are starting to change.

The bad news is that the shifts we see do not go nearly far enough or reach widely enough to solve the time crunch confronting working parents. When asked, "What is the biggest daily challenge you face as a parent?" the single most frequent response was balancing work and family. Thirty percent of parents—strikingly, the same percentage among fathers as mothers—said work-family balance was their greatest challenge. Clearly, this is no longer just a women's issue. William Thompson, a father we spoke to from Plain City, Ohio, put it like this, "Absolutely, it's an issue for fathers. Professionally and personally, work-family balance is the biggest issue I struggle with."

Among parents working full time, four out of ten cited "balancing work and family" as their toughest daily challenge—twice as many gave this response as the next oft-mentioned concern, "instilling moral values." The work-family time crunch looms large in parents' lives, and it is getting worse. In response to an open-ended question about their greatest worries, 19 percent of parents spontaneously mentioned coping with work and family and having time for their kids, up significantly from 6 percent four years ago.

For working parents, the lack of time for family and self is reaching crisis proportions. Moms working full time are especially overburdened. Nearly four-fifths of them don't have enough time for themselves and almost half say they lack enough time for their kids.

Table 14.1. Parents' Agreement on Issues Crosses All Boundaries: Gender, Race,

		Gender		Race		
Issues	All Parents %	Men %	Women %	White %	Black %	Hispanic %
GUNS						
Require trigger locks or safety devices	88	85	92	87	99	89
License/register all gun owners	84	80	88	83	88	86
Raise age of possession	82	79	85	82	88	83
EDUCATION						
Tax breaks for higher education	89	86	91	89	87	91
Federal funds for school construction and repair	85	81	88	84	88	88
Universal early childhood education	81	81	81	80	90	85
WORK-FAMILY						
Tax incentives to encourage family-friendly policies	90	88	91	91	85	88
Law to ensure 24 hours paid leave	84	80	87	83	94	88
HEALTH INSURANCE						
Health insurance for every child	88	83	93	88	90	93

Source: National Parenting Association, *What Will Parents Vote For? Update 2000,* May 2000.

While helpful, the transition we are beginning to see in the workplace does not reach everyone. Our data show that the folks left out tend to be lower-income and younger parents—precisely those who need help the most. Thirty percent of parents with family incomes over $60,000 a year, compared to only 6 percent of parents with incomes under $20,000, work for firms that rank high on an index measuring the availability of family-friendly options. Par-

Party, and Income (Percent Strongly Favor or Somewhat Favor)

Party			Family Income			Own Guns	
Dem. %	Ind. %	Rep. %	Under $20,000 %	$20,000–$60,000 %	Over $60,000 %	Yes %	No %
93	89	83	95	91	84	82	92
83	86	81	89	84	80	68	93
82	86	80	86	81	82	75	87
86	91	88	89	90	86		
84	87	81	92	86	80		
89	85	69	89	83	74		
92	89	89	92	90	90		
89	86	77	93	86	81		
90	90	82	94	93	78		

ents under age thirty-five, who generally have younger children, are also less likely to have on-the-job flexibility.

Apart from limited child-care subsidies and the passage of the Family and Medical Leave Act (FMLA) of 1993, the government has not done much to address the time bind squeezing today's families. The FMLA guaranteed that new parents could have twelve weeks of job-protected leave, but time off is

Table 14.2. Parties' Response to Interest Groups

Q. 9: To which of the following groups do you think Republicans listen most? (Read list, rotate start point.)			Q. 10: To which of the following groups do you think Democrats listen most? (Read list, rotate start point.)		
Republicans listen most to . . .	Parents	Nonparents	Democrats listen most to . . .	Parents	Nonparents
Business	28%	32%	Campaign Contributors	32%	26%
Campaign Contributors	27	13	Union Members	20	25
Parents	7	6	Parents	12	11
Christian Conservatives	7	12	Business	10	12
Union Members	6	7	Senior Citizens	6	8
Senior Citizens	6	9	The Gun Lobby	2	1
The Gun Lobby	4	6	Christian Conservatives	1	1

Source: National Parenting Association, *The Parent Vote: Moms _and_ Dads Up for Grabs,* October 2000.

unpaid and the law applies only to those working in firms with fifty or more employees. That means that people working for smaller firms—over half the parents in our sample—are excluded.

Work-life balance is just beginning to emerge on the political landscape, but it is potentially a huge issue. Millions of Americans—men as well as women—see this problem as their biggest daily struggle. But they have not

Figure 14.1. What's the Biggest Challenge Facing You as a Parent?

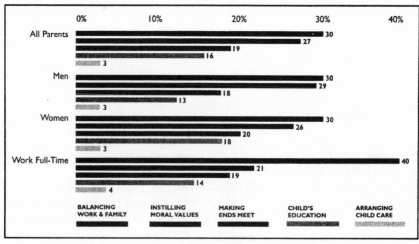

Source: National Parenting Association, *What Will Parents Vote For? Update 2000,* May 2000.

Table 14.3. Who Feels the Time Crunch the Most?

Percentage of parents who say . . .	Not enough time for self	Not enough time for kids
All Parents	56%	32%
Working full-time		
Women	79	48
Men	53	36
Working part-time		
Women	50	30
Men	58	35
Non-working		
Women	45	17
Men	40	14

Source: National Parenting Association, *What Will Parents Vote For? Update 2000,* May 2000.

yet demanded systemic changes to help them. Instead, parents try to cope as individuals, settling for lesser careers, patching together child-care arrangements, making tough either-or choices and then feeling guilty and exhausted at the end of the day. Although parents have not looked to the government for help, when specific public policies were proposed to them, the ideas drew broad support.

- Ninety percent favor (55 percent strongly favor) tax incentives to encourage family-friendly policies by employers, such as benefits for part-time workers and flexible working hours. This proposal drew the strongest favorable rating of any single measure we asked about in both our 1996 and January 2000 polls.
- Eighty-four percent favor (53 percent strongly favor) a law to ensure twenty-four hours' or three days' paid leave annually for family needs, like parent-teacher conferences or taking kids to the doctor.

Table 14.4. Which Parents Have Workplace Flexibility?

Availability of Family-Friendly Work Options*	Income		
	Under $20,000	$20,000–$60,000	Over $60,000
High	6%	19%	30%
Middle	32	33	38
Low	62	48	33

Source: National Parenting Association, *What Will Parents Vote For? Update 2000,* May 2000.
*Workplaces were ranked on an index based on positive responses to four items: being able to work fewer or flexible hours to meet family needs, availability of paid leave, and ability to work from home.

These measures were overwhelmingly favored across party affiliation, race, gender, and income (table 14.1).

We also asked parents their views on whether new mothers should be allowed to collect unemployment benefits while on maternity leave, an idea put forward by the Clinton administration. Federal regulations, issued June 13, 2000, allow states to use the unemployment insurance system to offer paid leave to working parents following the birth or adoption of a child. Even when presented with the opposing argument that this could draw down reserves that might be needed in times of recession, parents favored the idea by a margin of five to three (54 percent to 34 percent).

Parents would like to see this and other workplace practices adopted that would give them more time with their families. Three out of four parents (78 percent) favor letting workers take time off rather than get extra pay for overtime and being able to trade in ten days' pay for ten days' additional leave (76 percent).

Our survey found that job hours have become less rigid for many workers—and this is a helpful change. But such steps alone are unlikely to solve the magnitude of the time dilemma facing working parents. Despite the reported prevalence of flexible hours, work-family pressures are still intense for parents. It will take more fundamental changes to reorganize our lives of paid work so that we can give the unpaid job of parenting—a vital social investment—the attention it deserves. Our findings on parents' opinions suggest that the leaders who recognize this and articulate bolder ideas to combat the family time famine will tap into a market eager to spend their votes for this new political product.

Action to Combat Gun Violence.   Crime and violence continue to top the list of parents' worries and have intensified from 1996 to 2000. Forty percent of parents cite crime and violence as a major worry, up from 30 percent in 1996. The highly publicized wave of deadly school shootings in 1999 was undoubtedly weighing on parents' minds. Nearly seven out of ten parents (69 percent) told us they are worried that a school shooting, like the one at Columbine High School in Colorado, could happen at a school near them. Concern is pervasive; at least two-thirds of parents in every demographic group and region fear that such a shooting could take place locally. The fact that statistics show that, overall, school violence is actually down appears to offer little comfort to most parents. As a Detroit mother told *Offspring Magazine* in response to our findings, "Sure you can say the odds are against a school shooting. I'm sure that's what all the Columbine parents thought too. But if it happens to your child, odds don't matter much."

Parents do not sidestep their responsibility when it comes to gun violence. Over half (53 percent) put most of the blame for school shootings on "par-

Table 14.5. Parents' Support for Tougher Gun Control

	Percent in Favor			
	All Parents	Women	Men	Gun Owners	Nonowners
Legislation requiring gun makers and sellers to install trigger locks or safety devices to make it harder for kids to fire them	88%	92%	85%	82%	92%
Registering all guns and licensing all owners, as is done with cars	84	88	80	68	93
Raising the age of possession for handguns and assault weapons to 21*	82	85	79	75	87

* Federal law bans only private ownership of all assault weapons and ammunition clips with over ten rounds made after September 13, 1994.
Source: National Parenting Association, *What Will Parents Vote For? Update 2000,* May 2000.

ents' failure to teach and watch their kids." One in five think violent TV, movies, and computers are the most to blame, and 14 percent point to kids' access to guns. However, while parents may not see access to guns as the prime *cause* of youth violence, they certainly see restricting access to guns as an important *solution* to the problem. Parents—including the 32 percent in our survey who own guns—overwhelmingly support legislation requiring trigger locks, gun registration, and raising the age for gun possession. Just over half of parents (51 percent) would ban handguns altogether.

Once again, support cuts across party lines *when we look at parents' views.* All three measures were favored by at least eight out of ten parents, whether they identified themselves as Democrats, Republicans, or independents. Tougher gun control is another issue that unites parents from all backgrounds, income levels, and regions.

Better Schools. The schooling of their children is a paramount concern for parents. Many aspects of education absorb their attention: quality, school hours, meeting the costs of preschool and college, and, as we have seen tragically, safety. When asked what should be the next president's top priority, the most frequent answer by a sizable margin was "improving public schools." This was the case despite the fact that, historically, public schools have been primarily a local, not a federal, responsibility. Whether or not they make this distinction, it may be that parents are so dissatisfied and frustrated with the quality of education that they just want someone, somewhere, to fix the schools.

Table 14.6.   What Should Be the Next President's Top Priority?

Parents saying . . .	Jan. 2000	Sept. 2000
Improving public schools	29%	28%
Health insurance for all	17	18
Tax cuts	16	19
Strengthening moral values	16	19
Gun control	12	9
Family-friendly workplaces	5	3
Restricting abortion	3	2

Source: National Parenting Association, *What Will Parents Vote For? Update 2000,* May 2000, and *The Parent Vote: Moms and Dads Up for Grabs,* October 2000.

We probed parents' views on policies to address education in two different ways. In our January 2000 poll we asked about whether they favored several specific measures that have been advanced as strategies for strengthening education. In our follow-up September poll, we posed the question differently, asking parents to rank education plans. We said, "Here are some ideas that have been offered to improve our schools. Since federal funds are limited, tell me which one you think should be the top priority." Although parents favor

Table 14.7.   Improving Education: Priorities

	All	Candidate Choice			Gender		Race	
		Bush	Gore	Undecided	Mothers	Fathers	White	Black
More teachers to cut class sizes	53%	44%	62%	57%	54%	52%	52%	59%
Higher standards and accountability	49	53	47	38	47	51	50	41
Better paid and trained teachers	41	36	47	37	45	36	41	43
Ensuring students read by grade 3	14	12	14	20	15	13	13	21
Repairing and building more schools	12	14	9	16	11	13	11	11
Vouchers for public or private schools	11	18	4	7	9	13	12	7
Universal preschools	8	8	7	7	8	8	8	11

Numbers shown are top two choices combined.
Source: National Parenting Association, *The Parent Vote: Moms and Dads Up for Grabs,* October 2000.

using federal aid for rebuilding schools and expanding early childhood education—and by large margins of over eight out of ten—if forced to make a choice, they would put tax dollars first into hiring more teachers to reduce class size, raising standards, and improving teacher pay and training. These solutions come out far ahead of other proposals, from vouchers to ensuring students read by grade three, that were put forward in the 2000 presidential campaigns.

Some parent advocates have urged keeping schools open longer to better match the work day and year. Indeed, two-thirds of parents would like to see more afterschool programs, though this proposal is somewhat less popular than it was in 1996, when 75 percent of parents voiced their support. And parents are divided on whether the school year should be lengthened by a month, with 44 percent in favor and 49 percent opposed. Taken together with other findings from our survey, it suggests that given a choice between keeping kids in school more or cutting back their own work hours, many parents would prefer the latter. As Detroit mother Joyce Present told us, "The point is for me to spend more time with my daughter. Her being in a classroom doesn't achieve that."

Economic Means to Provide Their Children with Essentials. Although fewer than one in five parents thought that a general tax cut should be the president's top priority, we found substantial support for targeted tax breaks, particularly aimed at helping parents afford to provide their children with a good education, health insurance, and other basic needs:

- Eighty-nine percent favor (56 percent strongly favor) increasing tax deductions or credits to help more families pay for higher education.
- Eighty-eight percent favor (63 percent strongly favor) health insurance for every child, with a full or partial government subsidy to parents who can't afford it.
- Eighty-seven percent favor (59 percent strongly favor) eliminating state and local sales taxes on kids' necessities like diapers, school materials, and car seats.

The great majority of parents—86 percent—agree that the minimum wage should be raised so that all full-time workers are above the poverty level. Support for this idea unifies parents; it gets high levels of support from African Americans, whites, and Hispanics. Not surprisingly, 98 percent of those at the lowest end of the income ladder favor raising the minimum wage, but the proposal was also supported by 91 percent of middle-income parents, and 78 percent of those earning over $60,000 a year. Raising the minimum wage to lift families out of poverty enjoys greater support among Democrats

(90 percent) and independents (89 percent) than among Republicans (76 percent), but all favor it by substantial margins.

What Are the Political Implications? Parents comprise one of the largest groups in the electorate—much larger in fact than other voter categories that are given far more attention. According to the Voter News Service exit polls from the 2000 presidential elections, 39 percent of voters had children under eighteen. By comparison, 14 percent were seniors, sixty-five and older; 10 percent were African Americans; and 26 percent were members of a union household. Yet despite their numbers, parents are not perceived as a powerful voting bloc and do not tend to think of themselves that way.

On an individual level, however, parents see "parenthood" as a prime identity determining their voting decisions. When asked which factors would be the most important in their choice of a candidate, 38 percent of mothers and 33 percent of fathers ranked "being a parent" first, ahead of factors commonly believed to be more influential, including gender, race, income level, religion, and where they lived. This finding was confirmed in our focus groups.

Although mothers and fathers see "parenthood" as an important personal political identity, they do not make the jump to perceiving parents as a crosscutting group with a potentially powerful voice. The surveys reported in this chapter found that parents express similar priorities and wide support for fairly specific public policy measures to reduce gun violence, improve schools, and ease work-family time pressures. Yet even when presented with

Table 14.8. Interest Group Identification: Top Choice

Q. 4: We describe who we are in different ways: by where we're from, our religion, and so on. Now, if you think about the presidential election in November, which of the following factors will be the most important in your choice of a candidate? (Read list, rotate start point)

| | Parents | | | |
	All	Mothers	Fathers	Nonparents*
Being a parent	35%	38%	33%	15%
The city, suburb, or rural area where you live	13	11	16	16
Your gender	9	11	7	13
Your religion	8	10	7	13
How well off you are	8	8	9	9
Your race	3	2	3	3

* Nonparents are identified as adults without dependent children; some may have grown children.
Source: National Parenting Association, *The Parent Vote: Moms and Dads Up for Grabs*, October 2000.

this empirical data, parents in our focus groups found it hard to imagine themselves as a group with common interests that could wield clout in the civic arena.

COULD A PARENTS' MOVEMENT EMERGE?

Parents are not monolithic. But like women before the publication of *The Feminine Mystique,* seniors in the 1950s, African Americans before the civil rights movement, and gays before Stonewall, parents could become galvanized into a force for social change. Though parents are not facing the same kinds of discrimination as these groups before them, mothers and fathers do face a system that is stacked against them—at work, in the schools, on our streets, and all around us in the popular culture. Our research found striking evidence of far-reaching agreement among parents on measures needed to help them set their children on the right course. We also found that mothers and fathers already think of themselves as parents when they enter the voting booth. It is a leap from here to the genesis of a parents' movement, but a leap that is plausible and possible.

NOTES

1. *What Will Parents Vote For? Update 2000* (New York: National Parenting Association, May 2000) was conducted for the National Parenting Association from January 26 to February 8, 2000, by Charney Research, a New York–based polling firm. It consisted of a total of 650 telephone interviews, divided among a national random sample of 500 American parents and oversamples of 50 black parents, 50 Latino parents, and 50 parents who were welfare recipients. All respondents were American citizens 18 or older, with children who were living at home or as their dependents. The margin of sampling error for the national sample is ±4.5 percent.

The oversamples were conducted to provide subsamples large enough to allow comparison of separate findings concerning African Americans, Hispanics, and welfare beneficiaries. The oversamples are weighted down to their correct proportions of the national population in the data on all parents.

The sample structure is similar to that of the 1996 survey of American parents conducted for the National Parenting Association, except in one respect. The 1996 parents poll excluded welfare recipients, who then made up 5 percent of parents. They currently make up 3 percent of parents. Since they are so few, even if welfare recipients are excluded for the 2000 data, none of the national results change by more than one percentage point. Hence the 2000 findings, although they include welfare recipients, are comparable to the 1996 results.

The Parent Vote: Moms and Dads Up for Grabs (New York: National Parenting Association, October 2000) was conducted by Charney Research for the National Parenting

Association from September 8 to 15, 2000. A total of 750 telephone interviews were conducted, including a random sample of 500 parents, an oversample of an additional 50 African American parents, and a random sample of 200 nonparents. All were U.S. citizens aged 18 or older. Parents were defined as people who had children living at home or as their dependents. The margin of sampling error for the parents sample is ±4.5 percent and for the nonparent sample ±7 percent.

The black parents oversample was conducted in order to provide a black subsample large enough to allow comparison of attitudes between black and white. In the figures for all parents, the oversample is weighted down to its correct proportion of the national population.

The nonparent sample received an interview half as long as the parents' interview, to allow comparison of the views of parents and nonparents on some of the issues in the poll.

This analysis of the findings of the surveys is based on the work of Craig Charney and Joan Zacharias of Charney Research, and Nancy Rankin, Ruth Wooden, and Peggy Shiller of the National Parenting Association.

15

Fixing Social Insecurity:
A Proposal to Finance Parenthood

Nancy Rankin

Ask parents and many of them will tell you they would like to be able to take some time out from their jobs so they can devote more attention and energy to their kids. A recent study by Public Agenda, a nonpartisan public policy research organization, shows that most parents (68 percent) "would prefer to stay home with their children when they are young." Among parents with children under five, 80 percent of mothers say this and 52 percent of fathers.[1] Public Agenda's report set off a predictable outcry—especially among child-care advocates and some feminists. But before rushing to refute it, maybe it's time we listened carefully to what parents are actually saying.

Parents are not arguing that mothers shouldn't work—of course, they should be able to—or that we don't need better, more affordable child care. Of course, we do. But more and better child care is just part of the solution. We also need to re-engineer our work lives to create more time for parenting. Public Agenda's report confirms findings from the National Parenting Association and other public opinion polls.[2] Parents don't define their biggest struggle as finding child care; they see it as balancing work and family.[3] Even more striking is the finding that both *mothers and fathers* say that balancing job and family responsibilities is their toughest daily challenge. And almost half of full-time working mothers surveyed said they don't have enough time for their kids. Research by both Public Agenda and the National Parenting Association shows that given a choice of public policies, parents would much prefer to see tax breaks that make it easier for parents to cut back on job hours and incentives for businesses

---

Nancy Rankin is past executive director of the National Parenting Association and before that, director of research and programs.

to adopt flexible work policies, than massive new subsidies for a national child-care system.[4]

We are fed up with either-or choices of uninterrupted work from graduation to grave versus jettisoning hard-earned degrees and years of job experience if we choose to spend more time at home for a few years raising our kids. For lower-income and single parents the choice is even starker: the income to support your children versus the time to care for them in the way you deem best. It's time for a new paradigm that allows us to take a chunk of time out from our lives of paid work to give the unpaid, but no less important, work of parenting the attention it deserves.

If so many parents are yearning to stay home with their children during their earliest years, what stops them? One factor is certainly well-founded anxieties about returning to the labor market and visions of lifetime career setbacks. Some want the continued rewards of work, but with scaled-down hours. For many parents, though, the biggest barrier is practical: they can't afford to.

Here's a proposal to help them. Why not allow working parents to draw Social Security benefits for up to three years during their prime child-rearing years? This would give moms and dads a real choice about how much time to spend working and how much time to spend with their kids. Some parents would decide to stay at home or cut back to part-time work so they do not become entirely disconnected from the labor market. Those who elected to "borrow on their Social Security" would repay the system, at least in part. For example, they could increase the employee's share of the payroll taxes they pay in when they return to work, they could defer their age of retirement with full Social Security benefits on a year-for-year basis, or they could accept a reduced monthly benefit, as those who opt for early retirement do now.

Any of these options would still involve some subsidy; otherwise the required payback would take too steep a cut out of future paychecks or retirement benefits to make it an affordable choice. Given our "pay-as-you-go" system of financing senior benefits out of tax contributions from current workers, you can argue this is fair. Without parents devoting time and resources to raising children, there will not be productive employees in the future whose earnings will be taxed to pay the bill for the older generation. And that is, in fact, exactly the argument made in a recent decision by Germany's Constitutional Court. It ruled that workers with children should pay a lower premium for the country's compulsory long-term nursing care insurance plan than childless ones, on the grounds that future beneficiaries will depend on the premiums paid by coming generations of workers. "Those people who have not helped to maintain the number of future contributors—i.e., the childless—are getting an unfair financial advantage, says the court. So they should pay more."[5]

How much of a difference would this make for parents trying to make ends meet? Plenty, it turns out. Taxes and child-care costs take such a big bite out of parents' incomes that even modest Social Security benefits could largely replace the net income from an average job.[6] For example, a parent earning a second salary of $30,000 (assuming the spouse also makes $30,000) would net only about $10,065 after taxes, child care, and work expenses (see box 15.1). That works out to about the same as the average annual Social Security income for retirees of $10,140 in 2001. It's enough to make a real difference for American families.

Box 15.1   Net Income after Taxes, Child Care, and Work Expenses

Example: A two-earner couple, where each parent makes $30,000

The second salary:	$30,000
Subtract:	
Social Security and Medicare taxes	2,295
Additional state/local taxes (@ estimated rate of 5%)	1,500
Estimated additional federal income tax	6,180
Additional child care (estimated at $120/week)*	6,240
Commuting cost ($25/week times 50)	1,250
Cost of work clothing and dry cleaning	870
Cost of restaurant meals on work days ($25/week times 50)	1,250
Other (nonreimbursed expenses, paid help, meals out, etc.)	350
Net income	$10,065

---

*Based on U.S. Census figures for weekly total child-care costs per family (for families including a preschooler), adjusted for inflation. *Source: What Does It Cost to Mind Our Preschoolers?* U.S. Census, 1995. Calculations used in this example are adapted from a model appearing online in offspringmag.com on April 13, 2000. Estimates are based on federal tax rates at that time.

Among mothers or fathers taking advantage of this option, most would probably stay at home during their children's earliest years. Recent research and reporting about the importance of these first years for brain development have reinforced deeply held sentiments. But we also know that kids' needs don't magically disappear at age three. A struggling third-grader or a troubled teen can be just as demanding of parental attention. This proposal would let parents decide what makes sense for them and their families.

One issue that would need to be addressed is overcoming barriers to workforce reentry. It is unrealistic to expect that employers be asked to guarantee someone's job after a leave of a year or more. So fears of getting back on track are justified. The career highway is easy to exit, but difficult to get back on. We need to create more "on-ramps"—opportunities and recruitment strategies that give workers a path to accelerate back up to speed and full productivity. For example, employees on an extended parenting time-out could maintain an alumni-like status with their former employer, kept in the loop with regular contacts and invitations to participate in training and staff development. They would become a prime candidate pool for rehires. Incentives could be created to encourage professional associations, unions, and local colleges to offer transition training, placement, and on-the-job mentoring to returnees.[7] More fundamentally, we need messages to change the national mindset, so that nurturing children is seen as a respectable addition to lifetime accomplishments, not discounted as a brain cell–diminishing résumé gap.

Continuation of health insurance would also need to be addressed, although for married workers with a covered spouse this would not be a problem. Others could buy into their former employees' group plan or perhaps into Medicare.

Thinking of Social Security as a kind of savings account that parents could tap into is a natural offshoot of the current policy debate. Some companies offer employees 401(k) thrift plans that they can borrow against to make major purchases. But many working families don't have this benefit. It's hard for young parents to save early on during the stage of life when they are having children and also trying to buy their first home, pay back education loans, or start businesses. Indeed, economists have long recognized that young families are vulnerable to a type of "market failure." Banks are not likely to lend them money based on a hypothetical future earnings stream—but the Social Security trust fund could. It makes sense to think of our retirement system as a means to promote social investment—truly our national social security. Looking at it this way, we could also consider allowing Americans to draw Social Security benefits for limited periods for other valued social investments in addition to parenting, such as caring for an aging relative or midcareer retooling to obtain new job skills.

Even as medical science is creating time in our later years, we are increasingly starved for time during mid-life. True, the growing availability of work-life practices, like flextime and telecommuting, helps some workers balance job and family. But lower-income and younger workers, who need these policies the most, are the least likely to work for firms that offer such benefits. The National Parenting Association survey found that only 6 percent of parents in families earning under $20,000 a year worked for family-friendly firms, compared to 30 percent of parents with annual incomes over $60,000.[8] Employer flexibility is enormously important, but it is unlikely to sufficiently ease the time famine facing working parents and others trying to meet pressing personal responsibilities. If the problem is the need to "borrow time," one solution is to use our Social Security system as a "time bank." It is an idea worth serious consideration.

Adjusting the Social Security system we designed in 1935 to fit present-day needs of working people is not as radical as it first sounds. In fact, during the 2000 presidential campaign Al Gore proposed changing the way Social Security benefits are calculated to help offset what he called the current "motherhood penalty." When a parent, most often mom, takes time out of the paid labor force to stay home raising the children, she not only loses the income she would have earned then, but will have lower Social Security benefits in the future. Gore proposed crediting stay-at-home parents with $16,500 in income for up to five years. By his calculations that would give an average of $600 a year more in benefits to as many as eight million retirees.[9]

Gore's idea recognized the importance of parenting by acknowledging the contribution parents make to society through the unpaid work of nurturing children. And it offered modest financial benefits, primarily to older women. But the bolder proposal offered here—allowing parents to actually draw Social Security at two points in their lives—would offer real relief from the time crunch to the millions of Americans struggling to meet the dual demands of job and family every day. As Bryn Mawr economist Richard B. Du Boff explains, "The function of Social Security is one of social insurance. We pool our resources, and make transfer payments to ourselves at appropriate stages of the life cycle."[10] In the last century we addressed old age, when too many Americans suffered from impoverishment. Today, compelling needs have emerged earlier in our lives when we are raising our families. A transformed labor force faces policies that have not adequately changed to compensate for the massive entry of women into paid employment. Our Social Security system has long been thought of as providing a measure of financial security in return for a lifetime of work. What work is a more vital contribution to the future of our country than raising children well?

NOTES

1. Steve Farkas, Ann Duffett, and Jean Johnson, *Necessary Compromises* (New York: Public Agenda, 2000), p. 13.

2. Kathleen Sylvester summarizes much of this opinion research in an article, "Caring for Our Youngest: Public Attitudes in the United States," included in a September 2001 report by the David and Lucile Packard Foundation, *Caring for Infants and Toddlers*. In addition to the Public Agenda research, she cites a September 2000 election issues poll by the *Washington Post,* the Kaiser Family Foundation, and Harvard. Of 1,500 registered voters surveyed in that poll, 79 percent agreed with the statement: "It may be necessary for mothers to be working because the family needs money, but it would be better if she could stay home and take care of the house and children." A 1999 *Los Angeles Times* poll of 1,601 California parents found that 68 percent of fathers and 69 percent of mothers felt that it is "much better for the family" if the father works outside the home and the mother stays home with the children.

3. Ruth Wooden and Nancy Rankin, *What Will Parents Vote For?* (New York: National Parenting Association, 2000), pp. 2–3. In this national survey of American parents, when asked "What is the biggest daily challenge you face as a parent?" the single most frequent response was "balancing work and family," cited by the same percentage—30 percent—of mothers as of fathers. In contrast, only 3 percent of parents gave "arranging child care" as their response. Among parents working full time, 40 percent said balancing work and family was their biggest daily challenge. *What Will Parents Vote for in New York?*, the poll conducted by Charney Research for the National Parenting Association in June 2001, found views similar to those in the national survey. In the state poll 31 percent of mothers and fathers surveyed said "balancing work and family" was their biggest daily challenge, compared to 22 percent each for "their child's education" and "instilling moral values," the next most often mentioned concerns.

4. Public Agenda's 2000 survey found that if parents had to choose, "twice as many parents of children 5 or under say policy makers should concentrate on making it easier and more affordable for one parent to be home during a child's first few years (62%), rather than on improving the quality and affordability of outside-the-home child care (30%)." For a fuller discussion, see Farkas, Duffett, and Johnson, *Necessary Compromises*, p. 28.

Among the policies that drew the highest levels of support in national surveys of parents conducted for the National Parenting Association in 1996 and 2000 were proposals to ease work–family pressures by decreasing work hours.

Proposal	Percent strongly/somewhat favor	
	2000 Survey	1996 Survey
Tax incentives to encourage family-friendly policies by employers, such as benefits for part-time workers and flexible working hours	90	90
A law to ensure 24 hours or three days paid leave annually for family needs	84	87
Letting workers take time off instead of extra pay for overtime	78	79

5. "No German Children? Then Pay Up," *The Economist,* April 7, 2001, p. 54.

6. Median earnings of full-time, year-round U.S. workers in 1999 were $36,476 for men and $26,324 for women, according to the U.S. Census Bureau Current Population Survey.

7. New York City's Teaching Fellows program, created in 2000 to draw young professionals from other fields into teaching, is a prime example of an "on-ramps" concept. The program gives recruits accelerated, intensive pre-service training.

8. Wooden and Rankin, *What Will Parents Vote For?* p. 3.

9. James Dao, "Gore Proposes New Benefits for Parents and Widows," *New York Times,* April 5, 2000, p. A19.

10. Richard B. Du Boff, in a letter to the editor, *New York Times,* August 19, 2001, p. WK12.

CONCLUSION

16

Taking Parenting Public

Ruth A. Wooden

Few situations generate more passionate feelings among adults than being a parent. Parenting is one of the most intense experiences of our lives, yet most American parents find themselves today, at the beginning of the twenty-first century, living this experience mostly in private. It is time, in our view, to recognize that the vast majority of parents today, while still expecting to take primary responsibility for raising their children, would be well served by a movement toward greater public support for navigating through the long, tough job of parenting children in today's world. Parenting can be a frightening, worrisome, emotional roller-coaster, and adding loneliness and isolation to this endeavor can bring greater frustration and even hopelessness to the hard work of raising children well.

Child rearing is one of the few subjects in modern life that can bring very different people together to participate in animated, mutually supportive discussions and activities. No matter what other circumstances may divide adults, they can find common ground in talking about the issues that come with raising their children. I have heard it said that two people can find themselves stranded in a train station in Philadelphia, Pennsylvania: one a fifty-year-old divorced black man, a civil engineer living in Oakland, California, and the other a thirty-year-old married white woman who works part time at a restaurant in Spartanburg, South Carolina. They apparently have little in common to talk about, until they discover that they both have ten-year-old daughters. And then they can talk for hours.

Ruth A. Wooden is senior counselor at Porter Novelli and past president of the National Parenting Association. She was previously president of the Advertising Council for eleven years.

The problem is that we do not find ourselves as parents "stranded" that way very often, with other parents or interested people who can share our concerns about how to bring up our children. Modern life has evolved in such a way that our families are more private and isolated than ever. Parents, aunts, uncles, and siblings are often separated by geography. Homes are not as "open" to neighbors as they were in earlier decades, and families are not in their homes as much as they used to be. We are expected to fend for ourselves by a culture that increasingly devalues, or at the very least minimizes, the work we do as parents. Put it this way, it is certainly not valued in the same way that paid work is valued in our increasingly "market-centric" society. My colleague Sylvia Ann Hewlett, an economist and author of *When the Bough Breaks: The Cost of Neglecting Our Children,* offers an instructive look at how both liberal and conservative economic policies undermine families. She writes that "economic markets do not reward the non-market work of nurturing; but without nurturing the nurturers, our market economy will increasingly depend on a stressed out, overburdened workforce, raising the next generation of stressed out, overburdened workers." As long as our "social reward" system is focused on economic results, the work of parenting will be seen as a lesser contribution to the well-being of our society. What a sad commentary that is.

This isolation of parents is just one of the many challenges that confront today's parents. I have been known to refer to "parenting in the closet," and such a phrase connotes the discomfort many people find at talking about their parenting roles in public. All of us parents have read the signs that talking about one's parenting work is incompatible with talk about the workplace and careers. In a June 2000 article in the *Wall Street Journal,* columnist Sue Shellenbarger related the stories of several senior managers who found themselves distraught over the trials and tribulations of raising their teenagers and equally distraught about how to explain this to colleagues at work or to their management when they asked for leave or work schedule reductions. The worry was that they weren't "new" parents, they had "managed" up to now, they were experienced, mature employees. How could they explain that, in fact, raising teenagers is often just as difficult or more so than becoming a parent for the first time? Shellenbarger did note, however, that those employees who "did go public" with their parenting issues found an enthusiastic group of colleagues who were eager to share their own problems with raising teenagers!

But many people still remain uncomfortable with this kind of discourse. And some people are downright irritated. Several new publications suggest a new "backlash" against parents. *GQ Magazine* ran a story about "over zealous parents who bore the rest of the world with talk about cute Nathan." Journalist Elinor Burkett, in her book *The Baby Boon,* argues that nonparents are increasingly being asked to pick up the slack for parents who are shirking their work in favor of family responsibilities. These authors and others argue that nonparents are being discriminated against when policies such as flexible work rules apply only to parents. The thinking is that becoming a parent is one's personal "choice," and one should assume the cost and burden alone. It is remarkable and even a bit ironic that in the thirty-plus years that "reproductive choice" has been a factor in most adult lives, we may have seen the role of parenting move from a ubiquitous, yet valued, daily activity of community life to a strictly personal endeavor. Indeed, it has even been described by some as an "expensive private hobby."

On the political front, much of the rhetoric of candidates and the consultants and pollsters that advise them is full of references to supporting "hardworking families" and "putting families first." In the 2000 presidential election, hardly a day went by when one of the candidates wasn't photographed sitting cramped into a desk at a school somewhere, talking about making himself the "education" president.

The issues that count more in the social policy debate focus on what to do about the "entitlements" of Social Security and Medicare and, to a lesser extent, Medicaid and other supports for the very poor. This fosters a sense of impending intergenerational warfare—in other words, the image of younger employees supporting "greedy geezers"—but even more insidiously, this artificially polarized debate diminishes the political role of the vast majority of working parents, what Harvard professor Theda Skocpol calls the "missing middle."[1] Their voice is lost in the cacophony of skirmishes over preserving social supports for the elderly and liberal calls for new supports for the poorest children. Indeed, the parents of the vast majority of children in this country are missing from the political scene.

And finally, the cultural signs for parents are that they are increasingly seen as almost irrelevant in the lives of their children. Children, including not just teenagers, but also very young children, are now routinely marketed to as purchasers of a whole host of products that used to require at least some nod of recognition to the parent who presumably provides the money to buy these products. The media outlets that cater exclusively to teens (and also younger children) are too numerous to mention, and much of the entertainment appeal to their young audience is dismissiveness and even disdain for parents. As Bernice Kanner, the prominent writer about media culture featured in this collection, has written, "We have gone from *Father Knows Best* to Homer Simpson in just one generation."

Indeed, it seems that everywhere one turns, there is implicit or explicit criticism of the job that parents are doing in raising today's kids. And parents themselves are among some of the most vocal critics. In 1997, Public Agenda conducted a widely publicized public opinion study on behalf of the Advertising Council and Ronald McDonald House Charities called *Kids These Days: What Americans Really Think about the Next Generation.*[2] Public Agenda interviewed 2,000 adults, including both parents and nonparents, along with oversamples of Hispanic and African American parents. One of the most significant and surprising findings was the agreement among parents and nonparents alike as to the "diagnosis" of what is going on with "kids these days." They agree that our children are suffering from a "moral meltdown" that is perhaps more detrimental to their well-being than even some of the physical and material deficits facing the most vulnerable children in America.

What is this "moral meltdown"? The writers of the report, Steve Farkas and Jean Johnson, took great pains to describe this as a condition not of "family values" in the highly charged, ideological rhetoric of the past several years. Rather, it is more akin to the "home training" notion that Enola Aird discussed earlier in this volume. "Moral meltdown" refers more to what children learn at home than to any economic meltdown or deprivation. The survey suggests that the public sees children as lacking some of the basic values and virtues that most adults agree are essential to function as a competent adult—that is, character traits such as honesty, courtesy, empathy for others, and respect for authority.

Americans then look to the parents of these children and conclude that they are failing to do their job in providing this fundamental moral education. Not only are they not teaching these values, the Public Agenda study would suggest that parents are not "living" these values themselves. Only about one in five Americans (22 percent) said it was very common to find parents who are good role models for their kids. Again, the agreement between parents and nonparents on this point was striking.

Given this harsh assessment of parents' performance, it is not surprising to the authors of this report that the public is not more supportive of public and private efforts aimed at turning around troubled kids. "While the public is clearly worried about the future of these children, they see little they can do to change the course of their lives without changing the nature of the parenting these children receive at home." It's not the kids, it's the *parents* that keep the public away from supporting more investment in policies and programs that can work to help kids.

Furthermore, adults generally agree on a surprisingly clear set of recommendations. Public Agenda's findings show "a public that is anguished about our young people, but not without ideas about how to help them. The help they feel is needed is right in their own communities, and not where so many of the advocates for children focus much of their attention, i.e., on government programs and an out of control media and popular culture. Right at the top of the list is the need to strengthen the quality of parenting our children receive."

But as strong as the criticism is of the job that parents are doing, and despite the fact that parents themselves agree by and large with these assessments, these criticisms coexist with substantial levels of empathy for what people see as the enormously difficult and challenging undertaking that raising children in America has become. "These coexisting viewpoints may seem contradictory, but ordinary citizens seem to subscribe to two truths: These are tough times—maybe the toughest of times—to be a parent, but parents are not rising to the challenge."

The public is very mindful of the genuine struggles of many parents. More than half the public believes that parents who sacrifice and work hard for their kids are very common. People can easily imagine moments when the pressures of life can get to the most devoted parents. By almost a two to one margin (63 percent to 32 percent), Americans believe that "most parents face times when they can really need help raising their kids," instead of the proposition that "most parents can handle the job of raising their kids without help."

Finally, and most poignantly, the demoralization of parents is very real. Parents say they face the daunting task of raising respectful, helpful, morally grounded children in a world fraught with hazards and decidedly mixed messages (including the Homer Simpson image of Dad mentioned earlier). Unfortunately for many of them, they have not been able to find much emotional support for this task, including support among one of the groups that could help them the most—that is, other parents in the "same boat," facing the same task.

Certainly, the "privatization" of parenting has been a factor here in the lack of support by parents for each other—in other words, parenting is what you do "by yourself" and you "learn it by yourself." Unfortunately, our divisive political rhetoric and certain social policies have not been helpful either, as middle- and working-class parents felt "left out" by services that went only to the poorest families, who were frequently viewed as "undeserving" welfare cheats. Too many parents have been left out of the equation, as politicians and the press fight over whether to support their elderly parents or the poorest children. No wonder so many of them say that "what they do in Washington never makes much difference in their lives."

In light of this demoralization, we wondered about the effect this had on the voting behavior of parents. Parents have not been thought of as a powerful political constituency, certainly not in the same way as, for example, the women's vote, the African American vote, or the Catholic vote. Yet upon examination, they could in fact be much more important than many of these traditional political interest groups that politicians and pundits alike follow so diligently. In the 2000 national election, parents constituted 39 percent of the electorate, compared to, for example, seniors (aged sixty-five plus) who made up 14 percent of voters and households with union members who make up 26 percent.[3] Yet the prevailing assumption is that parents "can't be mobilized because they don't share a common agenda."

In September 2000 the National Parenting Association conducted research among parents and nonparents alike to look further at parents in the political arena. We went looking for an understanding of how parenthood impacted the political identity of likely voters. We wanted to know: Is being a parent as important as gender or race in motivating one's choice of candidates?

What did we learn from this research? First we learned that, indeed, parenthood is a powerful political identity. More than a third of parents, both mothers and fathers, identified "being a parent" as the prime identity when they went into the voting booth to pick a candidate. More than half of both mothers and fathers named parenthood as one of their two top identities. Surprisingly, in such a forced-choice question, neither race nor gender were high on the selection as first- or second-choice political identities, even among mothers or among African American parents. The primary identity among nonparents was "the city, state or region where they live." This was the second-highest rating for parents, and indeed, after parenthood, the results for parents were very similar to the results of nonparents.

Second, we confirmed the findings from our previous surveys that there is remarkable unity about issues and policies among parents, cutting across the usual divides of gender, race, income, religion, and even political party affiliation. Our study also revealed that parents have different priorities from nonparents. Nearly a third of them named "improving public schools" as their choice for the top priority of the next president, whereas nonparents put tax cuts at the top of list for the new president's priorities. Mothers and fathers also were identical in naming their top daily concerns—30 percent of mothers and fathers picked "instilling moral values" as the number one challenge and 29 percent said "balancing family and work." These both came ahead of "making ends meet," except among the lowest-income parents.[4]

The similarity among mothers and fathers was perhaps the most startling finding in our survey, but it speaks to what the NPA has found in other studies of parents: they are struggling mightily to do better by their kids and are frequently overwhelmed with the challenge. In our view, this issue of family-work balance is a potential "sleeper" issue on the public agenda, one that could well galvanize parents into a more potent public and political force. It is dominating the daily lives of millions of parents, yet it is not on the radar screen of either politicians or parents themselves as a "public" issue. It is still seen as a challenge that is "private" to parents. This is another example of the need to "take parenting public" in order to strengthen the value placed on the work of parenting and the skills of individual parents.

Given all these challenges to the public perception of the work of parenting today, we feel it is essential to embark on a major effort to enhance the cultural value and honor we place on the important contribution parents make to our society. To do this we must encourage parents to go public, that is, express their passionate, but mostly private, feelings of concern, caring, and commitment that most of them feel for their children. The demoralized, marginalized, even vilified parents of this country need to come together and cross the usual divides that have been exacerbated artificially by our politics and to use the powerful common ground they share as a platform for strengthening the tattered social fabric of our communities. In short, they must come together to come through for their kids.

What is needed is a new social movement that unites Americans, that seeks out the interests of a vast bloc of citizens, not just another special interest, Washington-based advocacy lobby fighting for its share of the pie. Instead, this should be a movement of "volunteer" parents from all walks of life that seeks to urge government and citizens alike to recognize that the most important prescription for helping parents do a better job is to make parenting a higher priority on the public agenda, as well as in our private lives. This should be a national movement, but it must start simultaneously in towns, cities, and states across America. It will need the support of like-minded professional organizations, but it must be fundamentally a citizen movement, happening right where families live, work, and go to school.

Helping to "spark" such a movement is the mission of the National Parenting Association. We seek to encourage the attitude that the needs of our children must be "put first" in the eyes of their families and the nation. Our work to date, much of which has been included in this edited volume, has sought to make the case for "reframing" the discussion of today's parenting role. There is no more urgent need at the outset of this movement than to bring the work of parents into greater public discussion, especially among parents themselves. For only when the earnest work of parenting is part of everyday talk and everyday life (when it makes it onto the stage of Jay Leno's monologue on the *Tonight Show*) will this work have the priority it needs and deserves. Our children's well-being, and the well-being of our families and neighborhoods, will be the greatest beneficiaries of a campaign and movement to "take parenting public."

But what does it mean to "take parenting public"? Why did we choose the metaphor of capital markets, when we have argued so strongly that, in fact, parenting is the ultimate nonmarket activity in our culture? It is precisely because the metaphor helps us look at parenting through a new lens. In a culture that values growing markets and building successful business enterprises, the work of parenting is very similar to the classic "undercapitalized" business, a business that must go to the public markets—in other words, go public—if it is to get the "capital" it needs to become the kind of business its founders envision. It can no longer grow much if it stays as a private company. It has long had undervalued assets, with the potential to grow tremendously with significant investment. With that new investment, it could potentially return an enormous profit to the investors, one that would build a long-term foundation for other new businesses to come.

The investment that is needed for a parenting movement is both human and financial "capital." And in our view, the human capital investment is an investment in developing more positive attitudes and stronger values and beliefs. The financial capital investment includes new social supports that can help parents come through better for their children. Human capital investments will help us change the way people see the work of parenting, especially in the new context facing most parents at the beginning of this century. We need to recognize that, in the words of the Oldsmobile commercial, "this isn't your parent's parenting any more." The actual tasks of parenting are much the same as our parents faced—that is, caring, education, and the transmission of values, family traditions, and customs—but the context is changed dramatically by the fast-changing economic and social environment.

Equally important is the need to generate greater financial capital for parents and build a movement that follows the pattern of previously successful social movements in this country, especially those efforts that led to important new social supports. Theda Skocpol, in her book *The Missing Middle,* articulates four crucial components of such social movements, the most successful of which have been Social Security and Medicare, but also the GI Bill of Rights, veterans' pensions, and child labor laws. (1) This parents' movement must cut across class, gender, and race lines and benefit the vast majority of citizens. (2) Its supports must be seen as a return for service to the community. (3) It must be nurtured and promoted by citizen associations. (4) It must seek tax and legislative support for the long term.

The first three elements of Skocpol's "recipe" can be put in place by the formation of a new civic collaboration of parents from across the country, working on behalf of the widest group of parents possible. The collaborative will seek to generate support for new attitudes and practices that honor and value the contributions of parents and new social policies that provide financial investments to parents in return for their service to the country. Critically important, especially early in the campaign, will be a major effort to challenge the image and the messages we have about parenting and to address the "cultural zeitgeist" in which these images and messages exist. This will require unusual patience by the parent movement, as these changes occur very slowly over years, with the expectation that it will require at least ten years to show significant changes in public attitudes. It is easy to lose heart for this important work of attitudinal and cultural change. It is essential that the movement enlist the guidance and help of other like-minded parents in the media and in the entertainment and marketing communities. They will be essential to building public support for this movement.

If one doubts that such support is there, one should pay heed to the work since 1998 of Andrea Alstrup, the corporate vice president for advertising at Johnson & Johnson, one of the largest television advertisers in the country. In a widely regarded speech to Advertising Women of New York in June 1998, Alstrup proposed the idea of a Family Friendly Programming Forum, a group of major advertisers that would work with the broadcast industry to create more family-appropriate programming. Alstrup's vision was to create more family viewing options in the critical 8:00 P.M. to 10:00 P.M. prime-time viewing period. She now has over forty major advertisers committed to the forum, which rewards existing family programming and has already produced at least one prime-time hit, the WB's *Gilmore Girls*. Alstrup "went public" with her particular parenting challenge, to great success.

In the end, this movement will be about giving voice to parents around this country who have not yet recognized the power they have to change things for themselves and their children. As the latest research from the National Parenting Association shows, parents are a larger constituency of voters than they and others think. Parents are more unified than divided in their views on public policy issues. Mothers and fathers have remarkably similar views. But most important of all, parents across all the usual classifications—that is, rich, middle class, or poor, Republican or Democrat, black, white, Latino or Asian, urban or suburban—share the most profound view of all: that being the parents of their children is the most important, passionate work of their lives.

Only when parents recognize and act on the potential they have to impact public attitudes and policies, when they "go public" with their urgent appeals to address the needs of all children, will we see new investments in the human capital of this country that will yield results not only for today's children, but for all the children yet to come in the twenty-first century.

NOTES

1. Theda Skocpol and Richard C. Leone, *The Missing Middle: Working Families and the Future of American Social Policy* (New York: Norton, 2000).

2. Steve Farkas and Jean Johnson, *Kids These Days: What Americans Really Think about the Next Generation* (New York: Public Agenda, 1997).

3. Figures from CNN Web site, http://www.cnn.com/ELECTION/2000/epolls/US/P000.html, from Voter News Service exit poll data, accessed November 8, 2000.

4. National Parenting Association, *The Parent Vote: Moms and Dads Up for Grabs* (New York: National Parenting Association, October 2000). In our previous survey, conducted in January and February 2000, parents ranked "balancing work and family" (30%), slightly ahead of "instilling moral values" (27%). But for both polls, looking at all parents, including stay-at-home parents, these two concerns are virtually tied within the polls' margin of statistical error. It is worth noting that among working parents "balancing work and family" is much more salient, named as the biggest daily challenge by twice as many parents (40%) as instilling values (21%). Nonetheless, the point being made here remains the same: in both surveys, responses by mothers and fathers were nearly identical (see figure 14.1).

Index

About the Contributors

Enola G. Aird is an activist mother and founder and director of the Mother-hood Project of the Institute for American Values. Trained as a lawyer, she spent several years in corporate law practice before leaving to devote her energies to her children and to family activism. She has served as talk-show host for a public radio station in New Haven, Connecticut, and as a member and chair of the Connecticut Commission on Children under two governors. During the mid-1990s she worked for the Children's Defense Fund in Washington, D.C., directing its violence prevention program and serving as an acting director of its Black Community Crusade for Children. She has served as a Lilly Leadership Workshop Fellow at the Yale Divinity School and currently serves on the board of directors and the executive committee of the National Parenting Association, where she is also an adviser to its Task Force on Revitalizing Parenting in the 21st Century. She is a member of the Waverly Extended Family and the Council on Civil Society.

Allan C. Carlson is president of the Howard Center for Family, Religion and Society and editor of *The Family in America*. He holds a Ph.D. in modern European history from Ohio University. From 1988 to 1993, he served via presidential appointment on the National Commission on Children. His books include *Family Questions: Reflections on the American Social Crisis, The Swedish Experiment in Family Politics, From Cottage to Work Station: The Family's Search for Social Harmony in the Industrial Age,* and *The New Agrarian Mind*. He served as general secretary of the World Congress of Families meetings in Prague (1997) and Geneva (1999).

David Elkind is currently professor of child studies at Tufts University in Medford, Massachusetts. His research has been in the areas of cognitive,

291

social, and emotional development where he has attempted to build on the work of Jean Piaget. He is perhaps best known for his popular books, *The Hurried Child, All Grown Up and No Place to Go, Miseducation, Ties That Stress,* and *Reinventing Childhood.* He lectures extensively at home and abroad and has appeared on many of the major network news and talk shows.

William A. Galston is a professor in the School of Public Affairs, University of Maryland, and director of the university's Institute for Philosophy and Public Policy. He is the author of five books and numerous articles on political theory, American politics, and public policy. He has published a number of articles on policies for children and families and on the laws governing marriage and divorce. From 1993 until 1995 he was on leave from the University of Maryland, serving as deputy assistant to President Clinton for domestic policy.

Sylvia Ann Hewlett is founder and chairman of the National Parenting Association. She was awarded a fellowship by the Center for the Study of Values in Public Life at the Harvard Divinity School for the academic year 1999–2000. The former executive director of the Economic Policy Council, she has also served on the faculty of Barnard College, Columbia University, and the New School University. Educated at Cambridge, Harvard, and London Universities, her books include *A Lesser Life*, the Robert F. Kennedy Award–winning *When the Bough Breaks, The War Against Parents* (co-authored with Cornel West), and the forthcoming *Creating a Life.*

S. Jody Heymann is founder and director of the Project on Global Working Families. A member of the faculty at the Harvard School of Public Health and the Harvard Medical School, she also chairs the Johnson Foundation Initiative on Work, Family, and Democracy. Her most recent book is *The Widening Gap: Why America's Working Families Are in Jeopardy and What Can Be Done About It.* She has served in an advisory capacity to the U.S. Senate Committee on Labor and Human Resources, the World Health Organization, and the U.S. Centers for Disease Control and Prevention, among other organizations. She received her Ph.D. in public policy from Harvard University and her M.D. with honors from Harvard Medical School. She trained in pediatrics at the Children's Hospital of Boston.

Wade F. Horn is the assistant secretary for the Administration for Children and Families in the U.S. Department of Health and Human Services (HHS). From 1994 until becoming assistant secretary, he served as the president of the National Fatherhood Initiative, a national nonprofit organization dedicated to increasing the number of children growing up with involved, committed, and responsible fathers. From 1989 to 1993 he served as the commissioner for Children, Youth and Families and chief of the Children's Bureau within HHS and from 1990 to 1993 he served as a presidential appointee to the National Commission on Children. He is the author of numerous books and articles on children and families.

Bernice Kanner is a marketing expert, author, and editor. She has been associated with Bloomberg LLC since 1994 as a columnist for radio, TV, and print and as a marketing adviser and new-product developer. She is the author of numerous books including *Are You Normal?*, *Lies My Parents Told Me*, *The 100 Best Commercials—And Why They Worked*, and *Women in Charge: Marketing to Women in the 21st Century*. A frequent contributor to many publications, she has been a marketing expert for the CBS *Morning News*, ABC, ESPN's *Business Times*, and other TV outlets. For thirteen years, through 1994, Kanner served up an intimate look at the marketing world with her award-winning weekly column "On Madison Avenue," for *New York* magazine.

Nancy Rankin is director of policy research and advocacy for the Community Service Society of New York. She has been a leading voice on parents and work–life balance. As executive director and head of research for the National Parenting Association she directed three national surveys of parents' concerns and political views and led development of the Parent Stress Index. She was project director for the NPA's Task Force on Revitalizing Parenting for the 21st Century, which formed the basis for this volume. Before joining the NPA, she was vice president of Ukeles Associates, providing consulting to nonprofit organizations and public agencies. Earlier in her career, she created and launched New York State's Enriched Housing program, one of the nation's first statewide efforts to offer the aging population alternatives to institutional care. She earned a master's in public affairs from Princeton University and graduated with honors from Cornell. She lives in New York City with her husband, economist Paul Bennett, and their two daughters.

Juliet B. Schor recently became professor of sociology at Boston College. Prior to that she taught economics and women's studies at Harvard University. She is the author of *The Overworked American: The Unexpected Decline of Leisure* and *The Overspent American: Why We Want What We Don't Need*. She is also a founding member of the Center for a New American Dream, an organization devoted to promoting environmentally and socially sustainable lifestyles.

Raymond Seidelman is a professor of political science at Sarah Lawrence College, where he teaches courses on U.S. political participation and the political economy of cities and suburbs. He is the co-author of *The Democratic Debate: An Introduction to American Politics*, now in a third edition, co-editor of *Debating Democracy,* a reader in American politics, as well as other books and articles. He has served as a Fulbright scholar in South Korea, taught at China's Nanjing University, and served as a consultant to the National Parenting Association.

Theda Skocpol is Victor S. Thomas Professor of Government and Sociology at Harvard University, where she also serves as director of the Center for American Political Studies. A leading scholar of American public policy and civic life, she was the elected president of the Social Science History Association in 1996 and will be president of the American Political Science Association in 2003. She writes for the educated public as well as scholarly audiences. Her book *Protecting Soldiers and Mothers: The Political Origins of Social Policy in the United States* won five major scholarly awards. Recent books include *Boomerang: Health Reform and the Turn Against Government*, *Civic Engagement in American Democracy* (co-edited with Morris P. Fiorina), and *The Missing Middle: Working Families and the Future of American Social Policy*. Her current research focuses on voluntary associations and political participation in American democracy, from the nineteenth century to the present.

Ruy Teixeira is a senior fellow at the Century Foundation and formerly director of the Politics and Public Opinion Program at the Economic Policy Institute. He is the author of several books, including *The Disappearing American Voter*, and numerous articles, both scholarly and popular. His latest book, with Joel Rogers, *America's Forgotten Majority: Why the White Working Class Still Matters*, was recently reissued in paperback. He is currently working on a new book, *The Emerging Democratic Majority* (co-authored with John Judis).

Cornel West is the Alphonse Fletcher Jr. University Professor at Harvard University. Previously he was the director of the African-American Studies Department and professor of religion at Princeton University. He is a magna cum laude graduate of Harvard, with an M.A. and Ph.D. from Princeton. He is a well-respected speaker and authority on issues of race and religion. He is the author of numerous articles and books including *Prophetic Fragments,* the best-seller *Race Matters*, and *The War Against Parents* (co-authored with Sylvia Ann Hewlett).

Peter Winn is professor of history at Tufts University in Boston. He is the author and editor of several books and numerous articles, including *Americas*, a comparative study that focused on the changing contexts of families over the past fifty years. He has also written or advised more than a dozen documentary films.

Edward N. Wolff received his Ph.D. from Yale University in 1974 and is currently professor of economics at New York University, where he has taught since 1974. He is also managing editor of the *Review of Income and Wealth*, a senior scholar at the Jerome Levy Economics Institute of Bard College, and a research associate at the National Bureau of Economic Research. He is president-elect of the Eastern Economics Association, a council member of the International Input-Output Association, and a past council member of the International Association for Research in Income and Wealth and has acted as a consultant with the Economic Policy Institute, World Bank, United Nations, and WIDER Institute. He is the author (or co-author) of *Growth, Accumulation, and Unproductive Activity: An Analysis of the Post-War U.S. Economy*; *Productivity and American Leadership: The Long View*; *Competitiveness, Convergence, and International Specialization*; *Top Heavy: A Study of Increasing Inequality of Wealth in America*; and *Economics of Poverty, Inequality, and Discrimination*.

Ruth A. Wooden is senior counselor at Porter Novelli and served as president of the National Parenting Association from July 1999 to July 2001. For the previous eleven years, she was president of the Advertising Council. In her work at the Ad Council, she was instrumental in the development and execution of the landmark multiyear public opinion survey exploring Americans' attitudes about children and teens, "Kids These Days" and "Kids These Days '99," conducted by Public Agenda. This study generated unprecedented interest as it identified important insights into public attitudes toward parents as well as kids and pointed to opportunities that need to be developed *on behalf of parents* to improve the conditions for kids in the United States. *Congressional Quarterly* selected the study as one of the most significant documents published in 1997.

The **National Parenting Association** works to make parenting a higher priority in Americans' private lives and on the public agenda through research, communications, and nonpartisan advocacy. It is a nonprofit organization. Survey reports can be found at the NPA Web site: www .parentsunite.org, or write to the NPA at P.O. Box 77, New York, NY 10113 (npa@nationalparenting.org).